T0312255

Population Economics

Population Economics

Assaf Razin and Efraim Sadka

The MIT Press
Cambridge, Massachusetts
London, England

This book was set in Palatino by Asco Trade Typesetting Ltd.

Library of Congress Cataloging-in-Publication Data

Razin, Assaf.
  Population economics / Assaf Razin and Efraim Sadka.
    p. cm.
  Includes bibliographical references and index.
    ISBN 978-0-262-18160-0 (hc. : alk. paper) — 978-0-262-51722-5 (pb. : alk. paper)
    1. Fertility, Human. 2. Population policy. 3. Economic development.
  4. Income distribution. 5. Social security. 6. Emigration and immigration.
  I. Sadka, Efraim. II. Title.
  HB901.R39   1995
  304.6—dc20   94-27773
                                                                                    CIP

Contents

Preface

This book provides a unified treatment of population changes based on solid microeconomic foundations. Since Gary Becker's pioneering analysis, which appeared in 1960, the implications of endogenous fertility coupled with parental altruism toward their own children for consumption, labor supply, savings and bequests, investments in human capital, and economic growth have been explored extensively in the literature. The purpose of this book is to analyze these and related new issues (e.g., migration, inter- and intragenerational income redistribution) in an integrated microeconomic framework.

The book can serve as a text for a graduate course or an advanced undergraduate course in population economics. It can also be used as a supplementary text for courses in public economics, labor economics, international trade, development economics, and demography. The only prerequisite is intermediate microeconomics. The reader who is not technically equipped may skip the more technical parts of chapters 3, 9, 11, 12, and 13.

This book is a follow-up of an earlier volume, written jointly with Marc Nerlove, *Household and Economy: Welfare Economics of Endogenous Fertility*, Academic Press (1987). We are grateful to Marc Nerlove for permitting us to draw extensively on this volume.

This study integrates and extends, in addition to the aforementioned volume, scattered work written jointly with colleagues that has appeared in various journals and other publications. We are indebted to Marc Nerlove, Larry Kotlikoff, Robert von Weizscaeker, and Chi-Wa Yuen, and to the editors and publishers, for permission to use material from the following:

Kotlikoff, Lawrence, and Assaf Razin (1988). "Making Bequests without Spoiling Children: Bequests as an Implicit Tax Structure and the Possibility that Altruistic Bequests Are Not Equalizing." NBER Working Paper no. 2735.

Nerlove, Marc, Assaf Razin, and Efraim Sadka (1987). *Population Policy and Individual Choice: A Theoretical Investigation.* Research Report, International Food Policy Research Institute, Washington, D.C.;

Nerlove, Marc, Assaf Razin, and Efraim Sadka (1988), "Bequest Constrained Economy: Welfare Analysis," *Journal of Public Economics* 37: 293–320;

Nerlove, Marc, Assaf Razin, Efraim Sadka, and Robert von Weizscaeker (1993), "Income Distribution and Efficiency: The Role of Social Security," *Public Finance* 47:462–475.

Razin, Assaf, and Efraim Sadka (1992). "International Migration and International Trade." NBER Working Paper no. 4230, December, 1992.

Razin, Assaf, and Chi-Wa Yuen (1993). "Convergence in Growth Rates: A Quantitative Assessment of the Role of Capital Mobility and International Taxation," In Leonardo Leiderman and Assaf Razin (eds.), *Capital Mobility: The Impact on Consumption, Investment, and Growth.* Cambridge: Cambridge University Press, Cambridge,

Razin, Assaf, and Chi-Wa Yuen (1994). "Utilitarian Tradeoff Between Population Growth and Income Growth," *Journal of Population Economics*, forthcoming.

In addition, chapter 14 is a reprint of T. N. Srinivasan's survey "Development in the Context of Rapid Economic Growth: An Overall Assessment" (United Nations, 1993; except for his original section 3). We thank T. N. Srinivasan and the publisher for permitting us to print his work.

The work on this book was performed in various academic institutions: The Eitan Berglas School of Economics, Tel-Aviv University; University of Michigan (1986); University of Chicago (1986–1987);

University of Bonn (1989); Center for Economic Studies, University of Munich (1992); Institute for Advanced Studies; Vienna (1993); and the Institute for International Economic Studies, University of Stockholm (1993).

Finally, our thanks to Mrs. Stella Padeh for efficient typing of the manuscript.

1

Introduction

The ultimate difficulties of any arbitrary, artificial, moral, or rational reconstruction of society center around the problem of social continuity in a world where individuals are born naked, destitute, helpless, ignorant, and untrained, and must spend a third of their lives in acquiring the prerequisites of a free contractual existence. The distribution of control, of personal power, position, and opportunity, of the burden of labor and of uncertainty, and of the material produce of social industry cannot easily be radically altered, whatever we may think ideally ought to be done. The fundamental fact about society as a going concern is that it is made up of individuals who are born and die and give place to others; and the fundamental fact about modern civilization is that it is dependent upon the utilization of three great accumulating funds of inheritance from the past, material goods and appliances, knowledge and skill, and morale. Besides the torch of life itself, the material wealth of the world, a technological system of vast and increasing intricacy and the habituations which fit men for social life must in some manner be carried forward to new individuals born devoid of all these things as older individuals pass out. The existing order, with the institutions of the private family and private property (in self as well as goods), inheritance and bequest and parental responsibility, affords one way for securing more or less tolerable results in grappling with this problem.

Frank H. Knight (1921, pp. 374–375)

Malthus and the classical economists combined a very simple model of family decision making with an equally simple model of the operation of the economy. In essays published in 1798 and 1830 Malthus saw, for the family, procreation without bound except possibly by "a foresight of the difficulties attending the rearing of a family ... and the actual distress of some of the lower classes, by which they are disabled from giving the proper food and attention to their children" (Malthus 1798, p. 89). For the economy, Malthus said that a high level of capital accumulation induced by a high level of profits—representing the difference between output and the rent of land (natural resources) and wages—permitted a continual increase in output and population, albeit at the cost of using land of increasingly poorer quality. As a result of the model of family decisions, there was not a rising standard of living for most people, but eventually a falling one.

Nevertheless, Malthus's hypothesis was rebuffed in modern history. Essentially, it failed because it ignored what was termed by Becker in his Nobel lecture (1993) "the economic way of looking at behavior." As Becker puts it:

The failure of Malthus's simple model of fertility persuaded economists that family size decisions lay beyond economic calculus. The neoclassical growth model reflects this belief, for in most versions it takes population growth as exogenous and given....

However, the trouble with the Malthusian approach is not its use of economics per se, but an economics inappropriate for modern life. It neglects that the time spent on child care becomes more expensive when countries are more productive. The higher value of time raises the cost of children and thereby reduces the demand for large families. It also fails to consider that greater importance of education and training in industrialized economies encourages parents to invest more in the skills of their children, which also raises the cost of large families. The growing value of time and the increased emphasis on schooling and other human capital explain the decline in fertility as countries develop, and many other features of birth rates in modern economies.

Becker's new way of looking at behavior emphasizes that fertility should be treated as an endogenous economic variable that responds to economic constraints and incentives. Parents care about the number of children and their welfare (or "quality"). Their choice of how many children to have and how much to spend on their welfare (via their nutrition, health, education, etc.) is determined by a process of preference maximization subject to economic constraints. This is not meant to say that cultural, ethnic, sociological, and other factors do not play a major role in fertility and child quality decisions. It is merely meant to say that these noneconomic factors play a crucial role in shaping parental preferences. But once preferences are shaped (and they could change over time), economics comes into play. At this stage, fertility and child quality decisions are amenable to economic analysis. The recognition that much economic investment is made in human beings rather than in physical capital and that fertility itself is shaped in important ways by economic considerations—a recognition crucial to the understanding of long-term growth—has led in recent years to a renewed interest in the economics of household decisions. It is at this level that decisions about consumption, savings, labor force participation, migration, investments in human capital, and even fertility are made.

In this book we systematically explore the microeconomic-based implications of endogenous fertility and child quality for population trends and many social issues of population policy. The organization of the book is as follows.

Chapter 2 presents a survey of some summary indicators of population dynamics. These stylized facts, so to speak, provide a background for the choice of topics and issues analyzed in the book. Part I reformulates within a modern microeconomic framework the determinants of fertility. A distinction is made between two fundamental drives of fertility: a parental altruistic motive that gives rise to a trade-off between the quantity and the welfare (or quality) of children, and an old age security motive in which children serve merely as a capital good. Part II surveys various social welfare objectives for population size. It also analyzes the menu of policy instruments required to enhance these objectives. Part III explores the implications of endogenous fertility and parental altruism for market failure, that is, the failure of the laissez-faire market mechanism to achieve Pareto efficiency. We show how endogenous fertility and parental altruism can internalize the much-discussed Malthusian externality. Because parental altruism generates other externalities, including those associated with marriage of children and the allocation of bequests and investments in education among children, we also discuss noncoercive social policies to correct or offset the effects of such externalities. Part IV is devoted to the analysis of the intragenerational, interfamily, and intergenerational, intrafamily roles of a social security system. The two-way interactions between long-run economic growth and population growth are analyzed in part V, which also assesses the empirical findings about these interactions and the relevance of publicly debated policy recommendations. Part VI, devoted to migration as a source for population changes, places particular emphasis on whether trade in goods and capital flows can relieve the pressure for labor migration and provides an anatomy of gains and losses from migration, both in laissez-faire-oriented economies and welfare-oriented economies.

2

Population Dynamics: Summary Indicators

Economics and fertility interact. It is a widespread phenomenon that the poor have many children. As the World Bank (1984) succinctly puts it:

All parents everywhere get pleasure from children. But children involve economic costs; parents have to spend time and money bringing them up. Children are also a form of investment—providing short-term benefits if they work during childhood, long-term benefits if they support parents in old age. There are several good reasons why, for poor parents, the economic costs of children are low, the economic (and other) benefits of children are high, and having many children makes economic sense.

The rich may prefer to spend their money on the quality of their children rather than on having many children. In this book we lay down the microeconomic foundation for this phenomenon.

International comparisons clearly indicate that poor countries have higher population growth rates than rich countries. Table 2.1 shows that the average population growth rates ranged between 2.0 and 2.5 percent per year in the poor countries during the period 1965–1990. This range is somewhat lower for middle-income countries (1.8–2.5% per year). In the rich countries the average population growth rates are markedly lower, ranging between 0.6 and 1.0 percent per year. Because the low-income countries provide the lion's share (about 60%) of the world population, the population growth rates in these countries dominate the world population growth rates. Given the high crude mortality rate in the poor countries relative to the rich countries, the differences in crude birth rates are even higher than the differences in population growth rates.

Table 2.1
Annual population growth rates: International comparisons (percent)

	1965–73	1978–80	1980–90	Population in 1990 (millions)	1991 GNP per capita (dollars)
Low-income economies	2.5	2.1	2.0	3,066	350
Middle-income economies	2.3	2.2	1.8	1,379	2,480
High-income economies	1.0	0.8	0.6	817	20,570
World	2.2	1.8	1.7	5,262	4,010

Source: World Bank (1993, table A.1).

Malthus (1798) posited that "population, when unchecked, increases in a geometrical ratio ... subsistence increases only in arithmetical ratio." Thus population could be only stabilized by food shortage at the subsistence level, which leads to higher mortality rates. Malthus's prediction was contradicted by the economic and population changes associated with the "demographic transition" during and following the industrial revolution. This was a transition from high to markedly lower fertility rates, which together with the accelerated growth of agricultural and industrial production provided a check to population growth farther away from the subsistence population level, despite the contemporaneous decline in mortality rates.[1]

As already indicated, the rich tend to substitute quality for quantity of children. Child quality is a multidimensional construct, consisting of nutrition, education, skill development, health care, and so forth. Among other things, improved child quality may be reflected in prolonged life expectancy at birth. This trade-off between quantity and quality is nicely illustrated in figures 2.1 and 2.2, reproduced from the World Bank (1984). The first figure plots the average total fertility rate[2] in about 100 developing countries against income per capita, while the second figure plots the average life expectancy in the same countries against income per capita. In general, higher

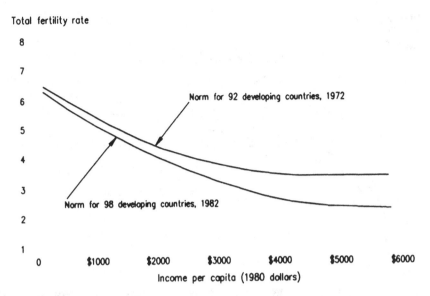

Total fertility rate

Figure 2.1
Fertility in relation to income in developing countries, 1972 and 1982
Source: World Bank (1984).

income per capita is associated with lower fertility and higher life expectancy.[3] Fertility generally fell and life expectancy generally rose between 1972 and 1982, reflecting a growth of per capita income. While the aforementioned data reveal the interaction between fertility and income levels, they do not relate to the relationship between the *rates* of population growth and per capita income growth.

Figure 2.3, reproduced from Razin and Yuen (1993), plots the correlation between per capita income growth rates and population growth rates, incorporating countries at *all* stages of development. The downward-sloping regression line filled through the points (roughly) confirms the negative correlation between the two growth rates. As a further confirmation, Razin and Yuen find that the correlation coefficient is −0.27.

In the last three centuries the *natural* growth rates of population were partly siphoned off through international migration. More than

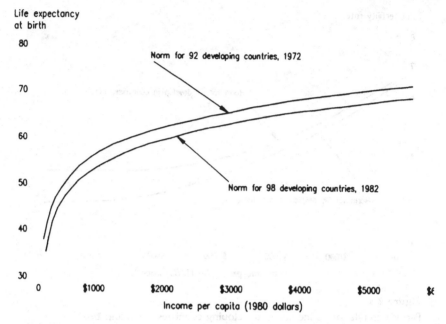

Figure 2.2
Life expectancy in relation to income in developing countries, 1972 and 1982
Source: World Bank (1984).

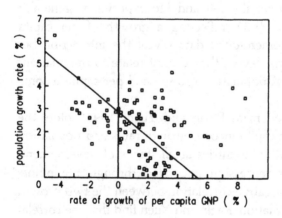

Figure 2.3
Correlation between population growth and per capita income growth
Source: Razin and Yuen (1993), based on 1965–1987 data for the 120 countries
(excluding those with the missing data) listed in tables 1 and 26 of the *World
Development Report* (World Bank 1989).

Table 2.2
Permanent emigration as a percentage of increase in populations of emigrants' countries

Period	Europe	Asia[a]	Africa[a]	Latin America[a]
1851–1880	11.7	0.4	0.01	0.3
1881–1910	19.5	0.3	0.04	0.9
1911–1940	14.4	0.1	0.03	1.8
1940–1960	2.7[b]	0.1	0.01	1.0
1960–1970	5.2	0.2	0.10	1.9
1970–1980	4.0	0.5	0.30	2.5

Source: World Bank (1984).
a. The periods from 1850 to 1960 pertain to emigration only to the United States.
b. Emigration only to the United States.

60 million people left Europe for Australia, Canada, the United States, and New Zealand. At its peak, 1881–1910, emigration from Europe was equivalent to 20 percent of the increase in its population, as we see in table 2.2, reproduced from the World Bank (1984). More recently, international capital mobility and trade in goods have interacted considerably with international migration.

The stylized facts outlined here motivate the selection of this book's topics, whose treatment is analytical.

I

The Microeconomics of Fertility
and Child Quality

3

Number and Quality of Children

A distinguishing feature of our approach to population economics is the thesis that parents care about both the welfare and number of their children. This idea that parents derive positive utility from both the number and the well-being of their offspring was first formulated and applied to the microeconomics of household behavior by Gary S. Becker and Greg H. Lewis (1973). It then became a pillar of positive and normative analysis, both in theoretical and empirical applications, of population and human resource economics.

The conventional theory of consumer behavior posits that the household derives a positive utility from a bundle of goods and services that parents choose to buy and consume from a set of alternative bundles constrained by a given budget. The novelty of the Becker-Lewis approach is that the household ("parents") allocates its budget not only for purchasing traditional consumer goods and services but also for investment in the present and future well-being of the children. Furthermore, because parents also care about the number of their children, their *total* spending on children becomes a product of two *choice* variables: the number of children and the well-being of each child (or the "quantity" and "quality" of children, respectively, in the language of Becker and Lewis). The improvement in the quality of a child can be done in a variety of ways: spending on the current consumption of the child, investing in the child's health and education ("investment in human capital"), and providing for the child's future consumption ("bequest"). This approach yields a unified theory of the allocation of time (among work, leisure, education, child rearing, etc.), fertility, consumption, savings, investment in human capital, and bequests.

For the ease of exposition, we posit in this chapter a static model that combines bequests, investments in human capital and so on into one aggregate variable called quality of children and that abstracts from this variable's both intra- and inter temporal time allocation. Subsequent chapters refine this model by gradually introducing such features as time allocation, bequests, investment in human capital, and other dynamic elements.

Our focus here is on the quantity-quality trade-off, analyzed as much as possible within the familiar model of consumer behavior. We pay special attention to the effect of household income on the choice of the quantity and quality of children, employing only familiar consumer theory concepts such as substitution effects, income elasticities, and the like.

3.1   The Quantity-Quality Trade-off: A First Look

Consider a pair of parents as an individual decision maker (henceforth, "parent") who consumes units of single composite consumption good (c). The parent also extracts utility from the number of her children (n) and the quality, or well-being (z), of each one of them. This quality is measured by the units of the single composite good spent on these children (e.g., on their education, health, etc.). For the sake of simplicity, we treat n as a continuous variable. In addition, we assume that all children are identical and that the parent treats them symmetrically, so we use the symbol z for the quality of each and every child.

The parent has an ordinary utility function,

$$u(c, z, n), \tag{3.1}$$

where the marginal utility u_i is positive, $i = 1, 2, 3$. This means that the parent extracts positive utility from all three variables—consumption (c), quality of children (z) and quantity of children (n). The parent chooses both z and n, in addition to c. Let the parent's income, in terms of the single composite good, be I. She spends c on herself and a total of zn on her children. The parent's budget constraint is therefore

$$c + zn \leq I. \tag{3.2}$$

Notice that the expenditure side of the budget constraint (the left-hand side of equation 3.2) is not of the familiar type where the expenditures on each consumption good are added together in order to get total expenditure. Here both z and n are quantities of "consumption goods" ("quality" and "children," respectively). On the expenditure size of (3.2), z and n appear together as a product. Thus, in some sense, z can be viewed as the price of n and n as the price of z. Indeed, the quality, as measured by the money expenditure on the well-being of each child, is the price that the parent pays for each additional child and vice versa. Furthermore, these "prices" are determined by the parent rather than being given to the competitive household in the standard theory of consumer behavior. This special form of (3.2) yields a nonlinear budget constraint, and we can no longer talk about a budget line.

The unique specification of the budget constraint produces a subtle ambiguity with respect to the effect of income on the demand for children. Suppose children were a normal good in the conventional sense that a rise in income, when their "price" is *fixed*, induces a larger demand for children. Even in this case, the income effect on the number of children need not be positive, because a rise in income might plausibly induce parents to spend more on their quality, thereby raising their "price." This *self-determined* increase in the price of children might induce parents to have fewer children. Furthermore, the lower number of children in turn would make the "price" of quality cheaper, thereby generating more spending on quality. Thus, an increase in income could very well be spent on quality rather than on quantity of children. Quality might substitute for quantity of children as income rose.

These considerations are presented diagramatically in figure 3.1 within the familiar framework of indifference curves and budget constraints. In order to allow the use of a two-dimensional diagram, suppose that the parent's consumption (c) has already been determined (at the optimal level), say $\bar{c}$, so that she is left with a budget of $I - \bar{c}$ which she can choose how to spend on quantity (n) and quality (z) of children: $zn \leq I - \bar{c}$. Let the rectangular hyperbola BB represent this budget constraint, so that the parent chooses point A where the indifference curve UU is tangent to the budget curve. Now

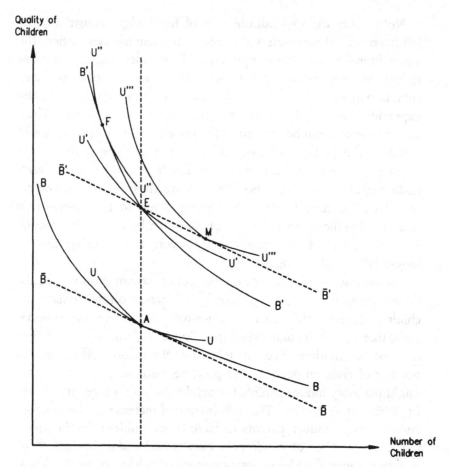

Figure 3.1
The quantity-quality trade-off

suppose income rises by ΔI. The parent's consumption, being a normal good, rises also by some Δc that is smaller than ΔI, so that some extra money is left to spend on children. The budget constraint then shifts outward to $B'B'$. The normality of n in the conventional sense implies that the indifference curves become steeper and steeper as we move upward along any vertical line. Were the budget curves linear, such as $\bar{B}\bar{B}$ and $\bar{B}'\bar{B}'$, then a rise in income would produce a new optimum at point M (where the indifference curve $U'''U'''$ is tangent to the budget curve $\bar{B}'\bar{B}'$) with a larger number of children. A rise in income in our case, however, not only shifts the budget constraint upward but also makes it steeper. Thus, as we move from point A to point E, both the budget curve and the indifference curve become steeper, and it could well be the case that at point E the budget curve becomes steeper than the indifference curve. This is indeed the case depicted in figure 3.1, where, at point E, the indifference curve $U'U'$ is steeper than the budget curve $B'B'$. In this case, the new optimum is at point F, where the indifference curve $U''U''$ is tangent to the budget curve $B'B'$. At the new optimum (point F) the number of children is smaller than at the old optimum (point A), that is, the increase in income reduced the number of children and raised their quality.

This first look at the quantity-quality trade-off suggests that the effect of income on fertility is not clear-cut. It thus requires a more formal analysis to which we now turn.

3.2   The Effect of Income on Fertility: A Second Look

The formal optimization problem faced by the parent is to choose c, z, and n so as to maximize the utility function (3.1) subject to the budget constraint (3.2). The optimal c, z, and n in this problem all depend on income I. Denote the optimal c, z, and n by $C(I)$, $Z(I)$, and $N(I)$, respectively. One is interested in the sign of the elasticity of N with respect to I. As we noted, this is not the standard question as to whether a certain good is a normal good, and one cannot use the standard conditions for normality. We therefore form a hypothetical problem that is a standard consumer optimization problem; we explain below how it is related to our true problem (3.1)–(3.2).

Consider the following problem:

$$\max_{c,z,n} u(c, z, n), \tag{3.3}$$

subject to

$$c + p_n z + p_n n \leq I + M,$$

where $p_z > 0$, $p_n > 0$, and M are parameters. One can interpret p_z and p_n as the "prices" of quality and quantity of children, respectively; M is interpreted as a lump-sum transfer. Now (3.4) is a standard consumer optimization problem, and one denotes the optimal bundle of c, z, and n by $\bar{C}(p_z, p_n, I + M)$, $\bar{Z}(p_z, p_n, I + M)$, and $\bar{N}(p_z, p_n, I + M)$, respectively. The latter functions are conventional Marshallian demand functions; in particular, it is assumed that they exhibit normality:

$$\bar{C}_3, \bar{Z}_3, \bar{N}_3 > 0.$$

Comparing (3.1)–(3.2) with (3.3), it is straightforward to establish the relationship between (C, Z, N), and $(\bar{C}, \bar{Z}, \bar{N})$. Evaluated at $p_z = N(I)$, $p_n = Z(I)$ and $M = N(I)Z(I)$, the bundle $(\bar{C}, \bar{Z}, \bar{N})$ is equal to (C, Z, N):

$$\bar{C}(N(I), Z(I), I + N(I)Z(I)) = C(I), \tag{3.4a}$$

$$\bar{Z}(N(I), Z(I), I + N(I)Z(I)) = Z(I), \tag{3.4b}$$

$$\bar{N}(N(I), Z(I), I + N(I)Z(I)) = N(I). \tag{3.4c}$$

Differentiating totally the last two relationships with respect to I:

$$(\bar{Z}_1 + Z\bar{Z}_3)\frac{dN}{dI} + (\bar{Z}_2 + N\bar{Z}_3 - 1)\frac{dZ}{dI} = -\bar{Z}_3, \tag{3.5a}$$

$$(\bar{N}_1 + Z\bar{N}_3 - 1)\frac{dN}{dI} + (\bar{N}_2 + N\bar{N}_3)\frac{dZ}{dI} = -\bar{N}_3. \tag{3.5b}$$

Employing the Hicks-Slutsky equations appropriate to the hypothetical problem (3.3), one sees that $\bar{Z}_1 + Z\bar{Z}_3$ is the Hicks-Slutsky substitution effect of the "price" of the quality of children on the quality of children, denoted by $\bar{S}_{zz}$. $\bar{Z}_2 + N\bar{Z}_3$ is the Hicks-Slutsky substitution effect of the "price" of the quantity of children on the quality of children, denoted by $\bar{S}_{zn}$. Similarly, $\bar{N}_1 + Z\bar{N}_3$ is denoted by $\bar{S}_{nz}$, and $\bar{N}_2 + N\bar{N}_3$ is denoted by $\bar{S}_{nn}$. By the symmetry of the Hicks-Slutsky substitution effects, $\bar{S}_{zn} = \bar{S}_{nz}$. Substituting these relationships into (3.5) and solving for dN/dI yields

$$\frac{dN}{dI} = \frac{\bar{N}_3(1 - \bar{S}_{nz}) + \bar{Z}_3 \bar{S}_{nn}}{(1 - \bar{S}_{nz})^2 - \bar{S}_{zz} \bar{S}_{nn}}. \tag{3.6}$$

In elasticity terms, (3.6) becomes

$$\eta_{nI} = k \frac{\bar{\eta}_{nI}(1 - \bar{\varepsilon}_{nz}) + \bar{\eta}_{zI} \bar{\varepsilon}_{nn}}{(1 - \bar{\varepsilon}_{nz})^2 - \bar{\varepsilon}_{zz} \bar{\varepsilon}_{nn}}, \tag{3.7}$$

where

$\eta_{nI} = \dfrac{dN}{dI} \cdot \dfrac{I}{N}$ is the income elasticity of $N(\cdot)$,

$\bar{\eta}_{nI} = \bar{N}_3 \dfrac{I + \bar{N}\bar{Z}}{\bar{N}}$ is the income elasticity of $\bar{N}(\cdot, \cdot, \cdot)$,

$\bar{\eta}_{zI} = \bar{Z}_3 \dfrac{I + \bar{N}\bar{Z}}{\bar{Z}}$ is the income elasticity of $\bar{Z}(\cdot, \cdot, \cdot)$, with

$k = \dfrac{I}{I + \bar{N}\bar{Z}} < 1,$

$\bar{\varepsilon}_{nn} \equiv \dfrac{\bar{S}_{nn} p_n}{\bar{N}} = \dfrac{\bar{S}_{nn} \bar{Z}}{\bar{N}}$ is the own-substitution elasticity of $\bar{N}(\cdot, \cdot, \cdot)$,

$\bar{\varepsilon}_{zz} \equiv \dfrac{\bar{S}_{zz} p_z}{\bar{Z}} = \dfrac{\bar{S}_{zz} \bar{N}}{\bar{Z}}$ is the own-substitution elasticity of $\bar{Z}(\cdot, \cdot, \cdot)$,

and

$\bar{\varepsilon}_{nz} \equiv \dfrac{\bar{S}_{nz} p_z}{\bar{N}} = \bar{S}_{nz}$ is the cross-substitution elasticity.

(Note that the standard income elasticities, $\bar{\eta}_{nI}$ and $\bar{\eta}_{zI}$, are assumed positive.) Similarly, we find that

$$\eta_{zI} = k\frac{\bar{\eta}_{zI}(1 - \bar{\varepsilon}_{nz}) + \bar{\eta}_{nI}\bar{\varepsilon}_{zz}}{(1 - \bar{\varepsilon}_{nz})^2 - \bar{\varepsilon}_{zz}\bar{\varepsilon}_{nn}}. \tag{3.8}$$

Thus one can see from (3.7) that if there is a unitary substitution elasticity between the quantity and quality of children (i.e., $\bar{\varepsilon}_{nz} = 1$), then $\eta_{nI} = -(k/\bar{\varepsilon}_{zz})\bar{\eta}_{zI} > 0$, by the negativity of own-substitution elasticity ($\bar{\varepsilon}_{zz}$). In this case an increase in income increases fertility (and, as can be seen from equation 3.8, child quality as well).

Now assume that the substitution elasticity between the quantity and quality of children is larger than one (i.e., $\bar{\varepsilon}_{nz} > 1$). Also assume that total expenditure on children increases with income (i.e., $N(I)Z(I)$ increases in I). This means that at least one of the components of this expenditure, $N(I)$ or $Z(I)$, must be increasing income. Suppose then that $\eta_{zI} > 0$. Since it is assumed that $\bar{\varepsilon}_{nz} > 1$, it follows that the numerator on the right-hand side of (3.8) is negative. Hence the denominator must also be negative. But it then follows from (3.7) that η_{nI} is positive. Thus, under the assumption that total expenditure on children increases in income, a high degree of substitutability between child quality and quantity (i.e., $\bar{\varepsilon}_{nz} > 1$) implies that income has a positive effect on both the quantity and the quality of children (i.e., both η_{nI} and η_{zI} are positive).

However, as this quantity-quality problem is not a standard consumer choice problem, one can extract from (3.7) many cases in which income has a negative effect on fertility (i.e., $\eta_{nI} < 0$). If the substitution elasticity between the quantity and quality of children is smaller than one (i.e., $\bar{\varepsilon}_{nz} < 1$), there are two possibilities.

One possibility is that the denominator of (3.7) or (3.8) is positive. This occurs when the own-substitution elasticities (i.e., $\bar{\varepsilon}_{zz}$ and $\bar{\varepsilon}_{nn}$) are relatively low. In this case one can see from (3.7) that if the income elasticity of quality in the hypothetical problem (3.3) (i.e., $\bar{\eta}_{zI}$) is substantially higher than the income elasticity of quantity in the same problem (namely, $\bar{\eta}_{nI}$), then child quantity falls with income (i.e., $\eta_{nI} < 0$), while child quality rises (i.e., $\eta_{zI} > 0$).

The other possibility is that the denominator of (3.7) or (3.8) is negative. This occurs when the own-substitution elasticities (i.e., $\bar{\varepsilon}_{zz}$ and $\bar{\varepsilon}_{nn}$) are relatively high. In this case if $\bar{\eta}_{zI}$ is substantially lower than $\bar{\eta}_{nI}$, then, again, $\eta_{nI} < 0$ and $\eta_{zI} > 0$.

3.3   Conclusion

Introducing the quantity and quality of children into the parent's utility function yields a nonlinearity in the budget constraint. The principal result is that, even if the demand for both quantity and quality of children is normal in the conventional sense, the observed elasticity of fertility (numbers of children) with respect to income may be negative. Whether or not this occurs depends in part on the elasticity of substitution between quantity and quality of children in the parent's utility function. This result may explain empirical findings (in international cross-section comparisons and in time-series data) that higher standards of living are associated with lower fertility and higher spendings on quality of children (medical care, education, etc.).

4

Children as a Capital Good

The preceding chapter focused on a certain important motive of endogenous fertility namely, that parents have children because they are altruistic: they care about children, both about their number and their welfare. We have abstracted from another motive for bringing children (which is very important in less developed countries) the so-called old age security motive, which essentially views children as a capital good. The latter motive is analyzed in this chapter. In the words of T. W. Schultz (1974), "children are 'the poor man's capital'" in developing countries. Becker (1960) writes that "it is possible that in the mid-nineteenth century children were a net producer's good, providing rather than using income." Neher (1971) and Willis (1980) develop the idea that parents in less-developed countries are motivated, in part, to bear and rear children because they expect children to care for them in old age.

When the motive for having children is their role as a capital good, requiring investment in the present and providing income for old age, it is natural to expect that better access to capital markets will unambiguously reduce the demand for children because children will then be a less important means of transferring income from the present to the future. For instance, Neher (1971) writes that "the good asset (bonds) drives out the bad asset (children)." This is indeed the essence of the old age security hypothesis.

The first section of this chapter describes a simple model of old age security, with children being the sole form of capital. In section 4.2.1. we introduce physical capital and allow parents to choose between investing in children and in physical capital. In this case the old age security hypothesis is confirmed: the introduction of physical capital reduces the number of children. In section 4.2.2 we introduce a financial capital market in which parents can lend and borrow. In this case, the old age security hypothesis, somewhat surprisingly, does not hold: access to financial capital markets may plausibly increase rather than decrease the number of children. Finally, in section 4.3 we reexamine the old age security hypothesis when there is also an altruistic motive for having children, in addition to the old age security motive.

4.1   A Simple Model of Old Age Security with No Capital

In this section we portray a simple, stripped-down model of the old age security motive for bringing children, where children serve as the sole form of "capital," the sole means for parents to transfer income from their productive years to their old age, unproductive years.

Suppose that the parent lives for only two periods, productive and fertile youth and unproductive old age. There is a single all-purpose good that is produced by labor alone. Each parent is endowed with an amount of labor capable of producing k_1 units of this all-purpose good in the first period. A parent brings children during the first period, each endowed with an amount of labor capable of producing k_2 units of the good in the second period, when the child grows up. Each child consumes x_1 units in the first period and x_2 units in the second period. For the moment, assume that the parent does not care about the welfare of her children. She merely views them as a capital good intended to provide for her old age consumption in the second period of her life, when she can no longer work. Consequently, the utility of the parent is assumed to depend only on c_1 and c_2, her first-period and second-period consumption, respectively:

$$u = u(c_1, c_2). \tag{4.1}$$

Thus x_1 and x_2 are assumed to be exogenously given (at conventional or subsistence levels).

A parent can thus use the output she produces in the first period for consumption (c_1), for investment in n children (nx_1), and for investment in physical or financial capital (S). Recall that in this section it is assumed that no other capital exists so that children are the sole form of capital and are the only means of transferring consumption from the present to the future. Consequently, S is set equal to zero in this section. This S is only introduced in this section in order to facilitate the analysis of the effects of capital discussed in later sections. Thus a parent faces the following budget constraint in the first period:

$$k_1 = c_1 + nx_1 + S. \tag{4.2}$$

The investment in each child yields a "return" of $(k_2 - x_2)$ units of the all-purpose good in the second period. This return is simply the output of the child less its consumption. It is assumed that $k_2 - x_2 > 0$, for otherwise it does not pay to invest in children. Thus the parent's consumption in the second period (c_2) is given by

$$c_2 = n(k_2 - x_2) + (1 + r)S, \tag{4.3}$$

where r is the real return on capital. (Recall again that $S = 0$ in this section.)

Solving equation 4.2 for n,

$$n = (k_1 - c_1 - S)/x_1, \tag{4.4}$$

and equation 4.3 for n,

$$n = [c_2 - (1 + r)S]/(k_2 - x_2), \tag{4.5}$$

then equating the right-hand side of equation 4.4 to the right-hand side of equation 4.5 (recalling that $S = 0$) yields the parent's budget constraint between c_1 and c_2:

$$c_2 = (k_2 - x_2)(k_1 - c_1)/x_1. \tag{4.6}$$

The interpretation of equation 4.6 is straightforward: the maximum amount that the parent can consume in the second period is obtained when she consumes nothing in the first period $(c_1 = 0)$. In this case she can invest all of the endowment, k_1, in k_1/x_1 children, which, in turn, yield $(k_2 - x_2)(k_1/x_1)$ in the second period. Notice also that $(k_2 - x_2)(k_1/x_1)$ is the future value of the parent's lifetime income measured in units of future consumption. A unit of present consumption (c_1) is a unit of forgone investment in children; therefore, it has an opportunity cost in terms of future consumption. This cost, $(k_2 - x_2)/x_1$, is the return to a unit of investment in children: investing one unit of the all-purpose good in children means bearing $1/x_1$ children, who each yield $(k_2 - x_2)$. The parent's budget line between present and future consumption is depicted in figure 4.1.

The parent chooses that point on the budget line that maximizes her utility function. This is the point (c_1^*, c_2^*) in figure 4.1, where an indifference curve, $u(c_1, c_2) = \text{constant}$, is tangent to the budget line.

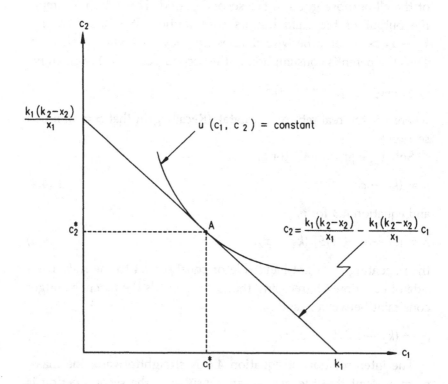

Figure 4.1
Equilibrium demand for consumption over two periods

Once the parent chooses the optimal consumption bundle (c_1^*, c_2^*), the optimal number of children (n^*) is determined from equations 4.4 or 4.5:

$$n^* = (k_1 - c_1^*)/x_1 = c_2^*/(k_2 - x_2). \tag{4.7}$$

Observe that an increase in the cost of children, x_1, reduces the slope of the budget line in figure 4.1 and the intercept with the vertical axis, leaving unchanged the intercept with the horizontal axis. Therefore, if c_2 is not a Giffen good, then c_2 falls, and by (4.5) the number of children, n, also falls. However, the effect of a decrease in the payoff to investment in children $(k_2 - x_2)$ on the number of children is ambiguous. Such a change has the same effect on the budget line as before (making c_2 more expensive relative to c_1), and again c_2 must fall, if it is not a Giffen good. Whether n rises or falls, however, depends on whether the decrease in c_2 is proportionally higher or lower than the decrease in $(k_2 - x_2)$; see (4.5). Because the return to their investment through children falls, families may need to invest more (i.e., have more children) even if they are content with consuming less in the future. By contrast, an increase in the parent's endowment, k_1, has a pure income effect. The budget line shifts upward without any change in its slope; c_2 increases if it is a normal good and thus, by (4.5), the number of children, n, must also rise. Here the income effect, in the absence of any trade-off between quality and quantity of children, is unambiguously positive.

We conclude this section with a simple example. Suppose the utility function (equation 4.1) is of the Cobb-Douglas form:

$$u(c_1, c_2) = c_1^\alpha c_2^{1-\alpha}, \tag{4.8}$$

where a fraction, α, of lifetime income, $k_1(k_2 - x_2)/x_1$, is spent on present consumption, c_1, and the remaining fraction, $1 - \alpha$, is spent on future consumption, c_2. Consequently, the parent chooses

$$c_1^* = \alpha\{[k_1(k_2 - x_2)/x_1]/[(k_2 - x_2)/x_1]\} = \alpha k_1, \tag{4.9}$$

$$c_2^* = (1 - \alpha)\{[k_1(k_2 - x_2)/x_1\}, \tag{4.10}$$

and

$$n^* = (k_1 - c_1^*)/x_1 = (1 - \alpha)k_1/x_1. \tag{4.11}$$

In this simple example, an increase in k_1 raises c_1, c_2, and n. An increase in x_1 lowers c_2 and n but does not affect c_1. An increase in $(k_2 - x_2)$ raises c_2 but has no effect on c_1 and n.

4.2 Old Age Security with Capital

4.2.1 Physical Capital

Now suppose there is physical capital in which parents can invest their savings, that is, we drop the constraint that $S = 0$. There is now an alternative to children for transferring present to future consumption. We assume that this form of investment yields a constant real return of r. But there is still no financial capital market through which borrowing can take place, that is, we assume $S \geq 0$.

Recall that for now the parent does not derive utility from the number or welfare of her children. Therefore the parent will not invest in children if the return that they yield, $(k_2 - x_2)/x_1$, is lower than $1 + r$, the alternative payoff per unit of investment in physical capital. In order to analyze the effect of introducing physical capital on the old age security hypothesis, assume that k_2, x_2, and x_1 vary by family. Parents will choose to have no children if x_2 or x_1 is sufficiently high or if k_2 is sufficiently low, so that

$$(k_2 - x_2)/x_1 < 1 + r. \tag{4.12}$$

Instead, they will transfer consumption from the present to the future by investing in physical capital (i.e., they will choose a positive S). On the other hand, parents for whom the inequality is reversed, so that

$$(k_2 - x_2)/x_1 > 1 + r, \tag{4.13}$$

will not invest in physical capital, thus $S = 0$. These parents are not affected by the introduction of physical capital and consequently they will choose the same number of children as before.

If there is physical capital, some families (those for whom equation 4.12 holds) will choose to have no children, while other families (those for whom equation 4.13 holds) will choose to have the same number of children as they would if there were no physical capital. It therefore follows that the total population must be smaller with physical capital than without. This is the essence of the old age security hypothesis.

4.2.2   Financial Capital

The analysis of the preceding subsection demonstrates that the old-age security hypothesis holds in a model with investment in physical capital as a substitute to investment in children. This model essentially captures a one-sided capital market, where people can lend (by investing in physical capital), but they cannot borrow. In this subsection a perfect financial capital market is introduced in which people can both lend and borrow and in which the interest rate is determined to clear the market at equilibrium. Total savings equal total dissavings, that is, the total supply of funds of those who save is equal to the total demand for funds of those who dissave.

In this case some families may indeed, as in the preceding subsection, choose to have no children if the capital market offers them an investment opportunity with a higher yield, but other families may now use the capital market for borrowing in order to invest more in children. Thus the introduction of a financial (two-sided) capital market may well increase rather than decrease the number of children, contrary to the old age security hypothesis. In the absence of a capital market, all families transfer resources from the present to the future through their children. With physical capital, only families with high rates of return on children (relative to the interest rate) continue to use children as a means of transferring resources from the present to the future. The other families invest in physical capital. But, with a financial capital market, these other families with low rates of return on their children can also enjoy the high rates of return on children by lending to the families that have these high rates and letting them invest in children. Thus families with a high rate of return on children invest in children not only for themselves but also for families with a low rate of return. The introduction of a financial capital market allows the economy to use children as a capital good more efficiently. Consequently, the economy may invest more in children. This is exactly what happens in the next example.

Suppose that there are only two types of families (A and B) who both have the Cobb-Douglas utility function of equation 4.8. The two families have the same endowments (k_1 and k_2), the same second-period child consumption (x_2), but different first-period child consumption (x_1^A and x_1^B). Assume that $x_1^A > x_1^B$, so that the return on investment in children is higher for family B than for family A:

$$(k_2 - x_2)/x_1^A < (k_2 - x_2)/x_1^B.$$

The earlier example showed that in the absence of a capital market the number of children in each family (see equation 4.11) is given by

$$n^{*i} = [(1 - \alpha)k_1]x_1^i, \tag{4.14}$$

where $i = A$, B. (Note that the family with the higher return on children chooses to have more children.) The aggregate number of children, in this case (N^*), can be found from equation 4.14:

$$N^* = n^{*A} + n^{*B} = (1 - \alpha)k_1(1/x_1^A + 1/x_1^B). \tag{4.15}$$

Now, a financial capital market is introduced that allows both lending ($S > 0$) and borrowing ($S < 0$) at the market-determined real interest rate of r. The equilibrium occurs when the savings of one family are equal to the dissavings of the other family. If, for some family, $(1 + r)$ is lower than the return on investment in children, $(k_2 - x_2)/x_1^i$, then it pays that family to borrow (and invest in children) indefinitely, thereby increasing future consumption indefinitely. But this cannot be an equilibrium. Thus, the equilibrium interest rate (r^{**}) cannot fall short of the rate of return on investment in children for any family:

$$1 + r^{**} \geq (k_2 - x_2)/x_1^B > (k_2 - x_2)x_1^A. \tag{4.16}$$

Now, if the first inequality in equation 4.16 is strict, then both families have zero demand for children (because the rate of return on children is lower than the rate of interest), and both families will want to save. But the capital market cannot be in equilibrium when both families save. Thus, at equilibrium,

$$1 + r^{**} = (k_2 - x_2)/x_1^B > (k_2 - x_2)/x_1^A. \tag{4.17}$$

In this case, family A will choose to have no children, $n^{**A} = 0$, because it is better for it to invest in the capital market. For this family, the first- and second-period budget constraints, equations 4.2 and 4.3, now become

$$k_1 = c_1 + S \tag{4.18}$$

and

$$c_2 = (1 + r)S. \tag{4.19}$$

These two constraints can be consolidated into one present-value, lifetime budget constraint:

$$k_1 = c_1 + c_2(1 + r). \tag{4.20}$$

Maximization of the utility function, equation 4.8, subject to the budget constraint, equation 4.20, yields the optimal levels of c_1, c_2, and S for family A:

$$c_1^{**A} = \alpha k_1, \tag{4.21}$$

$$c_2^{**A} = (1 - \alpha)k_1(1 + r^{**}), \tag{4.22}$$

and

$$S^{**A} = k_1 - c_1^{**A} = (1 - \alpha)k_1. \tag{4.23}$$

Family B is indifferent between investing in the capital market and investing in children (because $(k_2 - x_2)/x_1^B = 1 + r^{**}$). The consumption of this family is given by

$$c_1^{**B} = \alpha k_1 \tag{4.24}$$

and

$$c_2^{**B} = (1 - \alpha)k_1(1 + r^{**}).\tag{4.25}$$

For equilibrium in the capital market, family B must dissave, that is, family B must borrow in the capital market in order to invest in children (because family A has a positive S). Accordingly,

$$S^{**B} = - S^{**A} = -(1 - \alpha)k_1.\tag{4.26}$$

In order to find the number of children of family B, substitute equations 4.24 and 4.26 into the first-period budget constraint, equation 4.2, to obtain

$$n^{**B} = (k_1 - c_1^{**B} - S^{**B})/x_1^B = [2(1 - \alpha)k_1]/x_1^B.\tag{4.27}$$

The aggregate number of children, N^{**} in this case, is found from equation 4.27, recalling that $n^{**A} = 0$:

$$N^{**} = n^{**A} + n^{**B} = [2(1 - \alpha)k_1]/x_1^B.\tag{4.28}$$

Comparing N^* to N^{**} from equations 4.15 and 4.28, it can be seen that

$$N^{**} = [2(1 - \alpha)k_1]/x_1^B = (1 - \alpha)k_1(1/x_1^B + 1/x_1^B)$$

$$> (1 - \alpha)k_1(1/x_1^A + 1/x_1^B) = N^*.\tag{4.29}$$

Thus the introduction of a capital market increases, rather than decreases, the number of children, contrary to the old age security hypothesis.[1]

4.3   Old Age Security with Endogenous Fertility

So far it has been assumed that neither the number of children nor the children's welfare entered the parent's utility function. If, however, the parent does care about her children, it can again be shown that there is no presumption that the existence of capital will lead to a smaller demand for children than the absence of capital.

Suppose, then, that the utility function is

$$u = u(c_1, c_2, x_1, x_2, n),\tag{4.30}$$

so that the parent cares about the number of her children, n, and her children's welfare, which, in turn, depends on the children's consumption, x_1 and x_2. The parent now chooses x_1 and x_2 as well as n, c_1, and c_2.

In this case even the introduction of physical capital, enabling the parent to transfer present into future consumption, may plausibly increase the demand for children. This is because the presence of better or more means for transferring resources from the present to the future increases welfare and thus may create a positive income effect on the desired number of children. This effect may dominate the negative substitution effect (as shown in subsection 4.2.1) that the introduction of physical capital may have on the number of children.

In the absence of capital the parent chooses c_1, c_2, x_1, x_2, and n so as to maximize (4.30), subject to (4.2) and (4.3), where S is set equal to zero. With capital she is not constrained to have S equal to 0. Comparing the optimal n in these two cases does not yield an unambiguous result. Some insight into the source of this ambiguity may be obtained by assuming that children are born in the second period (i.e., $x_1 = 0$) and that u is weakly separable between the first-period variable (c_1) and the second-period variables (c_2, x_2, n), that is, present consumption (c_1) does not affect preferences over future consumption (c_2) and quality (x_2) and quantity (n) of children. Formally, it is assumed that u can be written as

$$u(c_1, c_2, x_2, n) = f(c_1, v(c_2, x_2, n))\qquad(4.31)$$

(see Goldman and Uzawa 1964 for a formal definition and discussion of weak separability). In this case c_2, x_2, and n must maximize $v(\cdot)$ subject to the second-period budget constraint $(1 + r)S = c_2 + nx_2 - nk_2$. Thus one can see that the difference between the optimal c_2, x_2, and n in the absence of capital ($S = 0$) and in the presence of capital ($S > 0$) results only from an income effect.

Here we can draw on the work of Becker and Lewis (1973) that we discussed in chapter 3. (The only difference is the new term $-nk_2$ in the budget constraint. This term can be interpreted as some child allowance in the framework of Becker and Lewis without changing their results.)

As noted in chapter 3, quality is part of the "price" of a unit of the quantity of children, and conversely, quantity is the "price" of a unit of the quality. Since these "prices" are control variables (controlled by the parent), the income effect in this household optimization problem is coupled with an endogenous price effect. As illustrated in chapter 3, no unambiguous conclusion can be reached about the effect of an increase in income on the quality of children.

In chapter 3 we established conditions on certain demand elasticities that guarantee that income has a negative effect on the quantity of children. In this case the old age security hypothesis may indeed hold; however, this result is indeed special. In general, if $x_1 \neq 0$, if the weak separability assumption does not hold, or if the aforementioned elasticity conditions are not satisfied, then the introduction of a capital market may well cause an increase in the number of children.

Let us, for example, continue to maintain the weak separability assumption and to hold $x_1 = 0$. If the elasticities of substitution between c_2 and x_2 and n are sufficiently low and if a family is induced to invest in physical capital by the introduction of such capital, that family will also increase c_2, x_2, and n. Or consider the extreme case in which the elasticities of substitution between c_2 and x_2 and between x_2 and n are zero. In this case the utility function (4.31) is written as

$$u(c_1, c_2, x_2, n) = f(c_1, \min\{c_2, \gamma x_2, \delta n\})$$

for some $\gamma > 0$ and $\delta > 0$.

Clearly, the parent chooses to have $c_2 = \gamma x_2 = \delta n$ in this case. For those families who continue not to save after the introduction of capital, n will be unchanged; however, all three variables, c_2, x_2, and n, increase in the same proportion if there is saving in physical capital. The old age security hypothesis is thus invalid in this case.

II

Ethical Considerations

Ethical Considerations

5

Social Evaluation of Population Size

In the preceding chapters we analyzed the issue of individually efficient fertility, that is, the individual parent was assumed to choose the number of her children so as to maximize her own utility (which may or may not take into account her children's well-being). The question of whether the population size is socially optimal when it is determined by unfettered fertility decisions by the individual parent is the subject of this chapter. Whether an economic allocation is optimal depends of course on the criteria used by society to evaluate its welfare (the so-called social welfare function). We review here several social welfare criteria and the policies needed to support them; we examine their implications for optimal population sizes.

5.1 Criteria for Social Optima with Variable Population

Welfare economics theory has traditionally considered given sets of individuals (societies) without regard to population growth. As Sumner (1978, p. 95) notes, "most of the traditional moral theories ... were devised in and for a world in which population was not a pressing problem." Traditional welfare economics is concerned with the allocation of resources among the existing population; it deals with what is referred to as fixed pool problems. In this book, however, we determine the number of persons as part of the analysis; we are concerned with what can be referred to as variable pool problems.

It is not clear whether a social welfare function that works nicely for a fixed pool problem would also work reasonably well for variable pool problems. Sumner (1978, p. 96) claims that "many classical theories are incomplete in just this sense: they imply little or nothing for population problems. Utilitarianism is an exception to this rule: it may generate what one regards as the wrong solution, but it at least generates a solution."

The utilitarian theory has two versions. The original one (classical utilitarianism) was first enumerated in modern form by Bentham and given further refinement by Sidgwick. Bentham and Sidgwick argued that if additional people enjoy, on the whole, positive happiness (utility), population ought to be allowed to increase to the point at which total utility (the sum of the utilities of all people) is at a maximum. A revised version of the classical theory, known as average utilitarianism, is concerned with maximization of the average, or per capita, utility. Edgeworth (1925) attributes this revised version to Mill, who used a per capita utility maximization argument to justify limits to the size of population.[1] In the remainder of this section we give a brief summary of the literature concerned with the debate between the advocates of the two theories—classical (total) utilitarianism and average utilitarianism.

To begin with, there is of course no difference between the two theories where the choice is among alternatives that have the same effects on population levels: if population levels are the same, the average utility differs from the total utility by a multiplicative constant. Thus, it is only in a situation in which different alternatives would produce different population levels that the two theories can diverge. Consider the following example from Sumner (1978, p. 100): Suppose that the question is whether to add an additional person to the existing population. If the utility added by the additional person is positive but less than the status quo average, "then expanding the population by this one person will produce a greater sum but a lesser average than the status quo. It will therefore be preferred by the classical theory but not by the average theory. It is no accident that the average theory was devised strictly to handle questions of population."

In the modern welfare economics literature, Harsanyi (1953, 1955) and Vickrey (1960) have presented the foundations for utilitarianism in terms of a contractual theory. Because they consider a fixed population, they do not distinguish between classical and average utilitarianism, so that one can view them as advocates of both theories. They envisioned a situation similar to what Rawls (1971) later termed the "original position," which is characterized by a "veil of ignorance." There are two societies (both of size n) for you to choose to be in. You know the list of utility levels that each society has:

$$U^1 = (U_1^1, \ldots, U_n^1) \text{ and } U^2 = (U_1^2, \ldots, U_n^2).$$

You are denied any information about where in this list ("in whose shoes") you will be, so you assume that you have an equal probability to be anywhere. If your behavior under risk satisfies the von Neumann–Morgenstern axioms, you will choose the society in which the expected utility ($\sum_{i=1}^{n} U_i^1/n$ or $\sum_{i=1}^{n} U_i^2/n$) is higher. Note that the expected utility in this case is also the average utility. Since n is a constant in the Harsanyi-Vickrey framework, it provides a justification for either classical or average utilitarianism.

If the two societies differ in size, it would seem that the Harsanyi-Vickrey approach still leads to average utilitaranism. As Sumner (1978, p. 100) puts it: "you will always opt for the higher average; the prospect of larger numbers living at a lower average will hold no attraction for you." But Summer also maintains that the Harsanyi-Vickrey approach may well lead to the classical utilitarianism if the framework of the original position is slightly modified. Suppose that the two societies are of different sizes, n_1 and n_2, and that $n_1 > n_2$. Assume further that the number of the hypothetical contractors (the individuals who are searching for the society to belong to) is known to you and that it is equal to n_1. In this case the second society is overbooked and if you choose the second society you will first have to participate in a lottery to determine whether you have a place at all in this society. The probability of having a place is n_2/n_1. Therefore, by choosing the first society you obtain an expected utility of $1/n_1 \sum_{i=1}^{n_1} U_i^1$; by choosing the second society you obtain an expected utility of

$$\frac{n_2}{n_1} \frac{1}{n_2} \sum_{i=1}^{n_2} U_i^2 = \frac{1}{n_1} \sum_{i=1}^{n_2} U_i^2.$$

Thus, you will compare $1/n_1 \sum_{i=1}^{n_1} U_i^1$ with $1/n_1 \sum_{i=1}^{n_2} U_i^2$. Eliminating $1/n_1$ yields the sum-of-utilities criterion, or classical utilitarianism.

Some further support for classical utilitarianism may be obtained from the work of Arrow and Kurz (1970), who consider an intergenerational allocation of resources, with population changing from one generation to the next (although at an exogenously given rate). Addressing the question whether the social welfare function should depend on the average utility in each generation or the total utility in each generation, Arrow and Kurz argue convincingly in favor of the latter criterion.

Suppose that there are two generations of sizes n_1 and n_2 and an exhaustible resource capable of producing k units of consumption. All members of all generations have the same utility function $u(\cdot)$, which exhibits diminishing marginal utilities (i.e., u is concave). Let c^i be the consumption of each member of generation i, where $i = 1, 2$.

If the social welfare function W depends on the total utility of each generation, that is, $W = W(n_1 u(c^1), n_2 u(c^2))$, the optimal allocation is obtained by solving the following program:

$$\max_{c^1, c^2} W(n_1 u(c^1), n_2 u(c^2)), \tag{5.1}$$

subject to

$$n_1 c^1 + n_2 c^2 \leq k.$$

The latter inequality describes the overall resource constraint facing the two generations.

The first-order conditions for this optimization problem yield:

$$n_1 W_1 u'(c^1) - \lambda n_1 = 0, \tag{5.2a}$$

$$n_2 W_2 u'(c^2) - \lambda n_2 = 0, \tag{5.2b}$$

where $\lambda \geq 0$ is a Lagrange multiplier, W_i is the partial derivative of W with respect to its ith argument ($i = 1, 2$), and u' is the derivative of u.

Dividing (5.2a) by (5.2b), one obtains

$$\frac{W_1 u'(c^1)}{W_2 u'(c^2)} = 1. \tag{5.3}$$

Assume that W is symmetric (i.e., $W(a, b) = W(b, a)$). This means that the society is indifferent to the order by which generations come onto the stage of life. It then follows from (5.3) that $c^1 = c^2$, so that the social welfare function does not discriminate against any generation.

If the social welfare function depends on the average utility of each generation, however, it will discriminate against the generation with the large population. To see this, note that for average utilitarianism, one has to solve the following optimization problem:

$$\max_{c^1, c^2} W(u(c^1), u(c^2)), \tag{5.4}$$

subject to

$$n_1 c^1 + n_2 c^2 \leq k.$$

The solution is depicted in figure 5.1.

By the symmetry of W, the slope of the social indifference curve, $W(u(c^1), u(c^2)) = $ constant, is one (in absolute value) along the 45°-line. The slope of the consumption possibility frontier, $n_1 c^1 + n_2 c^2 = k$, is n_1/n_2 (in absolute value), which is smaller than one, assuming a positive rate of population growth (i.e., $n_1 < n_2$). Thus, the social optimum must lie to the right of the 45°-line, implying that $c^1 > c^2$. Hence average utilitarianism discriminates against the generation with the larger population.

Sumner suggests still another argument against average utilitarianism: it gives priority to existing individuals over potential individuals. Consider, for instance, a society of two individuals, Shelly and Ron, having utility levels of 1 and 0, respectively. Suppose that one contemplates adding Gil to the society and transferring the one unit of utility from Shelly to him. Classical utilitarianism will be indifferent with respect to this addition since total utility remains 1. Because, however, average utility falls from 1/2 to 1/3, average utilitarianism

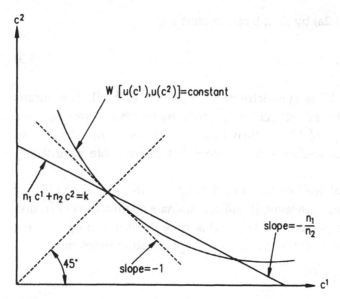

Figure 5.1
Socially optimal population size when social welfare depends on the average utility of each generation

will reject the addition of Gil to the society. At the status quo ante there was one individual (Shelly), who had one unit of utility. After the addition, there would also be just one individual (the potential person Gil) with one unit of utility. By rejecting the addition of Gil, average utilitarianism favors the existing person, Shelly, over the potential person, Gil.

There are also some objections to classical utilitarianism. Dasgupta (1984), referring to his earlier work (Dasgupta 1969), points out that "the application of classical utilitarianism in a world with finite resources often implies a large population size; by this we mean that the average standard of living is embarassingly low." As long as the average utility does not fall too rapidly when population is increasing (i.e., as long as the elasticity of average utility with respect to population size is less than one in absolute value), population ought to be increased indefinitely even though the average utility may approach zero. Parfit (1984) calls this "the repugnant conclusion."

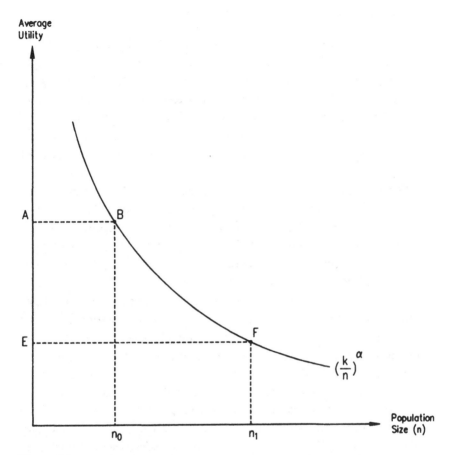

Figure 5.2
Illustration of the "repugnant conclusion"

For instance, suppose that the utility function of a representative individual is

$$u(c) = c^\alpha, \tag{5.5}$$

where $0 < \alpha < 1$. Further suppose that there is an exhaustible resource capable of producing k units of consumption. If the population size is n, average utility is $(k/n)^\alpha$ and is depicted by the downward sloping curve in figure 5.2. Multiplying average utility by n yields total utility $(k/n)^\alpha n = k^\alpha n^{1-\alpha}$, which is depicted by the area of the rectangle under the average utility curve. Thus, total utility increases without bounds as population grows larger. For instance, as population grows from n_0 to n_1, average utility falls from OA to OE in figure 5.2, while total utility rises from the area of the rectangle $OABn_0$ to the area of the rectangle $OEFn_1$. Therefore, according to classical utilitarianism, population ought to be increased indefinitely, but when this happens, average utility (namely, $(k/n)^\alpha$) approaches zero. On the other hand, according to average utilitarianism, the optimal population size should be as small as possible; this is also an embarassing conclusion.

Such implausible conclusions of either a zero or an unbounded population size can be eliminated by introducing public goods characterized by economies of scale and diminishing returns to labor. Such models are common in the local public finance literature, where community sizes are endogenously determined (e.g., Berglas and Pines 1983; Wildasin 1986; and Krugman 1990).

The basic idea underlying the determination of the optimal population size in these models is that there are some factors that yield advantages to size and others that generate disadvantages to size, and an optimal population size is obtained when the two groups of factors just balance each other. In the first group, there are commonly mentioned increasing returns to scale, public goods (jointly consumed by all members of the community, and whose cost can thus be shared), and the like. In the second group, we can cite diminishing marginal productivity of labor due to the existence of some fixed factor of production such as land, costs of transportation from the marketplace or the production site to the consumption place, congestion effects in the consumption of public goods or utilization of public inputs (e.g., road congestion), and the like.

The interaction between these factors can be most neatly seen in a model in which there is just one force pushing for higher size and another force pushing in the opposite direction. Suppose that there is a pure public good that generates an advantage to population size and a fixed factor of production (say, land) that causes labor to have a diminishing marginal product, thereby generating a disadvantage to population size. To simplify, suppose that all individuals are alike and that there is, in addition to the public good, only one other good which is privately consumed.

5.1.1   Average Utilitarianism

The optimal population size according to average utilitarianism is obtained by maximizing the average utility level

$$u(G, c), \tag{5.6}$$

subject to the resource constraint

$$F(T, n) \geq nc + G, \tag{5.7}$$

where G and c are, respectively, public and private consumption, F is a constant returns-to-scale production function, T is the fixed endowment of land, and n is the size of population. The resource constraint simply states that total output ($F(T,n)$) must be divided between public consumption (G) and total private consumption (nc), which is equal to the private consumption of a representative individual (c) times the number of people in the community (n). The determination of the optimal population size is graphically depicted in figure 5.3. For each given population size (n), we first find the optimal levels of private and public consumption and, consequently, utility. The efficient allocation of resources between private and public consumption is of course governed by the familiar Lindahl-Samuelson rule, which states that the sum over the population of the willingness to pay for the public good (i.e., nu_G/u_c, where u_G and u_c are the marginal utilities of public consumption and private consumption, respectively) is equal to the marginal cost of the public good, which is one. The maximized level of utility (for a given n) is now a function of n (namely, $u = u^*(n)$). The curve $u = u^*(n)$ is as shown in Figure 5.3. The slope of this curve is equal to $u_G(F_n - c)$, where F_n is the marginal product of labor. The explanation is straightforward: an additional person contributes a marginal product to society, but takes out private consumption, leaving a net contribution of $F_n - c$ to the rest of the society, which can be expressed by $u_G(F_n - c)$ in utility terms.

Notice that the additional person takes out only *private* consumption, and not *public* consumption because, by definition, that person is a free rider on the collectively consumed public good. Because the marginal product is diminishing (due to the fixed endowment of

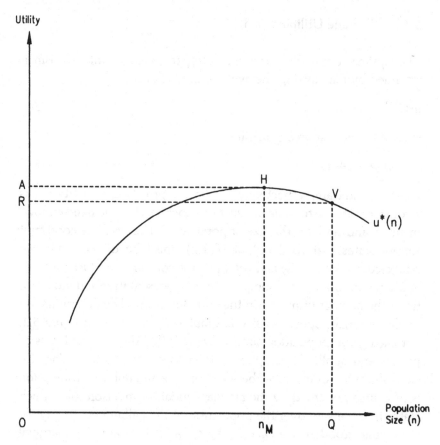

Figure 5.3
Efficient population sizes under average and classical utilitarianism
Note: The slope of the $u^*(n)$-curve is $(F_n - c)u_G$. At point H, we have $F_n = c$.

land), the net contribution to the rest of the society of an additional person is first positive and then becomes negative. The optimal population size is obtained when the marginal product of labor equals private consumption. This occurs at $n = n_M$ in figure 5.3.

An interesting implication of the rule determining the optimal population size under average utilitarianism is that each person privately consumes only a marginal product. Thus, the whole land rent is left to finance public consumption, and a community that has an optimal population size provides an optimal public consumption at a level fully covered by a 100-percent tax on land rents—the so-called Henry George rule; see Henry George (1914).

5.1.2 Classical Utilitarianism

The objective is now to maximize total utility, which is

$$nu(G, c). \tag{5.8}$$

In figure 5.3 this total utility is measured by the area of the appropriate rectangle under the average utility curve, $u^*(n)$. For instance, when population size is n_M, total utility is measured by the area of the rectangle OAHn_M. Because the curve is flat at point H, it follows that the area of the rectangle ORVQ is larger than the area of the rectangle OAHn_M, if Q is sufficiently close to n_M. Thus it is optimal to increase population size beyond the average utilitarianism level, n_M. Average utility does not typically fall to zero. Because the optimal population size occurs somewhere along the negatively sloped segment of the average utility curve, it follows that $F_n < c$. Hence the marginal person consumes privately more than a marginal product, and the Henry George rule does not apply: a 100-percent tax on land rent more than suffices to finance an optimal level of public consumption.

We reexamine below optimal population sizes in the presence of parents' altruism towards their children. We show that, in such a case as well, classical utilitarianism does not typically imply embarrassingly low standards of living, while average utilitarianism does not typically imply an embarassingly low population size.

5.2 Individual Choice and Social Optima

The key feature of the analysis in this book is the endogenous fertility of altruistic parents. By this we mean that parents care about both the number and welfare of their children, choosing both the number of their children and how much to provide for their welfare (through investment in their human capital, bequests, etc.), subject to a budget constraint. Thus population size cannot be controlled directly by government or social planners. This does not mean of course that the government cannot have a policy regarding the size of the population, but rather that the government has to base its population policy on setting the right economic incentives for parents to follow the socially desired population growth path. This means that fertility (parents' decisions about how many children to have) is the endogenous source of population growth.

That parents care about their children's welfare and number is a feature that appears to be absent from other studies of optimal population growth, such as Dasgupta (1969), Lane (1975, 1977), Samuelson (1975), Deardorff (1976), Meade (1976), and others, who assume that population size is determined by society (but see Lane 1977, pp. 111–119). To the extent that individual preferences are extraneous to fertility determinations, one cannot formulate a laissez-faire solution to the problem of optimal population size, which is the solution that results from utility-maximizing parents in the absence of any government fiats or incentives.

In this section we compare optimal population sizes (or growth rates) for classical utilitarianism (the Benthamite social welfare function) and average utilitarianism (the Millian social welfare function) with each other and with the laissez-faire solution.

Edgeworth (1925) conjectures that the Benthamite criterion leads to a larger population than the Millian criterion. Koopmans (1975), with slightly different versions of the two criteria, makes a similar conjecture. We confirm these conjectures in a more general framework with endogenous fertility: the socially optimal rate of population growth must be larger for a Benthamite than for a Millian social welfare function.[2]

We also find that no unambiguous conclusions can be drawn with respect to the laissez-faire solution versus the socially optimal solution according to either the Benthamite or the Millian criterion. It is not necessarily true that unfettered individual choice will lead to a smaller population than the Benthamite criterion, as Sidgwick thought, or to a larger population than the Millian criterion, as Mill thought.

Notice that with parental altruism, the aforementioned "repugnant conclusion" (see section 5.1), which states that the Benthamite criterion may lead to an embarrassingly low standard of living for future generations, is obviously not tenable. When the welfare of each child is an essential argument in the parent's welfare, the child's standard of living will never be driven to zero. This observation is evident in the simplified fixed resources analysis employed below. This "repugnant conclusion" may be less likely to be supported in a more dynamic context with an endogenously growing pool of resources (see chapter 13).

Consider an economy with two generations, each consisting of just one type of consumer. In the first period there is only one adult parent. She (together with her children) consumes a single private good (c^1). She also raises identical children, who will grow up in the second period. She dies at the end of the first period and bequeaths b to each one of the children. The number of children (n) that are born in the first period is a decision variable of the parent then living. The number of persons living in the second period is n. Each one consumes a single private good (c^2). It is assumed that the parent cares about both the number and welfare of the children. Therefore, the children's utilities are included in the parent's utility function. In a reduced form, the parent's utility can be written as

$$u^1 = u^1[c^1, n, u^2(c^2)], \tag{5.9}$$

where u^1 is concave in c^1 and u^2; u^2 is increasing and concave in c^2; both u^1 and u^2 are nonnegative. That is, people enjoy positive happiness, but there are diminishing marginal utilities: u^1 is also increasing in c^1 and u^2, but is not necessarily increasing in the number of children, n. This is because increasing n, ceteris paribus, gives by itself more happiness to parents but, on the other hand, lowers the quality of each child when total spending on parents and children in the first period (c^1) is constant. Assume that the parent who lives only one period has a budget constraint of

$$c^1 + nb = k; \qquad c^1, n \geq 0, \tag{5.10}$$

where k is the parent's initial endowment, which is nonrenewable and does not depreciate over time. This is like having an exhaustible resource capable of producing k units of consumption. The exact specification of the resource side of the economy is not crucial for the analysis in this section.

Assume that children are born with no endowment. Thus the exhaustible resource has to suffice for the consumption of the current generation and all future generations. The children's per capita consumption is therefore equal to their per capita inheritance:

$$c^2 = b. \tag{5.11}$$

Although the bequest, b, is not restricted to being nonnegative, it is immediately seen from equation 5.11 that it will never be negative. Thus institutional arrangements that do not allow b to be negative— parents cannot obligate their children to pay their debts—are superfluous here.

The constraints given by equations 5.10 and 5.11 can be consolidated into one budget constraint for the parent:

$$c^1 + nc^2 = k. \tag{5.12}$$

A competitive or laissez-faire allocation (LFA) is obtained when the parent's utility function, equation 5.9 is maximized with respect to c^1, c^2, and n, subject to the budget constraint of equation 5.12. This allocation is denoted by (c^{1L}, c^{2L}, n^L).

In this model the Benthamite (sum-of-utilities) social welfare function is defined by

$$B(c^1, c^2, n) = u^1[c^1, n, u^2(c^2)] + nu^2(c^2). \tag{5.13}$$

As mentioned, it is assumed that there is diminishing marginal utility of c^1 and c^2, that is: u^1_{11}, $u^2_{11} < 0$, where the subscripts stand for partial derivatives. A Benthamite optimal allocation (BOA) is obtained by maximizing equation 5.13 with respect to c^1, c^2, and n, subject to the economy-wide budget constraint, equation 5.12. This allocation is denoted by (c^{1B}, c^{2B}, n^B).

The Millian social welfare function, namely, the per capita (or average) utility, is

$$M(c^1, c^2, n) = \{u^1[c^1, n, u^2(c^2)] + nu^2(c^2)\}/(1 + n)$$

$$= [B(c^1, c^2, n)]/(1 + n) \tag{5.14}$$

because there are one parent and n children, or $(1 + n)$ people altogether, in our population calculus.

The Millian optimal allocation (MOA) is obtained by maximizing equation 5.14 with respect to c^1, c^2, and n, subject to the resource constraint of equation 5.12. This allocation is denoted by (c^{1M}, c^{2M}, n^M).

It is important to emphasize that the parent's utility function is assumed to represent her interest (e.g., happiness from being a parent, guilt relief in providing for the children, etc.) rather than her moral (social) preferences (e.g., believing that it would be wrong to have children and let them starve). This is why the term $nu^2(c^2)$ is added to $u^1[c^1, n, u^2(c^2)]$ when the Benthamite and Millian social welfare criteria are defined. In this way, children are seen as having more than just an instrumental role in society, that is, they are persons and individuals and not just the means or instruments by which parental welfare is affected.

One would expect that when the total happiness of society is maximized rather than the average happiness of its members, optimal population size will be larger. This is indeed the case: $n^B > n^M$. To prove this, observe that both the BOA and the MOA satisfy the same resource constraint, equation 5.12. Since the Millian allocation maximizes M and since $M = B/(1 + n)$, it follows that

$$B(c^{1M}, c^{2M}, n^M)/(1 + n^M) \geq B(c^{1B}, c^{2B}, n^B)/(1 + n^B). \tag{5.15}$$

Since (c^{1B}, c^{2B}, n^B) maximizes B, it follows that

$$B(c^{1B}, c^{2B}, n^B) \geq B(c^{1M}, c^{2M}, n^M). \tag{5.16}$$

Therefore

$$(1 + n^M)/(1 + n^B) \leq B(c^{1M}, c^{2M}, n^M)/B(c^{1B}, c^{2B}, n^B) \leq 1, \tag{5.17}$$

from which it follows that $n^B \geq n^{M}$.[3]

Because the Millian criterion calls for maximization of the average utility, intuition suggests that laissez-faire results in overpopulation relative to this criterion. Although this may be true under some circumstances, it does not hold in general. Since the LFA satisfied the same resource constraint as the MOA, equation 5.12, it follows from the definition of the MOA that

$$M(c^{1M}, c^{2M}, n^M) \geq M(c^{1L}, c^{2L}, n^L). \tag{5.18}$$

Since $M = B/(1 + n)$, it is implied by equation 5.14 that

$$B(c^{1M}, c^{2M}, n^M) \geq [(1 + n^M)/(1 + n^L)]B(c^{1L}, c^{2L}, n^L). \tag{5.19}$$

Since $u^2 > 0$, it also follows that

$$B(c^{1L}, c^{2L}, n^L) = u^1[c^{1L}, n^L, u^2(c^{2L})] + n^L u^2(c^{2L})$$

$$\geq u^1[c^{1L}, n^L u^2(c^{2L})] \geq u^1[c^{1M}, n^M, u^2(c^{2M})] \tag{5.20}$$

because (c^{1L}, c^{2L}, n^L) maximizes u^1, subject to the overall resource constraint, equation (5.12). Thus it can be concluded from equations 5.19 and 5.20 that

$$B(c^{1M}, c^{2M}, n^M) \geq [(1 + n^M)/(1 + n^L)]u^1[c^{1M}, n^M, u^2(2^{2M})],$$

so that

$$(1 + n^M)/(1 + n^L) \leq B(c^{1M}, c^{2M}, n^M)/u^1[c^{1M}, n^M, u^2(c^{2M})]$$

$$= \{u^1[c^{1M}, n^M, u^2(c^{2M})]$$

$$+ n^M u^2(c^{2M})\}/u^1[c^{1M}, n^M, u^2(c^{2M})]$$

$$= 1 + \{n^M u^2(c^{2M})/u^1[c^{1M}, n^M, u^2(c^{2M})]\}. \tag{5.21}$$

Because the extreme right-hand side of equation 5.21 is strictly greater than one, it is impossible to say anything about the ratio on the extreme left-hand side; in particular, it cannot be concluded that $n^L > n^M$.

Where the Benthamite criterion calls for a maximization of the total utility of parents and children, the competitive allocation maximizes the parent's utility only. Intuition therefore suggests that laissez-faire leads to a smaller population than the Benthamite optimum; however, this is not necessarily true. When $nu^2(c^2)$ is added to the parent's utility, as suggested by the Benthamite criterion, increasing the product $nu^2(c^2)$ is indeed desirable; but it does not follow that both n and c^2 need be increased.

To see this, observe that it follows from the definition of the LFA and the BOA that

$$u^1[c^{1L}, n^L, u^2(c^{2L})] \geq u^1[c^{1B}, n^B, u^2(c^{2B})]$$

and

$$u^1[c^{1B}, n^B, u^2(c^{2B})] + n^B u^2(c^{2B}) \geq u^1[c^{1L}, n^L, u^2(c^{2L})] + n^L u^2(c^{2L}).$$

Hence

$$n^B u^2(c^{2B}) \geq n^L u^2(c^{2L}).$$

Thus, indeed, the total utility from children (nu^2) must be larger at the BOA than at the LFA. But it does not follow that $n^B > n^L$.

Indeed, we provide an example in appendix 5.1 in which the population size in the MOA can bear any relationship to the population size in the LFA. In particular, the LFA can result in an under-populated world relative to the MOA. Similarly, we provide another example in which the LFA can result in an overpopulated world relative to the BOA.

5.3 Optimal Population Policies

The assumption that fertility is endogenous allows consideration of noncoercive policies aimed at moving the economy from the laissez-faire allocation (LFA) to either the Benthamite optimal allocation (BOA) or the Millian optimal allocation (MOA) by changing the incentives (prices) faced by parents. Notice that the need here for government action is not warranted because of a market failure, as in the familiar case of external economies or diseconomies reviewed in appendix 5.2. The LFA is indeed Pareto-efficient and is located on the Pareto frontier (of Pareto-efficient allocations). Government action is needed only to move to the socially optimal allocation, which is another point on this frontier.

All possible direct and indirect taxes and subsidies are considered candidates for the optimal policy. Notice that children themselves are a "commodity" and may be subject to a tax or a subsidy. There-fore, a head tax is not a lump-sum nondistortionary tax as in the traditional economic literature with exogenous population. Here such a head tax affects fertility decisions on the margin and is therefore distortionary.

Among the set of possible direct and indirect taxes and subsidies to achieve a social optimum, subsidies for future consumption and child allowances (positive or negative to encourage or discourage having children) are necessary. We show below that a subsidy for future child consumption (c^2), such as a bequest subsidy, is warranted under both the Benthamite and the Millian criteria; a positive child allowance is necessary under the Benthamite criterion, but the child allowance needed under the Millian criterion may be positive, zero, or negative. Notice that in order to achieve each one of these optima (Benthamite or Millian), two distortionary instruments are needed. While these instruments change the incentive to bear children and care for them, they nevertheless offset the distortionary effect of each other and move the economy from one distortion-free allocation (the LFA) to another distortion-free allocation (either the BOA or the MOA).

Although the remedies that are needed here are not necessitated by externalities, a similar apparatus (described in appendix 5.2) can nevertheless be employed to derive them. The difference between the Benthamite or the Millian social welfare functions (which underlies the BOA or the MOA, respectively) and the parent's utility function (which underlies the LFA) implies that marginal social benefits (as derived from the social welfare function) will, in general, be different from marginal private benefits (as derived from the parent's utility). This is why techniques can be used here that are similar to those used in the externality case. Consider first the BOA. It is obtained by maximizing

$$u^1[c^1, n, u^2[c^2]] + nu^2(c^2),$$

subject to the resource constraint

$$k - c^1 - nc^2 = 0$$

(see equations 5.13 and 5.12 above).

The marginal cost of c^2 is the same for the parent and society. It is derived from the budget constraint, equation 5.12, and is equal to the number of children. This means that the marginal social cost (MSC) curve and the marginal private cost (MPC) curve are identical

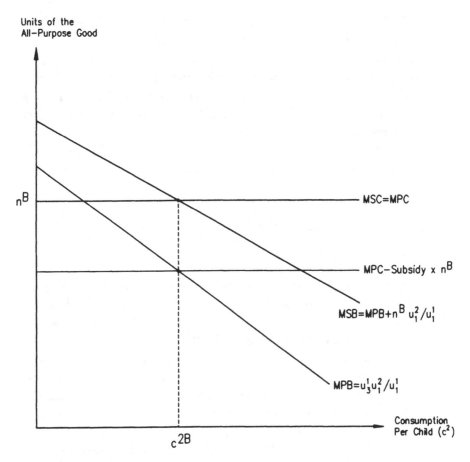

Figure 5.4
The Benthamite optimal allocation: Corrective policy instruments

and equal to n^B. Given the optimal number of children (n^B), these curves are flat (see figure 5.4). However, the social and private benefits differ. For the parent, the marginal benefit (MPB) is the marginal utility that the parent derives from c^2, which is $u_3^1 u_1^2$. Expressed in units of the all-purpose good, MPB $= u_3^1 u_1^2/u_1^1$. However, society extracts utility from children not only via the parent's utility, but also directly via the term nu^2. Hence MSB $=$ MPB $+ nu_1^2/u_1^1$. Thus the Benthamite optimum consumption per child is at c^{2B}, where MSB $=$ MSC. To support this amount of consumption, the parent's cost of c^2 should be lowered by a *bequest subsidy* of size u_1^2/u_1^1 per unit of c^2, so that the MPC curve will intersect the MPB curve at c^{2B}. (Recall that the parent's decision is governed by her private costs and benefits.) Similarly, the marginal social benefit of children exceeds the marginal private benefit of children because of the term nu^2, which is added to the parent's utility, u^1. Hence a positive *child allowance* is needed in order to support the BOA. The magnitude of this child allowance is derived in appendix 5.3.

Consider next the policy instruments that are needed to support the MOA, which is obtained by maximizing

$$[u^1(c^1, n, u^2(c^2)) + nu^2(c^2)]/(1 + n),$$

subject to the resource constraint

$$k - c^1 - nc^2 = 0$$

(see equations 5.14 and 5.12 above, respectively). As in the previous case, the marginal social and private costs of c^2 are derived from the resource (budget) constraint (5.12) and are identical. Given the optimal number of children (n^M), the MPC = MSC curve is flat at the level n^M in figure 5.5. However, the social and private benefits differ. The marginal social welfare of c^2 is $(u_3^1 u_1^2 + nu_1^2)/(1 + n)$. Dividing this term by the marginal social welfare of c^1 (which is equal to $u_1^1/(1 + n)$), we obtain the marginal social benefit of c^2, in terms of c^1, as MSB $= (u_3^1 u_1^2 + nu_1^2)/u_1^1$. Similarly, MPB $= u_3^1 u_1^2/u_1^1$. Thus MSB $=$ MPB $+ nu_1^2/u_1^1$. The MSB and MPB curves are also drawn in figure 5.5. The Millian optimal level of c^2 is obtained at c^{2M}, where MSC $=$ MSB. To support this allocation, the corrective policy must lower the MPC curve so as to intersect the MPB curve at c^{2M}. This is done by a bequest subsidy equal to u_1^2/u_1^1 per unit of c^2. In this case, however, it is not clear whether the marginal social benefit of children exceeds or falls short of the marginal private benefit of children. The reason for this ambiguity is that the Millian objective differs from the parent's objective in two conflicting ways: on the one hand, a larger number of children increases total utility (through the additional term nu^2 in the Millian objective function), but on the other hand, a larger number of children reduces average utility as the latter is obtained by dividing total utility by the size of population

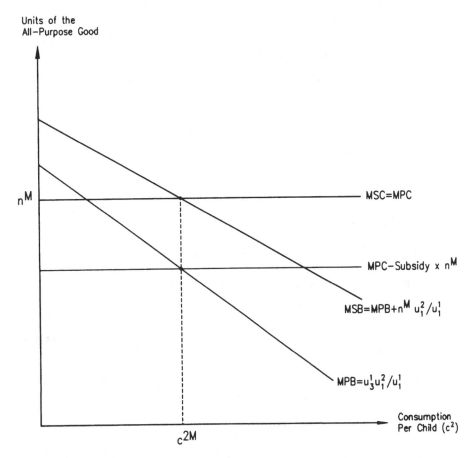

Figure 5.5
The Millian optimal allocation: Corrective policy instruments

Table 5.1
Benthamite and Millian optima: Corrective policy instruments

Policy instrument	Benthamite optimum allocation	Millian optimum allocation
Subsidy to children's consumption	$u_1^2/u_1^1 > 0$	$u_1^2/u_1^1 > 0$
Child allowance	$(u^2 - c^{2B}u_1^2)/u_1^1 > 0$	$u^2/u_1^1 - c^{2M}u_1^2u_1^1 - \dfrac{u^1 + n^M u^2}{(1 + n^M)u^1}$

$(1 + n)$. Therefore, the child allowance could be either positive or negative in the Millian case. The size and magnitude of this allowance are derived in appendix 5.3.

Table 5.1 summarizes the policy instruments that support the Benthamite and Millian allocations.

Appendix 5.1 Population Size: Comparison between MOA and LFA and between BOA and LFA

Example 1

Let the parent's utility function be

$$u^1(c^1, n, u^2(c^2)) = c^1 + an - \tfrac{1}{2}gn^2 + nu^2(c^2), \qquad a, g > 0, \qquad (5A.1)$$

where $u^2(c^2) = \log(1 + c^2)$.

The Millian criterion in this case is

$$\frac{u^1 + nu^2}{1 + n} = \frac{c^1 + an - \tfrac{1}{2}gn^2 + 2n\log(1 + c^2)}{1 + n}. \qquad (5A.2)$$

In order to find the MOA, substitute first the resource constraint $c^1 = k - nc^2$ into (5A.2), which becomes

$$\frac{an - \tfrac{1}{2}gn^2 + k + n[2\log(1 + c^2) - c^2]}{1 + n}. \qquad (5A.3)$$

Then maximize (5A.3) with respect to c^2 and n, subject to the constraint $nc^2 \leq k$ (so that $c^1 \geq 0$). Clearly, c^{2M} must maximize

$$2\log(1 + c^2) - c^2.$$

Hence we conclude that $c^{2M} = 1$. Substituting this into (5A.3), we can also conclude that n^M must maximize

$$\frac{an - \tfrac{1}{2}gn^2 + k + n[2\log 2 - 1]}{1 + n}.$$

Hence

$$n^M = \frac{-g + [g^2 + 2ag + 4g \log 2 - 2g(1 + k)]^{1/2}}{g}. \tag{5A.4}$$

We also have $c^{1M} = k - n^M c^{2M} = k - n^M$ (because $c^{2M} = 1$).

The LFA is found by maximizing

$$k - nc^2 + an - \tfrac{1}{2}gn^2 + n\log(1 + c^2)$$

$$= k + an - \tfrac{1}{2}gn^2 + n[\log(1 + c^2) - c^2] \tag{5A.5}$$

with respect to n and c^2. Clearly, c^{2L} must maximize

$$\log(1 + c^2) - c^2,$$

and hence we conclude that $c^{2L} = 0$. Substituting this into (5A.5), it is evident that n^L must maximize

$$k + an - \tfrac{1}{2}gn^2.$$

Hence

$$n^L = \frac{1}{g}, \tag{5A.6}$$

and we also have $c^{1L} = k - n^L c^{2L} = k$.

Comparing (5A.4) with (5A.6), we can conclude that

$$n^L \lessgtr n^M \tag{5A.7}$$

according to

$$\frac{a}{g} \lessgtr \frac{-g + [g^2 + 2ag + 4g \log 2 - 2g(1 + k)]^{1/2}}{g}.$$

With some simplifications, (5A.7) reduces to

$$n^L \lessgtr n^M$$

according to

$$a^2 \lessgtr 4g \log 2 - 2g(1 + k).$$

Thus, depending on a, g, and k, the Millian population size can be greater than, equal to, or smaller than the laissez-faire population size.

Example 2

Let the parent's utility function be

$$u^1(c^1, n, u^2(c^2)) = nc^1 - n^2 + nu^2(c^2), \qquad (5A.8)$$

where

$$u^2(c^2) = a\log(1 + c^2), \qquad a > 0.$$

Substituting $c^1 = k - nc^2$ into (5A.8), we can find the LFA by maximizing

$$n(k - nc^2) - n^2 + an\log(1 + c^2) \qquad (5A.9)$$

with respect to n and c^2. The first-order conditions are

$$k + a\log(1 + c^{2L}) - 2n^L(1 + c^{2L}) = 0 \qquad (5A.10)$$

and

$$-n^L + \frac{a}{1 + c^{2L}} = 0, \qquad (5A.11)$$

from which it follows that

$$n^L(1 + c^{2L}) = a. \qquad (5A.12)$$

Hence (5A.10) becomes

$$k + \alpha\log(1 + c^{2L}) - 2a = 0,$$

which yields

$$\log(1 + c^{2L}) = 2 - k/a.^4 \qquad (5A.13)$$

Taking the logarithms of both sides of (5A.12) yields

$$\log n^L + \log(1 + c^{2L}) = \log a. \qquad (5A.14)$$

Substituting (5A.13) into (5A.14), we get

$$\log n^L = \log a + k/a - 2. \qquad (5A.15)$$

The BOA is achieved by maximizing

$$n(k - nc^2) - n^2 + 2an \log(1 + c^2) \qquad (5A.9')$$

with respect to n and c^2. Note that (5A.9') differs from (5A.9) by only one term: $2a$ replaces a. Hence the solutions for c^{2B} and n^B are obtained by substituting $2a$ for a in (5A.13) and (5A.15):

$$\log(1 + c^{2B}) = 2 - k/2a \qquad (5A.13')$$

and

$$\log n^b = \log(2a) + k/2a - 2. \qquad (5A.15')$$

Comparing (5A.13') with (5.A13), one can indeed see that $c^{2L} < c^{2B}$, namely, that the BOA grants children more consumption than does the LFA. Depending on the parameter values (k and a), however, it may be that $n^B < n^L$. To see this, note from (5A.15') and (5A.15) that $n^B < n^L$ if and only if $\log(2a) + k/2a - 2 < \log a + k/a - 2$. Thus $n^B < n^L$ if and only if $\log 4 < k/a$. Obviously, one can choose k and a in such a way that $\log 4 < k/a$, so that $n^B < n^L$. Thus the Benthamite population size is smaller than the laissez-faire population size.[5]

Appendix 5.2   Externalities and Public Goods: A Diagrammatic Exposition

The fundamental results of welfare economics are the Pareto efficiency of competitive equilibria and the sustainability of Pareto-efficient allocation through competitive markets. The validity of these results, however rests on the absence of externalities and the nonexistence of public goods.

Externalities

The absence of externalities means that an action taken by any one of the agents (consumers or firms) in the market directly affects only that agent's utility or profit and that of no one else. In other words, all the costs and benefits resulting from the actions of that agent are fully perceived and accrue to that agent. We say that these costs and benefits are fully internalized: self-interested individual decisions lead to an efficient outcome, that is, a laissez-faire competitive equilibrium is Pareto-efficient.

There are many important instances, however, where actions taken by one agent have effects that are external to that agent. The action of one agent may directly affect the utility or profit of some other agent (or agents). In such cases we say that externalities exist. Perhaps the most famous example of externalities is that of the fable of the bees (Meade 1952). The owner of an apple orchard naturally produces apples, but as a by-product, apple trees also yield apple blossoms. A neighboring farmer raises bees to produce honey; however, the neighbor's bees consume nectar from the apple blossoms. In this case, the apple blossoms are an unpriced input into the production of honey. The action of the orchard owner generates an external effect on another agent—the honey producer—via the production of apple blossoms. The apple grower in this case does not capture the full benefit of her activity because she sells only the apples but not the apple blossoms. Her actions, motivated by maximizing her own profit, overlook the benefit to the honey producer. (Of course the bees also pollinate the apple trees, which is an unpriced benefit to the apple grower, but for simplicity we ignore this effect.) In any case, the marginal private benefit from apple production (accruing to the orchard owner) falls short of the marginal social benefit, which is the sum of the marginal private benefit of the orchard owner and the marginal benefit of the honey producer. Thus the action, of the apple producer, while "correct" from her perspective, is "wrong" from society's standpoint. A market failure occurs: a competitive laissez-faire market fails to achieve an efficient output of apples. In the apple blossom/honeybee example, the external effect is beneficial and is therefore called a positive externality or an external economy. Where the external effect is harmful, it is called a negative externality or an external diseconomy, as in the case of a chemical firm that dumps its waste into a river, thus reducing the catch of a fisherman downstream.

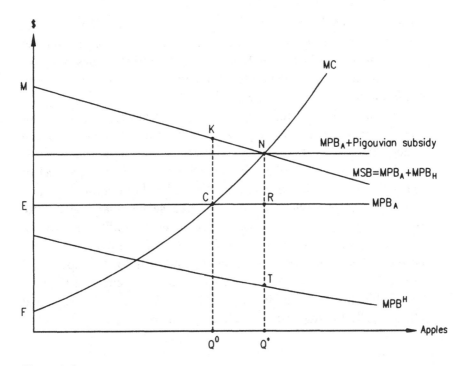

Figure 5.6
The apple blossom/honeybee example
Note: $NR = TQ^* =$ Pigouvian subsidy

Figure 5.6 shows why a market failure arises in the apple blossom/honeybee example. The curve MPB_A represents the marginal private benefit (revenue) accruing to the apple grower. Her marginal cost curve is the curve MC. The competitive decisions about how many apples to produce are made solely by the apple grower. Her private profit is maximized at Q^0, where her marginal private benefit is equal to her marginal cost (her profit is given by the area FEC). Q^0 is thus the competitive output of apples; however, apples also benefit honey production. The marginal value product of apples (via apple blossoms) in honey production is depicted by the curve, MPB_H. Thus the marginal social benefit of apples is given by the curve MSB, which is the vertical sum of MPB_A and MPB_H. The efficient output of apples is therefore Q^*, where MSB = MC and the total net benefit to society is FMN. (Compare this to FMKC, which is the net social benefit at the competitive equilibrium.) The cause of the market failure can be easily pinpointed: the apple producer does not take into account (and justifiably so from her standpoint) the benefit, MPB_H, accruing to the honey producer.

This discussion immediately suggests two kinds of remedies for the market failure. The apple grower can be induced to produce more if her MPB curve is raised by a subsidy. If the per-unit subsidy is equal to $NR = TQ^*$ (which is exactly the marginal value product of apples in honey production at the efficient level of output, Q^*), then the apple grower will produce Q^*, because her marginal private benefit curve will now be the curve labeled "MPB + Pigouvian Subsidy," and it intercepts her MC curve at Q^*. Such a subsidy is called a Pigouvian subsidy. Another remedy is for the apple and honey producers to merge. The marginal private benefit of the new firm will be just MSB and it will produce Q^*. In this case the external effect is fully internalized and no market failure arises.

Public Goods

Most goods are ordinary private goods in the sense that they can be parceled out among different individuals, or at least among different families. But there are many goods, such as basic research, general education level, national defense, television, or radio broadcasts, that "all enjoy in common in the sense that each individual's consumption of such a good leads to no subtraction from any other individual's consumption of the good" (Samuelson 1954). Such goods are called public goods.

From the point of view of the individual consumer, consumption of a public good entails utility in exactly the same way as consumption of an ordinary private good does. Therefore, as usual, one can derive a demand curve for a public good for each individual. This demand curve is also the marginal benefit curve. Consider two individuals, A and B, whose demand curves for a public good are, respectively, the curves $D_A = MPB_A$ and $D_B = MPB_B$ in figure 5.7. In this case, any output of the public good is consumed simultane-

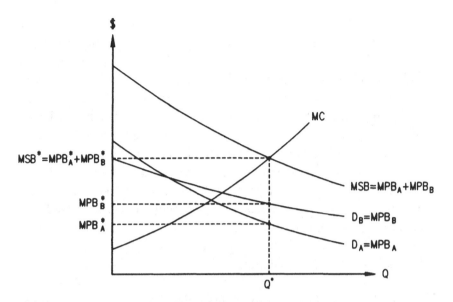

Figure 5.7
Marginal benefits and costs of public goods

ously by both A and B. Hence the marginal social benefit (MSB) at each level of output is the (vertical) sum of the marginal private benefit accruing to A (MPB_A) and the marginal private benefit accruing to B (MPB_B). If the marginal cost curve is plotted as the curve MC in figure 5.7, the efficient level of output of the public good can be seen to be Q^*, where the MSB $= \text{MPB}_A + \text{MPB}_B$ curve intersects the MC curve. This condition of Pareto efficiency is known as the Lindahl-Samuelson condition.

Can this output be reached in a competitive market? Generally, the answer is no. To induce a firm to produce Q^* it must be given the price $P^* \equiv \text{MSB}^*$. Individuals A and B will both purchase the quantity Q^*, if they pay the prices $P_A^* \equiv \text{MPB}_A^*$ and $P_B^* \equiv \text{MPB}_B^*$, respectively. That is, each individual must pay a price equal to that person's marginal private benefit (at the efficient level of output) and the firm must pocket the sum of all the individual prices. Such an equilibrium is called a Lindahl equilibrium. However, the problem of "free riding" makes the Lindahl equilibrium virtually impossible to achieve.

Usually once the public good is produced, exclusion of an individual from consuming it is prohibitively expensive. Realizing this, each individual attempts to free-ride and the firm will not be able to collect much revenue for its product; therefore, Lindahl equilibria are not viable. The government can of course provide public goods paid for by imposition of taxes, but whether it can provide efficient levels of public goods depends on its ability to measure the true individual valuations (the MPB curves) of the public goods.

The diagrammatic apparatus that were used in this appendix to derive Pigouvian corrective taxes/subsidies are very useful for analyzing other issues of market-based public policies. Indeed, we employed this apparatus in the text to derive the tax/subsidy policies that are needed to support the Millian optimal and the Benthamite optimal populations.

Appendix 5.3 Derivation of Formulae for Policies Needed to Support the Benthamite and Millian Optima

The Benthamite Optimal Allocation

The Benthamite optimal allocation (BOA) is obtained by maximizing

$$u^1[c^1, n, u^2(c^2)] + nu^2(c^2),$$

subject to the budget constraint

$$k - c^1 - nc^2 = 0.$$

Letting $\lambda \geq 0$ be the Lagrange multiplier, we may derive the following first-order conditions for an interior solution:

$$u_1^1 = \lambda, \tag{5A.16}$$

$$u_2^1 + u^2 = \lambda c^2, \tag{5A.17}$$

and

$$u_3^1 u_1^2 + nu_1^2 = \lambda n. \tag{5A.18}$$

Dividing equations 5A.17 and 5A.18 by equation (5A.16) yields

$$(u_2^1 + u^2)/u_1^1 = c^2, \tag{5A.19}$$

and

$$(u_3^1 u_1^2 + n u_1^2)/u_1^1 = n. \tag{5A.20}$$

Equation 5A.19 asserts that the social marginal rate of substitution of c^1 for n (the willingness of society to give up a parent's consumption for an additional child), which is $(u_2^1 + u^2)/u_1^1$, must be equated to the social "cost" of an additional child, which is equal to its consumption, c^2. Similarly, equation 5A.20 asserts that the social marginal rate of substitution of c^1 for c^2 must be equated to the social "cost" of a unit of the child's consumption, which is n, since each and every one of the n children consumes this unit.

In order to achieve the BOA allocation (via the market mechanism), it may be possible for the government to subsidize c^2 at the rate of α, to give child allowances (possibly negative) of β per child, and to balance its budget by a lump-sum tax (possibly negative) in the amount T. In this case, the parent's budget constraint becomes

$$c^1 + nc^2(1 - \alpha) = k + \beta n - T. \tag{5A.21}$$

Given this budget constraint, the parent maximizes

$$u^1[c^1, n, u^2(c^2)]$$

by choosing c^1, n, and c^2. Letting $\theta \geq 0$ be the Lagrange multiplier for this problem, we arrive at the following first-order conditions for an interior solution:

$$u_1^1 = \theta, \tag{5A.22}$$

$$u_2^1 = -\theta\beta + \theta c^2(1 - \alpha), \tag{5A.23}$$

and

$$u_3^1 u_1^2 = \theta n(1 - \alpha). \tag{5A.24}$$

Dividing equations 5A.23 and 5A.24 by equation 5A.22 yields

$$u_2^1/u_1^1 = c^2(1 - \alpha) - \beta, \tag{5A.25}$$

and

$$u_3^1 u_1^2 / u_1^1 = n(1 - \alpha). \tag{5A.26}$$

Equation 5A.25 states that the marginal rate of substitution of c^1 for n (i.e., a parent's willingness to give up her own consumption for an additional child) must be equated to the "price" of a child as perceived by the parent from the budget constraint (5A.21). The "price" consists of two components: the cost of providing the child with c^2 units of consumption, which is only $c^2(1 - \alpha)$ because of the subsidy α, and the tax on children, which is $-\beta$. Equation 5A.26 states that the marginal rate of substitution of c^1 for c^2 must be equated to the "price" of c^2, which is the number of children, times $(1 - \alpha)$.

If it is possible to achieve a BOA in this way, the optimal values of α and β can be found by comparing the first-order conditions for the BOA, namely, equations 5A.19 and 5A.20, with those of the individual parent's optimization problem, equations 5A.25 and 5A.26. First, compare equation 5A.20 with equation 5A.26 to conclude that

$$n(1 - \alpha) = n[1 - (u_1^2 / u_1^1)],$$

so that the optimal subsidy to children's consumption under the Benthamite criterion is

$$\alpha^B = u_1^2 [c^{1B}, n^B, u^2(c^{2B})] / u_1^1 [c^{1B}, n^B, u^2(c^{2B})]. \tag{5A.27}$$

Next, compare equation (5A.19) with equation (5A.25) to conclude that

$$c^2 (u^2 / u_1^1) = c^2 (1 - \alpha) - \beta,$$

so that the optimal child allowance under the Benthamite criterion is

$$\beta^B = \{u^2(c^{2B}) / u_1^1 [c^{1B}, n^B, u^2(c^{2B})]\} - \alpha^B c^{2B}. \tag{5A.28}$$

The interpretation of the formulae for α and β is straightforward. Because the term $nu^2(c^2)$ of the Benthamite criterion, equation 5.13, is ignored by the parent's objective, children's consumption (c^2) generates a difference between private and social evaluations; hence it ought to be subsidized in order to achieve the BOA. The optimal size of this subsidy has to be determined according to what the parent ignores (at the margin). When the parent considers increasing c^2, she ignores the social benefit nu_1^2 at the margin. This benefit is measured in utility units. Its equivalent in terms of the numéraire consumption good is nu_1^2/u_1^1. From the parent's budget constraint, equation 5A.21, it can be seen that if c^2 is subsidized at the rate α, then each unit of c^2 receives a subsidy of $n\alpha$. Thus the subsidy ought to be set so that $n\alpha = nu_1^2/u_1^1$, which explains the value of the optimal α in equation 5A.27.

For the same reason, n ought to be subsidized by u^2/u_1^1, so that the price of n for the parent will be $c^2 - (u^2/u_1^1)$. By the parent's budget constraint, equation 5A.21, the price of n is $c^2(1 - \alpha) - \beta$. It therefore follows that $c^2 - (u^2/u_1^1)$ must equal $c^2(1 - \alpha) - \beta$ and that $\beta^B = (u^2/u_1^1) - \alpha^B c^2$, as in equation 5A.28.

Note that $\alpha^B > 0$. To find the sign of β^B, observe that

$$\beta^B = (u^2/u_1^1) - \alpha^B c^2 = (u^2 - c^2 u_1^2)/u_1^1,$$

by substituting equation 5A.27 into equation 5A.28. Since u^2 is concave, it follows that

$$u^2(c^2) - u^2(0) \geq u_1^2(c^2)(c^2 - 0).$$

Since u^2 is assumed to be nonnegative, it follows that

$$u^2(c^2) \geq c^2 u_1^2(c^2),$$

so that $\beta^B > 0$. Thus the optimal child allowance under the Benthamite criterion must be positive.

Fixed α and β may not lead to the BOA because the parent's optimization problem is not convex; therefore, the second-order conditions may not hold. If they do not hold with fixed α and β, it is possible to achieve a BOA with nonlinear taxes, that is, with instruments α and β, which are functions of c^1, c^2, and n. In other words, the second-order conditions can always be satisfied by functions $\alpha(\cdot)$ and $\beta(\cdot)$. The values of $\alpha(\cdot)$ and $\beta(\cdot)$ at the optimum will be exactly α^B and β^B as given in equations (5A.27) and (5A.28), that is,

$$\alpha^B = \alpha(c^{1B}, n^B, c^{2B}),$$

and

$$\beta^B = \beta(c^{1B}, n^B, c^{2B}).$$

The Millian Optimal Allocation

We now turn to the Millian optimal allocation (MOA). This allocation is obtained by maximizing

$$\frac{u^1(c^1, n, u^2(c^2)) + nu^2(c^2)}{1 + n},$$

subject to the resource constraint

$$k - c^1 - nc^2 \leq 0$$

(see equations 5.14 and 5.12 above).

Letting $\lambda \geq 0$ be the Lagrange multiplier for this optimization problem, one derives the following first-order conditions for an interior solution:

$$\frac{u_1^1}{1 + n} = \lambda, \tag{5A.29}$$

$$\frac{(u_2^1 + u^2)(1 + n) - u^1 - nu^2}{(1 + n)^2} = \lambda c^2, \tag{5A.30}$$

and

$$\frac{u_3^1 u_1^2 + nu_1^2}{1 + n} = \lambda n. \tag{5A.31}$$

Dividing (5A.30) and (5A.31) by (5A.29), we obtain

$$\frac{u_2^1 + u^2}{u_1^1} - \frac{u^1 + nu^2}{(1 + n)u_1^1} = c^2, \tag{5A.32}$$

$$\frac{u_3^1 u_1^2}{u_1^1} + n\frac{u_1^2}{u_1^1} = n. \tag{5A.33}$$

These two equations, like equations 5A.19 and 5A.20, equate social marginal rates of substitution to social marginal costs. Following the procedure of the preceding subsection, we compare (5A.32) and (5A.33), respectively, with the first-order conditions, (5A.25) and (5A.26), for the parent's optimization problem in order to find the optimal α and β for the Millian criterion. First, compare (5A.33) with (5A.26) to conclude that

$$\alpha^M = \frac{u_1^2(c^{2M})}{u_1^1(c^{1M}, n^M, u^2(c^{2M}))}. \tag{5A.34}$$

Next, compare (5A.32) with (5A.25) to conclude that

$$c^2(1 - \alpha) - \beta = c^2 + \frac{u^1 + nu^2}{(1 + n)u_1^1} - \frac{u^2}{u_1^1}.$$

Hence

$$\beta^M = \frac{u^2(c^{2M})}{u_1^1(c^{1M}, n^M, u^2(c^{2M}))} - \alpha^M c^{2M}$$

$$- \frac{u^1(c^{1M}, n^M, u^2(c^{2M})) + n^M u^2(c^{2M})}{(1 + n^M)u^1(c^{1M}, n^M\, u^2(c^{2M}))}. \tag{5A.35}$$

These formulae for the optimal α and β under the Millian criterion could be given a similar interpretation of Pigouvian taxes or subsidies as we did for the Benthamite criterion (equations 5A.27 and 5A.28).[6] The subsidy to child consumption, namely α^M, is positive, as in the Benthamite case, but the sign of the optimal child allowance (β^M) is ambiguous in this case. The reason for this ambiguity can be seen by comparing the Millian social welfare, which is $(u^1 + nu^2)/(1 + n)$, with the parent's utility, which is just u^1. On the one hand, the Millian function adds nu^2 to the parent's function, and in this way n generates a positive externality; on the other hand, $(u^1 + nu^2)$ is also divided by $(1 + n)$, and in this way n generates a negative externality. Thus one cannot determine a priori whether n should be taxed or subsidized.

III

Externalities and Corrective Population Policies

6

Malthus's Hypothesis

Thomas Malthus (1798), in his well-cited, *Essay on the Principle of Population and a Summary View of the Principle of Population*, hypothesized that due to the phenomenon diminishing marginal productivity of labor on a fixed amount of land, uncontrolled fertility would cause population to increase to equilibrium at a subsistence level. In Malthus's words, "population, when unchecked, increases in a geometrical ratio ... subsistence increases only in an arithmetic ratio." Traditionally, this hypothesis has been refuted on the grounds that capital accumulation and productivity growth more than offset the law of diminishing returns. Becker (1960) pointed out that parents' altruism or endogenous fertility (see chapter 3) can also refute the Malthusian subsistence hypothesis even when capital formation and productivity growth are stagnant. Parents who substitute quality for quantity will opt for a family size that falls short of bringing the population size to a subsistence consumption level.[1] Nevertheless, there still remains the question whether smaller than the subsistence population size may not be excessive.

Consider this optimality issue associated with the equilibrium size of population. A fixed resource, such as land, that must be combined with labor to produce goods for consumption, leads Malthusian diminishing returns to a larger population size. This suggests a potential source of external diseconomies and market failure in relation to population size: the parent who has more children reduces the marginal product of *all* children, not only her own children. Thus it seems that unfettered Malthusian population growth is excessive.

Over the years, the Malthusian external diseconomy of larger population size has provided the focus of discussion of the inefficiency associated with population size and the grounds for a corrective population policy. It is remarkable, however, that this source of market failure is completely nullified when parents are altruistic toward their children; in that case, competition leads to Pareto efficiency from the standpoint of the present generation, as we shall see in this chapter.

Consider, for the sake of simplicity, a two-period model with one parent in the first period. It is assumed that the supply of land is fixed and that the supply of labor per capita is fixed as well (i.e., there are no labor-leisure decisions). Land is used in each period, together with labor, to produce a single good for private consumption in each period. We denote by c^1 the consumption by the parent in the first period. We denote by c_p^2 and c_k^2 the consumption of the parent and of each child, respectively, in the second period. Due to the Malthusian assumption that the amount of land is fixed, there is a diminishing marginal product of labor. Assuming that the labor endowment is equal to one unit, output is $f(1)$ in the first period, where f is a production function that exhibits diminishing marginal products of labor, that is, $f' > 0$ and $f'' < 0$. The parent in the first period bears n children; therefore, output is $f(n)$ in the second period.

The consumption possibilities of this economy can be described by the following two resource constraints:

$$c^1 + S = f(1) \tag{6.1}$$

and

$$c_p^1 + nc_k^2 = S + f(n), \tag{6.2}$$

where S is the quantity of consumption transferred from the first period to the second period. Equation 6.1 states that total output in period 1, $f(1)$, is used for private econsumption of the parent, c^1, and savings, S. Equation 6.2 states that output in the second period and savings from the first period are used for the parent's and children's consumption. Implicitly, it is assumed that the private good can be stored from the first to the second period without costs or returns. These two constraints are combined to yield a single constraint:

$$c^1 + c_p^2 + nc_k^2 = f(1) + f(n), \tag{6.3}$$

which specifies the overall resource constraint faced by society.

The parent's utility depends on her own consumption (c^1 and c_p^2), the consumption of each one of her children (c_k^2), and the number of her children (n):

$$u = u(c^1, c_p^2, c_k^2, n). \tag{6.4}$$

The parent's altruism is formalized above by letting c_k^2 and n be arguments in the parent's utility function. The parent in period 1 chooses c^1, c_p^2, c_k^2, and n so as to maximize her utility (6.4), subject to the budget constraint

$$c^1 + c_p^2 + nc_k^2 = w^1 + nw^2 + \pi^1 + \pi^2, \tag{6.5}$$

where w^i is the equilibrium wage rate and π^i is the equilibrium land rent (or pure profits) that accrues to the owners of the land in period $i = 1, 2$. The altruistic parent who cares about her children makes plans for their consumption, taking into account their earnings (nw^2) and the land rent (π^2) accruing in the second period.

To examine whether the competitive equilibrium is efficient, consider figure 6.1. In period 1, society consists of the single parent then living. To focus attention on the issue at hand, it is assumed that the objective of society coincides with the objective of this altruistic parent, which is to maximize her utility. Hence the marginal social benefit (MSB) from the number of children coincides with the private one (MPB) and they are both equal to u_n. Next consider the marginal social cost of children. As can be seen from the overall resource constraint of society, equation 6.3, the marginal cost of n is $c_k^2 - f'(n)$, where f' is the marginal product of labor. The marginal child consumes c_k^2 but also produces a marginal product of $f'(n)$. Hence society's net marginal cost is indeed $c_k^2 - f'(n)$. Because the marginal product is diminishing, the curve MSC $= c_k^2 - f'(n)$ is upward sloping.

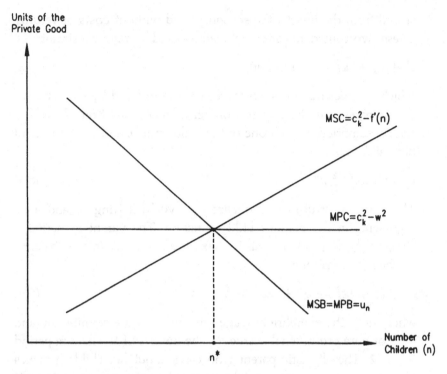

Units of the
Private Good

MSC=$c_k^2-f'(n)$

MPC=$c_k^2-w^2$

MSB=MPB=u_n

Number of
Children (n)

n^*

Figure 6.1
Marginal private and social costs of children

Now consider the marginal private cost of n. It can be seen from the parent's budget constraint, equation 6.5, that the marginal child consumes c_k^2, but also earns a wage of w^2. Hence the marginal private cost of children to the parent is MPC $= c_k^2 - w^2$. Since the parent and the children are assumed to behave as perfect competitors, that is, as price takers and wage takers, they consider w^2 to be constant. Hence the MPC curve is horizontal.

Thus the unfettered equilibrium number of children is n^*, where MPC $=$ MPB. The key point to observe here is that profit maximization requires that labor (children) be employed up to the point where the marginal product is equal to the wage. Since w^2 is the equilibrium wage, therefore $f'(n^*) = w^2$. Hence MSC equals MPC at the equilibrium number of children, n^*. Therefore, MSC is equal to MSB at n^*, so that n^* is also the efficient number of children. Denote by c_k^{2*} the optimal level of consumption of each child.

Were the parent not altruistic toward her children (as implicitly assumed by Malthus), she would care only about her own consumption (c^1 and c_p^2). She would let her children consume just some predetermined subsistence level, $\bar{c}_k^2$; she would obviously have children up to the point where her marginal net benefit from each additional child was brought down to zero: $w^2 - \bar{c}_k^2 = 0$. Since $f'(n) = w^2$, it follows that the unfettered Malthusian number of children (n^{**}) is determined by $f'(n^{**}) = \bar{c}_k^2$. Recall that the efficient number of children in the altruistic case is given by $f'(n^*) - c_k^{2*} = u_n > 0$. Since $\bar{c}_k^2$ (the subsistence consumption level) is obviously lower than c_k^{2*} (the efficient level of consumption of each child in the altruistic case), it follows that $f'(n^{**}) < f'(n^*)$. From the diminishing productivity of labor we conclude that $n^{**} > n^*$. Thus the Malthusian unaltruistic setup leads to overpopulation.[2]

We have shown that the Malthusian fixed land does not cause market failure from the standpoint of the present generation when parents are altruistic. On the other hand, endogenous fertility may create a new difficulty: the competitive equilibrium may fail to exist. The ability to control fertility may lead a mother who at first has a negligibly small effect on prices to believe she can increase her utility ad infinitum by increasing her fertility rate without bound. But if she adopts such a course of action, she will no longer have negligibly small effects; her behavior will start to influence prices, thus breaking down perfect competition. This point can be clearly seen if the parent's budget constraint, equation 6.5 is rewritten as

$$c^1 + c_p^2 = w^1 + n(w^2 - c_k^2) + \pi^1 + \pi^2.$$

Recall that the parent is unable to affect prices (w^2 is a constant parameter). Hence she must believe that by setting (if possible) c_k^2 below w^2, thereby making the net return from children, $w^2 - c_k^2$, positive, she can increase n, c^1, c_p^2, and consequently u to infinity. But for the economy as a whole, w^2 is not constant; it is equal to the marginal product of labor, $f'(n)$, which is diminishing. Therefore, no constant w^2 can be consistent with an arbitrarily large n. A competitive equilibrium may fail to exist.

Nevertheless, the possibility of the nonexistence of an equilibrium that arises in the present simplifying formulation seems not to be plausible in practice. For instance, the competitive equilibrium can be restored by assuming there is some cost of raising children (where the marginal cost is positive and increasing). In a reduced form model this cost could be built into the utility function, so that beyond a certain level, n stops being a "good" and starts being a "bad," implying that there will then be a disutility from children.

7

Bequests as a Public Good within Marriage

The traditional approach posits that the only way in which a bequest functions is to increase children's endowments at the expense of their own parents; however, when marriage is considered, the possibility arises that the consumption of a couple can also be increased by bequests from one spouse's parents. Because each family derives utility from the bequests of other families through marriages, Pareto efficiency can only be attained if the parents are free to bargain with one another about what each child's family will leave to its children.[1] Such bargaining was common in biblical times (and is still practiced in some less-developed countries), when parents negotiated *neduniahs* (doweries) and *mohars* (bride prices) with one another and when parents had certain property rights in their children. In modern societies, where much of parents' bequests is in the form of human capital (which belongs exclusively to the child) and where marriages are no longer "arranged," those kinds of property rights are difficult or impossible to enforce. If children are free to choose and marry for "love," that is, on the basis of considerations unrelated to bequests and if bequests are determined prior to their choices, the Pareto efficiency of laissez-faire marriages may break down. Because bequests benefit both partners in a marriage (as a public good within a marriage), parents may fail to include benefits to other children's parents in deciding on the amount of bequests to make to each of their own children. Thus there are external economies generated by bequests within a marriage, and there exists a scope for a corrective policy.

7.1   A Stylized Model

For the sake of simplicity, assume that there are only two families in the current generation and only two generations (periods), so that

c_i =   the consumption of family i in the first period,

n_i =   the the number of children family i,

b_i =   the bequest per child of family i,

k_i =   the resources available to family i for consumption and
             bequest, and

i =   1, 2.

The total bequest of two children who marry one another will be the sum of the bequests to each child, that is, $(b_1 + b_2)$. This sum is also assumed to be the consumption of the second generation. For the sake of simplicity, assume that the two families bring the same number of children into the world, so that the number of children available to marry each other will be identical.

Consider first the parent of family 1 in the first period. The parent derives utility from her own consumption (c_1), the number of her children (n_1), and the consumption $(b_1 + b_2)$ of the newly formed family of each child in the second period:

$$u^1 = u^1(c_1, n_1, b_1 + b_2). \tag{7.1}$$

Observe that b_2 is bequeathed by the parent of family 2, and is beyond the control of the parent of family 1, who therefore treats b_2 as a constant, choosing only c_1, n_1, and b_1 so as to maximize equation 7.1, subject to the budget constraint

$$c_1 + b_1 n_1 = k_1. \tag{7.2}$$

Similarly, the parent of family 2 chooses c_2, n_2 and b_2 (treating b_1 as an exogenous parameter), so as to maximize her utility:

$$u^2 = u^2(c_2, n_2, b_1 + b_2), \tag{7.3}$$

subject to her budget constraint

$$c_2 + b_2 n_2 = k_2. \tag{7.4}$$

The competitive equilibrium obtained by the above maximizations by the two families is denoted by

$$\bar{c}_1, \bar{c}_2, \bar{n}_1 = \bar{n}_2 \equiv \bar{n}, \bar{b}_1, \bar{b}_2. \tag{7.5}$$

Now we examine whether this allocation is Pareto-efficient. Consider figure 7.1. The per child bequest made by the parent of family 1 (b_1) is plotted on the horizontal axis and the units of the all-purpose good are plotted on the vertical axis. From the budget

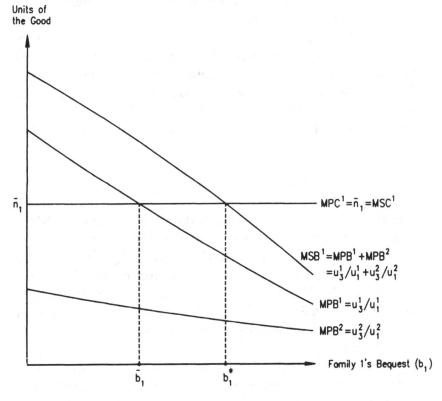

Figure 7.1
Marginal private and social benefits and costs of a bequest

constraint of parent 1, equation 7.2, it can be seen that the marginal private cost of b_1, denoted by MPC^1, is equal to $\bar{n}_1$ because increasing the bequest made to each child by one unit increases the total cost by the equilibrium number of children, $\bar{n}_1$. Increasing b_1 by one unit increases utility by the marginal utility of the children's consumption, u_3^1. To express this marginal utility in units of the all-purpose good, divide it by the marginal utility of the parent's consumption, u_1^1. Hence the marginal private benefit to the parent of family 1, denoted by MPB^1, is equal to u_3^1/u_1^1. Therefore, the unconstrained equilibrium amount of b_1 is $\bar{b}_1$, where $MPC^1 = MPB^1$.

Now we look at the marginal social cost and benefit curves in the same diagram. The marginal cost of a bequest made by the parent of family 1 to society (MSC^1) is the same as to the parent, that is, $MSC^1 = MPC^1 = \bar{n}_1$. However, b_1 also benefits the parent of family 2 because it increases consumption by her children who marry the children of the parent of family 1. Hence the marginal private benefit of b_1 to the parent of family 2, denoted by MPB^2, is equal to u_3^2/u_1^2. The marginal social benefit of b_1, denoted by MSB^1, is the sum of MPB^1 and MPB^2, that is, $MSB^1 = MPB^1 + MPB^2 = u_3^1/u_1^1 + u_3^2/u_1^2$. Hence the efficient level of b_1 will be b_1^* and not $\bar{b}_1$; a market failure therefore exists.

7.2 Pigouvian Remedy

The above discussion also suggests the Pigouvian remedy: MPC^1 should be lowered by a proper subsidy to bequests so that it will intersect MPB^1 at the efficient level of bequest, b_1^*. The rate of the subsidy (s^*) should be exactly equal to the proportion of the external effect in the MSB^1, $u_3^2/u_1^2(u_3^1/u_1^1 + u_3^2/u_1^2)$, at the efficient level of bequest, b_1^*. A similar subsidy should be applied to b_2 to induce the parent of family 2 to bequeath an efficient amount of b_2.

In the standard case of externalities discussed in chapter 5, the Pigouvian subsidy was all that was needed; here things are a bit different. The budget constraints given by equation 7.2 or 7.4 show that b is the price of n because each additional child costs his or her parent the amount b bequeathed to that child. (Similarly, n is also the price of b). Hence subsidizing b distorts the parent's decision about the number of children to have because it lowers their private cost (but not the social cost). For instance, the budget constraint facing the parent of family 1 now becomes

$$c_1 + b_1(1 - s)n_1 = k_1. \tag{7.6}$$

To correct this distortion, a direct tax must be put on children so that the marginal private cost of a child will equal the marginal social cost. To find the appropriate amount of the tax, consider figure 7.2, where the optimization of the number of children for the parent of family 1 is considered. The marginal private benefit of n_1 is the marginal utility of n_1, that is, u_2^1. Expressed in terms of units of the

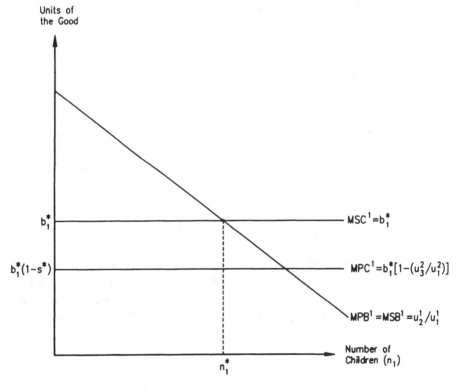

Figure 7.2
The marginal private benefits versus the marginal private and social costs of a child

all-purpose good, it is $\text{MPB}^1 = u_2^1/u_1^1$. This is also the marginal social benefit of n_1, MSB^1, since the number of children in family 1 does not affect the welfare of the other family. The marginal cost of n_1 to the parent of family 1 is the cost of the bequest to her children, which is $\text{MPC}^1 = b_1^*(1 - s^*)$. However, the marginal cost of n_1 to society is just b_1^*, that is, $\text{MSC}^1 = b_1^*$. Therefore, to induce the parent of family 1 to bear the efficient number of children, n_1^*, a tax of $b_1^* s^*$ must be put on each child.

In many parts of the world parents still bargain with each other about what they will give their children. The economics of dowry and bride price, which has been considered in discussions of polygamy, is related to this discussion.[2]

7.3   Assortative Mating

Another mechanism by which the externality effect is mitigated is through assortative mating. This was explored by Zhang (1994). Suppose that mating is likely to occur between children of families of similar social status as may be, for instance, indicated by income, education, etc. Thus a child receiving a large bequest is likely to marry a child who also receives a large bequest. The parent then realizes that if she makes a large bequest to her child, the child will receive a large bequest from the parent of her mate. Thus the utility function (7.1) of parent 1 now changes to

$$u^1 = u^1[c_1, n_1, b_1 + b_2(b_1)], \tag{7.1'}$$

where $b_2(b_1)$ is the function that describes the bequest of the parent of the mate of the child of parent 1. Turning to figure 7.1, the curve MPB^1 (the marginal private benefit of b_1 to parent 1) is now equal to $(u_3^1/u_1^1)(1 + b_2')$. With perfect mating (i.e., marriages between indentical-bequest families), $b_2' = 1$. Then MPB^1 coincides with MSB^1 (the marginal social benefit of b_1) in the symmetric equilibrium case, and Pareto efficiency obtains.

8

Bequests and Child Education: Full Information

Parents can transfer resources to their children in two major ways: direct transfers of consumption (bequests) and indirect transfers via investment in human capital (education) of their children, which enlarges the future consumption possibility sets of the children. The most efficient method of transfer may depend on the specific characteristics of a particular child, so that a parent may wish to use different methods for different children.

When children have different abilities, investments in their human capital are not equally productive. If parents cannot enforce transfers among their children, an egalitarian attitude may lead to inefficient allocation of education and bequests. For example, the parents may be led to invest too much in the human capital of low-ability children so that they will be equal (in their utility) to their more able siblings. Thus a source of potential market failure arises from the inability of parents to control the actions of their offspring after a certain point; in particular, parents cannot enforce transfers among siblings.

Although in some cases it may be more efficient to make transfers only via investment in human capital to some of the (more able) children and force them later in life to make cash transfers to the other siblings, this mode of transfer to children is impossible because the parents cannot enforce the required transfers. This poses a difficulty that cannot be eliminated by appeal to Becker's (1974) "rotten-kid theorem," which states that if the head of a household "cares sufficiently about all other members to transfer general resources to them, then distribution of income among members of the household would not affect the consumption of any member, as long as the head continues to contribute to all" (p. 1076). The difficulty is that the more able children may not receive any cash transfer from the altruistic parents.[1] This difficulty can neither be resolved by appeal to vaguely defined social norms. Becker and Tomes (1976) note the difficulty, but suggest in passing that "social and family 'pressures' can induce ... children to conform to the terms of implicit contracts with their parents." Such norms might be effective in some circumstances in some societies, but they have certainly not been generally effective even in ancient societies (as the biblical episode of Cain and Abel attests), let alone in modern societies.

When children differ in their abilities represents the most important case in which equal transfers to siblings are not efficient, even for parents conscious of equity among their children. It might be most efficient to invest only in the human capital of children with greater abilities if parents could guarantee that these children would later transfer part of the return to this investment to their less able siblings. If, however, the parents cannot enforce transfers among siblings, then they may not be able to take advantage of high rates of return to investment in the human capital of their more able children. In this case, transfers in the form of investment in human capital from parents to children will be too low relative to bequests; moreover, the investment in human capital will be inefficiently allocated among the children in the sense that the rates of return will not be the same for all children.

This chapter analyzes this potential market failure and puts forward a corrective policy.

8.1   The Model

Assume for the sake of simplicity that there are only two periods, two generations, and a single all-purpose composite good. The first generation consists of identical individuals (parents) who live for one period, but the second generation is not homogeneous: proportion p of children of each parent have high ability (indexed by A), and proportion $1 - p$ have low ability (indexed by B). Parents invest e^A and e^B units of the composite good in the education (human capital) of each one of the high ability and low ability children, respectively, and bequeath b^A and B^B units of the composite good to each child of high ability and each child of low ability, respectively.

The parent is endowed with k units of the composite good. Each child supplies one unit of adult labor in the second period. Investing e^i in the education of a child of ability level i augments the child's labor supply, as measured in efficiency units, to $g_i(e^i)$, $i = A, B$. The child then earns $wg_i(e^i)$, where w is the wage rate per efficiency unit. The difference between the two types of ability is reflected in the functions g_A and g_B. It is assumed that $g_A(e) > g_B(e)$ for all e, so that the able child is more productive than the less able. Furthermore, the marginal investment in the able child is also assumed to be more productive: $g'_A(e) > g'_B(e)$ for all e. We also assume that there are diminishing returns to investing in each child, i.e., $g''_i < 0$, $i = A, B$.

When the parent bequeaths b units of the composite good, we assume the bequest is invested (in physical capital) and yields bR units to the child as an adult in the second period, where $R \geq 1$ is the interest factor. For the sake of simplicity, w and R are assumed fixed.

We assume that parents treat their children's welfare symmetrically, irrespective of the child's ability, and plan their bequests to each child and investment in that child's education in such a way that each child will be able to consume the same amount, c^2, in the second period. As before, the parent's utility function depends on c^1, c^2, and n:

$$u(c^1, c^2, n). \tag{8.1}$$

The parent chooses c^1, c^2, and n so as to maximize (8.1), subject to the following budget constraints:

$$k = c^1 + pn(e^A + b^A) + (1 - p)n(e^B + b^B), \tag{8.2}$$

$$c^2 = wg_A(e^A) + Rb^A, \tag{8.3}$$

and

$$c^2 = wg_B(e^B) + Rb^B. \tag{8.4}$$

Constraint 8.2 is the budget constraint of the parent: consumption plus investment in the human capital of the children and the bequests to them cannot exceed the parent's endowment. Constraints 8.3 and 8.4 are the budget constraints facing each one of the more able and less able children, respectively, in the second period.

We assume a closed economy in which the total amount of bequests cannot be negative, that is,

$$pnb^A + (1 - p)nb^B \geq 0. \tag{8.5}$$

Such a constraint is natural because bequests form the economy's capital stock, and in a closed economy resources cannot be transferred backward from future to present generations. We further assume that no parent can enforce transfers from her offspring to herself. Formally:

$$b^A \geq 0, b^B \geq 0. \tag{8.6}$$

Constraint 8.5 will be binding whenever there is higher yield to investment in human capital than in physical capital. In this case, in order to equate the marginal yields on all forms of investment (i.e., $wg'_A(e^A) = wg'_B(e^B) = R$), parents may have to direct all investment to human capital and may even wish to transfer physical resources backward by borrowing (i.e., by making $pnb^A + (1 - p)nb^B$ negative), which we have ruled out. Therefore, relaxing constraint 8.5 will be welfare-improving in this case; however, (8.5) is a technological constraint that is imposed on the economy and neither individuals nor government can do anything about it. We assume henceforth that (8.5) is not binding. Chapter 10 analyzes the case where a constraint of this type is binding.

The situation is rather different with respect to constraint (8.6), which is essentially institutional. It stems from the inability of parents to enforce transfers among siblings. Note that constraints 8.3 and 8.4 disallow *direct* transfers among siblings: each child must consume exactly what the parents transfer to that child in the form of human capital or bequest. But (8.3) and (8.4) still leave open the possibility that parents make *indirect* transfers among their children.

For example, instead of asking child A to make a direct transfer of one dollar to child B, the parent can simply reduce the bequest to A (b^A) by one dollar and increase the bequest to B (b^B) by one dollar. These changes in the bequests (i.e., the *indirect* transfers among siblings) are possible as long as (8.6) is not binding. But if (8.6) is binding, as is the case when b^A is already zero, the parent cannot further reduce b^A and cannot therefore achieve a transfer among her children. Thus the constraint of no transfer among siblings is effective only when (8.6) is binding.

When constraint 8.6 is not binding, maximization of the utility function (8.6) subject to the budget constraints 8.2–8.4 implies that $wg'_A(e^A) = R = wg'_B(e^B)$. In this case both the *total* transfer of each child (i.e., $e^i + b^i$) and its *division* between education (e^i) and physical bequest (b^i) are efficiently determined. This outcome is achieved by the parent's investing in the child's human capital up to the point at which the marginal yield is equal to the interest factor (i.e., $wg'_i(e^i) = R$); the bs are then adjusted to maintain the egalitarian constraint $wg_A(e^A) + b^A = wg_B(e^B) + b^B$ (which is essentially required by constraints 8.3 and 8.4) and to achieve the total desired level of transfer ($e^i + b^i$) to each child. This case might be fairly common, but our main purpose is to analyze the case in which constraint 8.6 is binding; here the first-order condition $wg'_i(e^i) = R$ must be replaced by $wg'_i(e^i) \geq R$. As we show below, there is an aggregate misallocation between education and bequests: in particular, the parent is forced to invest too little in the human capital of her more able children.

We henceforth assume that (8.6) is binding, but because (8.5) is not binding, it cannot be the case that both inequalities of (8.6) are binding. Given our assumption about the relationship between g_A and g_B, we show that it is the second inequality that is not binding. Suppose to the contrary that $b^B = 0$. Hence $wg'_B(e_B) \geq R$. Because the first inequality is not binding in this case, it follows that $wg'_A(e^A) = R$. Since $g'_A \geq g'_B$ and both are diminishing (see figure 8.1), it follows that $e^B < e^A$ and hence that $g_B(e^B) < g_A(e^A)$. But since $wg_A(e^A) + b^AR = wg_B(e^B)$, it follows that $b^A < 0$, which is a contradiction. Therefore, $b^A = 0$ and $b^B > 0$.

Output

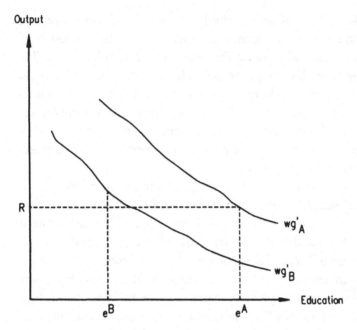

Figure 8.1
Return on investment in human capital in children of different abilities

This result means the rate of return on investment in the human capital of more able children is higher than that on investment in physical capital; given the amount of resources she is transferring, the parent would like to borrow from her able children (i.e., leave them negative bequests) in order to invest more in their human capital, but she cannot (see figure 8.2). If transfers among siblings were possible, constraint 8.6 would be effectively eliminated, thus permitting parents to equate rates of return.

In summary, the two ways in which parents might *collectively* enforce transfers among children by government action are only feasible if it is possible to discriminate among children by ability or to enforce obligations imposed upon children by parents. One method is by a system of lump-sum intragenerational transfers based on children's ability, but because individual ability is observable only by parents, such a system for achieving the first-best solution is infeasi-

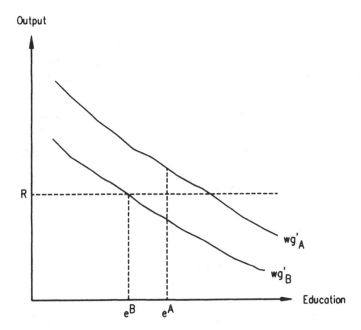

Figure 8.2
Returns to human capital for more able and less able children

ble. The other method is by a system of student loans that would enable parents to take out loans to finance the education of their more able children, while obligating those children to repay the loans in the next period. Such a system of loans achieves a first-best solution, but it rests on the ability of parents to obligate their children to repay loans the parents took on their behalf. In the next section we therefore consider only second-best solutions, namely, those which alleviate rather than eliminate constraint 8.6.

8.2   A Second-Best Corrective Policy

Among the second-best policy instruments that the government can use, we consider three: (1) a linear tax on the earned income of grown-up children in the second period with a marginal rate t and a demogrant T; (2) an inheritance tax at the rate τ, imposed on physical bequests only; and (3) an interest income tax at the rate θ. Other familiar policies are considered in the next section and shown to be either redundant or detrimental. It should be emphasized that taxes (head taxes or others) that discriminate on the basis of ability are not implementable and are thus excluded here. This is really the crux of the problem at hand. If such discriminatory taxes were allowed, then we could essentially eliminate constraint 8.6 and achieve a first-best allocation (continuing to assume that constraint 8.5 is not binding).

Given these policy instruments, constraints 8.2–8.4 facing the parent become

$$k = c^1 + pn(e^A + b^A) + (1 - p)n(e^B + b^B), \tag{8.2'}$$

$$c^2 = (1 - t)wg_A(e^A) + T + (1 - \theta')R(1 - \tau)b^A, \tag{8.3'}$$

and

$$c^2 = (1 - t)wg_B(e^B) + T + (1 - \theta')R(1 - \tau)b^B, \tag{8.4'}$$

where θ' is the tax rate on the interest factor (R), which is related to the tax rate (θ) on the interest rate $(R - 1)$ by $(1 - \theta')R = 1 + (1 - \theta)(R - 1)$ or $\theta' = \theta(R - 1)/R$. It is clear from (8.3') and (8.4') that either θ' or τ is redundant; therefore, we henceforth set $\theta' = \theta = 0$.

The parent maximizes $u(c^1, c^2, n)$, subject to the budget constraints 8.2'–8.4', and the nonnegativity constraint $b^A \geq 0$. The Lagrangian expression is

$$L = u(c^1, c^2, n) + \lambda_1[k - c^1 - pn(e^A + b^A) - (1 - p)n(e^B + b^B)]$$

$$+ \lambda_2[(1 - t)wg_A(e^A) + T + R(1 - \tau)b^A - c^2]$$

$$+ \lambda_3[(1 - t)wg_B(e^B) + T + R(1 - \tau)b^B - c^2] + \lambda_4 b^A, \tag{8.7}$$

where $\lambda_1 \geq 0$, $\lambda_2 \geq 0$, $\lambda_3 \geq 0$, and $\lambda_4 \geq 0$ are the Lagrange multipliers associated with (8.2'), (8.3'), (8.4'), and (8.6) respectively. The first-order conditions for c^1, c^2, b^A, b^B, e^A, e^B, and n, respectively, are given below:

$$u_1 - \lambda_1 = 0, \tag{8.8}$$

$$u_2 - \lambda_2 - \lambda_3 = 0, \tag{8.9}$$

$$-\lambda_1 pn + \lambda_2(1 - \tau)R + \lambda_4 = 0, \tag{8.10}$$

$$-\lambda_1(1 - p)n + \lambda_3(1 - \tau)R = 0, \tag{8.11}$$

$$-\lambda_1 pn + \lambda_2(1 - t)wg'_A = 0, \tag{8.12}$$

$$-\lambda_1(1 - p)n + \lambda_3(1 - t)wg'_B = 0, \tag{8.13}$$

and

$$u_3 - \lambda_1[p(e^A + b^A) + (1 - p)(e^B + b^B)] = 0. \tag{8.14}$$

The solution to this maximization problem yields c^1, c^2, n, b^B, e^A, and e^B as functions $\bar{c}^1(\mu)$, $\bar{c}^2(\mu)$, $\bar{n}(\mu)$, $\bar{b}^B(\mu)$, $\bar{e}^A(\mu)$, and $\bar{e}^B(\mu)$, respectively, of the government's instrument vector (t, T, τ). In addition, of course, $b^A = 0$, by assumption. The indirect utility function is denoted by

$$v(t, T, \tau) \equiv u(\bar{c}^1(t, T, \tau), \bar{c}^2(t, T, \tau), \bar{n}(t, T, \tau)).$$

Let us now turn to the government's budget constraint. In the first period, it has no expenditures or revenues. In the second period, the government collects $ntw[pg_A(e^A) + (1 - p)g_B(e^B)]$ from the marginal tax component of the linear earned income tax and $n(1 - p)\tau b^B R$ from the inheritance tax (recall that $b^A = 0$); it pays nT in demogrants. Thus the government must satisfy the following budget constraint:

$$T = tw[pg_A(e^A) + (1 - p)g_B(e^B)] + (1 - p)\tau b^B R. \tag{8.15}$$

Let the government choose its instruments (t, T, and τ) so as to maximize $v(t, T, \tau)$ subject to its budget constraint (8.15). A first-order characterization of the optimum is straightforward, but unfortunately not very informative. We therefore take up the more modest task of looking for welfare-improving directions of tax changes around the no-intervention state, $t = T = \tau = 0$ (the laissez-faire point).

In order to simplify the analysis, we substitute the functions $\bar{c}^1$, $\bar{c}^2$, $\bar{n}$, $\bar{b}^B$, $\bar{e}^A$, and $\bar{e}^B$ in the government's budget constraint (8.15):

$$T = tw\{pg_A[\bar{e}^A(t, T, \tau)] + (1 - p)g_B[\bar{e}^B(t, T, \tau)]\}$$
$$+ (1 - p)\tau R\bar{b}^B(t, T, \tau). \tag{8.16}$$

This equation defines T implicitly as a function $\bar{T}(t, \tau)$ of t and τ. This function means that, given the marginal tax rate on earned income (t) and the inheritance tax rate (τ), the government has just enough revenues from these taxes to pay a demogrant of $\bar{T}(t, \tau)$.

Total differentiation of (8.16) with respect to t and τ gives the partial derivatives of $\bar{T}$ with respect to t and τ (denoted by $\bar{T}_1$, and $\bar{T}_2$, respectively):

$$\bar{T}_1 = w[pg_A + (1 - p)g_B] + twpg_A'(\bar{e}_1^A + \bar{e}_2^A\bar{T}_1)$$
$$+ tw(1 - p)g_B'(\bar{e}_1^B + \bar{e}_2^B\bar{T}_1) + (1 - p)\tau R(\bar{b}_1^B + \bar{b}_2^B\bar{T}_1), \tag{8.17}$$

and

$$\bar{T}_2 = tw[pg_A'(\bar{e}_2^A\bar{T}_2 + \bar{e}_3^A) + (1 - p)g_B'(\bar{e}_2^B\bar{T}_2 + \bar{e}_3^B)]$$
$$+ (1 - p)R\bar{b}^B + (1 - p)\tau R(\bar{b}_2^B\bar{T}_2 + \bar{b}_3^B). \tag{8.18}$$

Evaluated at $t = \tau = \bar{T}(t, \tau) = 0$, the partial derivatives of $\bar{T}$ are found from (8.17)–(8.18) to be

$$\bar{T}_1 = w[pg_A + (1 - p)g_B] \tag{8.19}$$

and

$$\bar{T}_2 = (1 - p)R\bar{b}^B. \tag{8.20}$$

We can now evaluate the effects of changes in the marginal tax rate on earned income (t) and in the inheritance tax rate (τ), budget-balanced by a change in the demogrant (T), on welfare. That is, the changes in t, τ, and T are restricted by the government's budget constraint. Once the changes in t and τ are chosen, one is no longer free to make any change in T but is restricted to that change in T consistent with the function $\bar{T}(t, \tau)$.

Substituting $\bar{T}(t, \tau)$ for T in the indirect utility function $v(t, T, \tau)$ gives rise to

$$V(t, \tau) \equiv v(t, \bar{T}(t, \tau), \tau). \tag{8.21}$$

We next evaluate the effect of changes in t and τ (and the resulting necessary change in T, as dictated by the function $\bar{T}$) on the parent's welfare (V) at the laissez-faire point $t = \tau = \bar{T}(t, \tau) = 0$.

Differentiating (8.21) with respect to t and τ yields

$$V_1 = v_1 + v_2 \bar{T}_1, \tag{8.22}$$

and

$$V_2 = v_2 \bar{T}_2 + v_3. \tag{8.23}$$

Using the envelope theorem, we can calculate v_1, v_2, and v_3 by partially differentiating the Lagrangian expression (8.7):

$$v_1 = -w(\lambda_2 g_A + \lambda_3 g_B), \tag{8.24}$$

$$v_2 = \lambda_2 + \lambda_3, \tag{8.25}$$

and

$$v_3 = -R(\lambda_2 \bar{b}^A + \lambda_3 \bar{b}^B) = -R\lambda_3 \bar{b}^B. \tag{8.26}$$

Consider first a change in the marginal tax rate t (accompanied by a change in the demogrant T) at the laissez-faire point. Substituting (8.19), (8.24), and (8.25) into (8.22), we obtain

$$V_1 = -w(\lambda_2 g_A + \lambda_3 g_B) + (\lambda_2 + \lambda_3)w[pg_A + (1 - p)g_B]$$

$$= w(g_A - g_B)[\lambda_3 p - \lambda_2(1 - p)]. \tag{8.27}$$

Using (8.11) yields

$$(1 - \tau)R = \lambda_1(1 - p)n/\lambda_3. \tag{8.28}$$

Substituting (8.28) into (8.10) yields

$$-\lambda_1 pn + \lambda_2 \lambda_1(1 - p)n/\lambda_3 + \lambda_4 = 0.$$

Since $\lambda_4 \geq 0$, it follows that

$$\lambda_3 p - \lambda_2(1 - p) \geq 0. \tag{8.29}$$

Since $b^B > 0$ while $b^A = 0$, it follows from (8.3') and (8.4') that

$$g_A - g_B > 0. \tag{8.30}$$

Hence it follows from (8.27), (8.29), and (8.30) that $V_1 \geq 0$. Thus some tax on earned income (with a marginal rate t and a demogrant T) is welfare-improving.

In order to understand the rationale for this result, observe that because the constraint $b^A \geq 0$ is binding, the parent would have liked to increase e^A and to lower b^A. This is also evident from (8.10) and (8.12), which imply that

$$wg'_A = R + \frac{\lambda_4}{\lambda_2} \geq R,$$

which in turn means that the return to e^A (i.e., wg'_A) is greater than the return to b^A (i.e., R). But the parent cannot reduce b^A because b^A is already zero. Therefore, the parent cannot further increase e^A without increasing the transfer $npe^A + n(1 - p)(e^B + b^B)$ altogether because, by (8.3') and (8.4'), $(1 - t)wg_A(e^A)$ must be equated with $(1 - t)wg_B(e^B) + R(1 - \tau)b^B$, so that raising e^A must be accompanied by raising e^B or b^B as well. Since $g_A > g_B$, raising t takes more from the more able than from the less able children, while T is given equally to both kinds of children. Therefore, such an increase in t and T enables the parent to increase e^A without additional transfers to her children. Knowing that government is redistributing income among siblings enables the parent to channel the transfer of wealth to her offspring more efficiently, thus making the parent herself better off.

We next consider a change in τ (accompanied by the necessary change in T as dictated by the function $\bar{T}$). Substituting (8.20), (8.23), and (8.26) into (8.23), we obtain

$$V_2 = (\lambda_2 + \lambda_3)(1 - p)R\bar{b}^B - \lambda_3 R\bar{b}^B = [\lambda_2(1 - p) - \lambda_3 p]R\bar{b}^B \leq 0,$$

by (8.29). Thus some positive inheritance subsidy (a negative τ), financed by lowering the demogrant component of the tax on earned income, is welfare-improving. Here again the inheritance subsidy enables parents to overcome the deficiency in investment in the education of the able children without increasing the total transfer of wealth to their children: the required equality between $(1 - t)wg_A(e^A)$ and $(1 - t)wg_B(e^B) + (1 - \tau)Rb^B$ may be preserved when τ is made negative by increasing e^A and decreasing b^B.

8.3 Additional Policies

We have shown here that a linear tax on earned income and a subsidy to inheritance are useful in alleviating the constraint imposed by $b^A \geq 0$, which causes underinvestment in the human capital of able children. We could consider also direct government investment in human capital (free education), but as long as the values of e are positive, such a policy is redundant. Parents can always undo the effects of such policies by reducing their investments in human capital, dollar for dollar, in response to government investment. If public investment in human capital is so high as to make parents wish to have a negative e^A or e^B, it is even suboptimal.

Instead of direct government investment in human capital, one can consider a subsidy to education. A subsidy to education, in the first period, must also be financed by a lump-sum tax in the same period because the government cannot transfer resources from the future to the present. Such a subsidy does not help alleviate constraint 8.6; on the other hand, it creates a distortion by artificially lowering the cost of education to parents. Thus it reduces welfare because the parent can achieve the postsubsidy allocation under laissez-faire.[2]

Specifically, if there is a subsidy to education at the rate s and a lump-sum tax, Z, in the first period to finance it, the budget constraint of the first period (8.2') changes to

$$k = c^1 + pn[e^A(1 - s) + b^A] + (1 - p)n[e^B(1 - s) + b^B] + Z. \tag{8.2''}$$

Suppose that with this subsidy, the parent chooses $\hat{c}^1$, $\hat{n}$, $\hat{e}^A$, $\hat{b}^A$, $\hat{e}^B$ and $\hat{b}^B$. Since $Z = p\hat{n}\hat{e}^A + (1 - p)\hat{n}\hat{e}^B$, it follows (from 8.2'') that the postsubsidy allocation $(\hat{c}^1, \hat{n}, \hat{e}^A, \hat{b}^A, \hat{e}^B, \hat{b}^B)$ satisfies the laissez-faire budget constraint (8.2′). Hence the subsidy cannot be welfare-improving; because the subsidy distorts the relative price of education, it is actually welfare-reducing.

8.4 Conclusion

A social planner who can identify ability can devise a system of taxes and transfers based on ability in order to achieve an efficient allocation of resources. However, when identification of more able and less able children is impossible or prohibitively expensive for all except the parents themselves, a Pareto-efficient solution to the problem of optimal investment in human capital and bequests cannot be achieved.

We have shown that a linear tax on earned income and a subsidy to inheritance are Pareto improvements even though they do not provide a first-best solution. Such second-best corrective policies make the parent better off because they redistribute income from more able to less able siblings and allow the parent to allocate the investments in human and physical capital that she makes on her children's behalf more efficiently. Other policies, such as public investment in human capital or a tax/subsidy for education, were shown to be either redundant or Pareto-inferior relative to the laissez-faire solution. Public investment in human capital (e.g., free education) is redundant as long as the parent invests positive amounts in children of all abilities; the parent can always undo the effects of such a policy by reducing her investments in the human capital of her children, dollar for dollar. Instead of direct government investment in human capital, a subsidy to education might be considered. Such a subsidy in the first period, however, must be financed by a tax in the same period if the government cannot transfer resources from the future to the present; moreover, it creates a distortion by artificially lowering the cost of education to the parent. This distortion was shown to lower the welfare of the parent.

Interestingly, we propose here an income tax as a partial remedy to the inefficiency of the laissez-faire solution that arises when the parent cannot enforce transfers among her children. We have shown that such a tax improves the efficiency of the laissez-faire outcome. Recall that a progressive income tax is usually supported on equity grounds; it is viewed as a second-best tool of redistributing income from the rich to the poor, as in the optimal income tax literature.[3] There, a smaller pie is traded for a better (more equal) division of the pie by means of the income tax. In the present case, however, the income tax is justified purely on the grounds of efficiency!

9

Bequests and Child Education: Imperfect Information

In chapter 8 we analyzed the issue of allocating the transfers by parents between education and bequests and among their (heterogeneous) children. The heterogeneity of children manifested itself in different innate abilities, which generated different absolute, as well as marginal, productivities of investments in human capital. It was assumed that parents could directly and a priori identify the abilities of their children, even though most often parents cannot a priori (before investment in human capital is made) observe the abilities of their children. They can only observe the earnings of their children after the investment in human capital has taken place, and even then they cannot decompose differences in earnings among children into their two potential sources: differences in innate abilities and differences in work efforts.

When altruistic parents do not know their children's abilities and cannot observe their work effort, they will condition their transfers on the level of their children's labor earnings. To keep their children from pretending (by working less and earning less) to be of low ability in order to garner a larger transfer, parents are likely to make larger transfers to high-earning children and smaller transfers to low-earning children. In this case, parents cannot ensure perfect equality in consumption by their children without annihilating any incentive for work effort. Therefore, we no longer maintain the requirement of chapter 8 of a strict equality among children's consumption. We rather suppose that parents have a general egalitarian utility function that shows preference for greater equality among children but is not necessarily of the max-min type that requires perfect equality as in chapter 8.

Indeed, in addressing their information problem, altruistic parents may produce more inequality in their children's final consumption than would arise if they were not altruistic. To help keep their children from freeloading, parents may also make their transfers, at the margin, an increasing function of their children's labor earnings. Indeed, there are now some fairly good data showing that parental transfers are positively related to earning (e.g., Cox 1987).

Those familiar with the optimal income tax literature (Mirrlees 1971; Sadka 1976; Stiglitz 1987) may sense a parallel between a parent who redistributes among children of unobserved abilities and a government that redistributes among citizens of unobserved abilities. Indeed, the two problems are essentially isomorphic. An immediate implication of this proposition is that if government and parental preferences about the distribution of welfare coincide and if differences in abilities are exclusively intrafamily, there may be no optimal income tax role for the government, that is, parental choice of average and marginal bequests may substitute perfectly for the government's optimal tax structure.

9.1 The Choice of Transfers under Imperfect Information

A static model suffices to clarify the problem of an altruistic parent who wishes to transfer to a child, but does not know the child's ability and cannot observe the child's work effort. The parent's utility depends on the parent's own consumption and the utility of the child. The utility of the child, in turn, is a concave function of the child's own consumption and the child's effort. Prior to observing the child's labor earnings, the parent announces a set of transfers to the child conditional on the child's labor earnings; hence the parent maximizes her expected utility over the different possible states corresponding to different levels of the child's ability.

To illustrate the problem in the simplest manner, let the child have two possible ability levels, A_1 and A_h, where $A_1 < A_h$. Earnings of the low- and high-ability children are denoted by E_1 and E_h, respectively. The relationships between earnings, ability, and effort of the low- and high-ability children, L_1 and L_h, are given by

$$E_1 = A_1 L_1,$$
$$E_h = A_h L_h. \tag{9.1}$$

In equation 9.1 the wage per unit of effective labor supply is normalized to one; the expected utility function of the parent is given by

$$W_p = q[u(c_{p1}) + \beta v(c_{k1}, E_1/A_1)] + (1 - q)[u(c_{ph}) + \beta v(c_{kh}, E_h/A_h)], \tag{9.2}$$

where q is the probability the child is of low ability; c_{p1} and c_{ph} are the consumption values of the parent if the child turns out to have low or high ability, respectively; $v(\cdot)$ is the utility function of the child, which depends on that child's consumption (c_{k1} for the low-ability child and c_{kh} for the high-ability child) and effort, L_1 or L_n; $u + \beta v$ is the parent's utility function, which includes the child's utility (v); and $\beta \geq 0$ is a coefficient representing the intensity of the parent's altruism. In (9.2) the effort levels (L_1 and L_H) are replaced (using equation 9.1) by earnings divided by ability (E_1/A_1 and E_h/A_h, respectively).

The parent's problem is to maximize (9.2) with respect to c_{p1}, c_{k1}, c_{ph}, c_{kh}, E_1, and E_h subject to the budget constraints given in (9.3) and (9.4) that combine the family's total resources and consumption, and the self-selection constraints given in (9.5) and (9.6). In the budget constraints k stands for the parent's income. Note that $(k - c_{p1})$ is the parent's transfer to the low-ability child, and $(k - c_{ph})$ is the parent's transfer to the high-ability child. We assume that the non-negativity constraints on bequests (i.e., $k - c_{pi} \geq 0, i = 1, h$) are not binding and we therefore ignore them:

$$k + E_1 \leq c_{p1} + c_{k1}, \tag{9.3}$$

$$k + E_h \geq c_{ph} + c_{kh}, \tag{9.4}$$

$$v(c_{kh}, E_h/A_h) \geq v(c_{k1}, E_1/A_h), \tag{9.5}$$

and

$$v(c_{k1}, E_1/A_1) \geq v(c_{kh}, E_h/A_1). \tag{9.6}$$

The self-selection constraints, (9.5) and (9.6), deserve some explanation. The parent cannot directly choose the action of the child (i.e., c_k and L). She can only offer a transfer consumption-earning schedule that specifies for each earning level the amount of the transfer and consequently the child's consumption, which is the sum of her earning and the transfer. Each child then chooses that child's most preferred consumption-earning (via that child's effort) bundle among all the bundles on the consumption-earning schedule offered by the parent. Since there are only two ability levels, there are essentially only two bundles on the consumption-earning schedule that are relevant. These are (c_{k1}, E_1) and (c_{kh}, E_h), which are the bundles offered for the low- and high-ability levels, respectively. Notice that the high-ability child earns an income of E if that child's work effort is E/A_h. Notice also that a high-ability child will choose the bundle (c_{kh}, E_h) if and only if this bundle is preferred over the other bundle, (c_{k1}, E_1). This explains the inequality in (9.5). A similar explanation holds for (9.6).

Let us associate the Lagrangian multipliers θ_1 and θ_h with the constraints 9.3 and 9.4, respectively, and the multipliers λ_1 and λ_h with the constraints 9.5 and 9.6, respectively. Equations 9.7–9.12 present the first-order conditions for the choices of c_{p1}, c_{ph}, c_{k1}, c_{kh}, E_1, and E_h under the assumptions that (9.5) is binding and that (9.6) is not binding: (Indeed, figure 9.1 shows that these assumptions must hold.)

$$qu'(c_{p1}) - \theta_1 = 0, \tag{9.7}$$

$$(1 - q)u'(c_{ph}) - \theta_h = 0, \tag{9.8}$$

$$q\beta v_1(c_{k1}, E_1/A_1) - \theta_1 - \lambda_h v_1(c_{k1}, E_1/A_h) = 0, \tag{9.9}$$

$$(1 - q)\beta v_1(c_{kh}, E_h/A_h) - \theta_h + \lambda_h v_1(c_{kh}, E_h/A_h) = 0, \tag{9.10}$$

$$q\beta v_2(c_{k1}, E_1/A_1)\frac{1}{A_1} + \theta_1 - \lambda_h v_2(c_{k1}, E_1/A_h)\frac{1}{A_h} = 0, \tag{9.11}$$

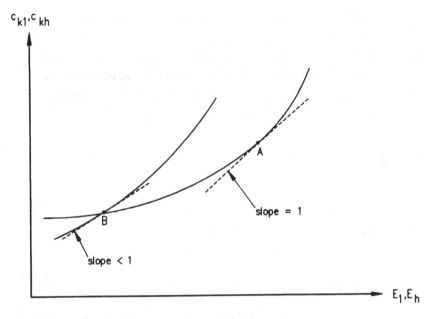

Figure 9.1
Using bequests as an implicit tax to sort children

and

$$(1 - q)\beta v_2(c_{kh}, E_h/A_h)\frac{1}{A_h} + \theta_h + \lambda_h v_2(c_{kh}, E_h/A_h)\frac{1}{A_h} = 0. \qquad (9.12)$$

The combinations of (9.7) and (9.9) and of (9.8) and (9.10) indicate that the parent equates her marginal utility of consumption to β times the child's marginal utility of consumption plus a term indicating how an increase in the child's consumption through an increase in transfers (transfers equal k minus parent's consumption) affects the self-selection constraint (9.5). In the case of equation 9.9, transferring another dollar to the child (increasing the child's consumption by a dollar) raises the high-ability child's utility when that child pretends to be of low ability; this makes the self-selection more difficult to satisfy and therefore raises, at the margin, the cost of transferring to the child. The opposite occurs with respect to equation 9.10.

The addition of equations 9.10 and 9.12 indicates that the high-ability child's marginal rate of substitution (v_2/v_1) between consumption and effort is equated to that child's marginal productivity (A_h). This is not the case for the low-ability child. The addition of (9.9) and (9.11) indicates that the low-ability child faces an implicit marginal tax at rate τ, where τ is given by

$$\tau = \frac{\lambda_h}{(q\beta - \lambda_h)v_1(c_{k1}, E_1/A_1)}H \tag{9.13}$$

and

$$H = v_1(c_1, E_1/A_h) - v_1(c_1, E_1/A_1) + v_2(c_{k1}, E_1/A_h)\frac{1}{A_h}$$

$$- v_2(c_{k1}, E_1/A_1)\frac{1}{A_1}. \tag{9.14}$$

If $v_{12} \leq 0$, that is, the marginal utility of consumption decreases with the amount of effort (increases with the amount of leisure), then $q\beta - \lambda_h$ (from equation 9.9) and H (from equation 9.14) are positive. Hence the tax rate on the high-ability child is positive because λ_h is positive.

Figure 9.1 illustrates why only the self-selection constraint on the high-ability child is binding. The diagram is, except for symbols, identical to that in Sadka (1976) and plots the utility of the child in consumption earnings space, assuming $v_{12} \leq 0$. At any point in this space the slope of the high-ability child's indifference curve is smaller than that of the low-ability child. At the optimum, the high-ability child is at point A and faces no implicit marginal tax (i.e., the slope of that child's indifference curve is one). At point A the high-ability child is indifferent between truthfully revealing that child's ability and pretending to be of low ability by earning E_1 and consuming c_{k1} at point B. The low-ability child ends up at point B with the slope of that child's indifference curve less than one, indicating a positive implicit marginal tax.

In the case of perfect information there are no self-selection constraints, so the solution can be found by simply setting λ_h or λ_1 equal to zero in the first-order conditions for the choice of c_{p1}, c_{ph}, c_{k1}, c_{kh}, E_1, and E_h. In this case there is of course no distortion of each child's work effort, and the parent equates her marginal utility of consumption to β times the child's marginal utility of consumption.

9.2 Comparisons of the Imperfect and Perfect Information Solutions

The log-linear utility function given in equation 9.15 is useful for illustrating differences between the full information and imperfect information problems.

$$W_p = q[\log c_{p1} + \beta(\log c_{k1} - \alpha(E_1/A_1))]$$
$$+ (1 - q)[\log c_{ph} + \beta(\log c_{kh} - \alpha E_h/A_h))]. \qquad (9.15)$$

From the first-order conditions it is easy to confirm the following relationships, where the superscript F stands for the case of full information and the superscript I stands for the case of imperfect information.

$$c_{p1}^I > c_{p1}^F$$

$$c_{k1}^I < c_{k1}^F$$

$$c_{ph}^I < c_{ph}^F$$

$$c_{kh}^I = c_{kh}^F \qquad (9.16)$$

$$E_h^I < E_h^F$$

$$E_1^I \; ? \; E_1^F.$$

We see that in the imperfect information case the parent of the high-ability child consumes less and makes a larger transfer (since transfers equal $k - c_{ph}$), while the parent of the low-ability child consumes more and makes a smaller transfer. Hence transfers are less equalizing for this utility function when information is imperfect; as presently described, under imperfect information the transfer to the high-ability child can exceed that of the low-ability child, while the

Table 9.1
Calculations based on the log-linear utility function

	Benchmark		$\beta = .75$		$q = .25$		$\alpha = .40$		$A_h = 1.25$	
	I	F	I	F	I	F	I	F	I	F
c_{p1}	1.96	1.58	2.43	2.00	2.20	1.58	2.46	1.97	2.26	1.58
c_{ph}	1.66	2.10	2.15	2.67	1.87	2.10	2.09	2.63	1.75	2.63
c_{k1}	1.36	1.50	1.39	1.50	1.30	1.50	1.72	2.24	1.07	1.50
c_{kh}	2.00	2.00	2.00	2.00	2.00	2.00	2.50	2.50	2.50	2.50
E_1	.34	.08	.83	.50	.50	.08	1.18	.85	.33	.08
E_h	.67	1.11	1.15	1.67	.87	1.11	1.58	2.13	1.25	2.13
T_1	1.04	1.42	.57	1.00	.80	1.42	.54	1.03	.74	1.42
T_h	1.34	.09	.85	.33	1.13	.90	.91	.37	1.25	.37
τ_1	.09	.00	.07	.00	.13	.00	.08	.00	.28	.00

Note: Except where indicated, all parameters are the benchmark parameters. The benchmark parameters are $k = 3$, $A_1 = .75$, $A_h = 1$, $q = .5$, $\beta = .95$, $\alpha = .50$. T_i is the transfer from the parent to the child of ability $i = h, 1$, that is, $T_i = k - c_{pi}$. τ_1 stands for the implicit marginal tax on the low-ability child. It is defined by $\text{MRS}_1 = A_1(1 - \tau_1)$ for $i = 1, h$, where MRS is the marginal rate of substitution between consumption and effort.

reverse holds under full information. The inequalities in (9.16) also indicate that the high-ability child consumes the same but earns less in the imperfect information case, with increased transfers making up for the lower earnings. The low-ability child consumes less in the imperfect information case, but her earnings may be larger or smaller.

Table 9.1 compares the imperfect and full information solutions for this utility function for a range of parameter values. The quantitative results are quite striking. For each of the sets of parameters imperfect information leads the parent to transfer more to the high-ability child than to the low-ability child, that is, transfers are not equalizing. For example, for the benchmark parameters the transfers, under full information, are 1.42 to the low-ability child and .9 to the high-ability child. With imperfect information, however, the transfers are almost the reverse, with only 1.04 going to the low-ability child and 1.34 going to the high-ability child. The counterpart of these differences in transfers is that the consumption of parents will be quite different when information is imperfect than when it is not. For the benchmark parameters the parent of the high-ability child consumes 2.10 under full information but only 1.66 under imperfect information, while the parent of the low-ability children consumes 1.58 under full information but 1.96 under imperfect information.

The low-ability child's consumption in the benchmark case is 1.50 with full information, but only 1.36 with imperfect information; the high-ability child's earnings adjust to maintain the same consumption level under full and imperfect information. Hence, compared with the case of full information, the high-ability and the low-ability child's consumption is less equal when information is imperfect. Indeed, when information is imperfect, the parent's transfers to her children can lead to more inequality in her children's consumption than would occur if the parent were not altruistic and made no transfers to her children. For the benchmark parameters, but with $\beta = 0$, the high-ability child's consumption is 2.00, while the low-ability child's consumption is 1.50 (as in the full information case, with $\beta = .95$).

The implicit marginal tax rates on the low-ability child listed in table 9.1 range from 7 to 28 percent. The 28 percent figure is particularly interesting. This implicit tax rate arises when A_h equals 1.25 while A_1 remains at .75. Compared with the benchmark case the implicit marginal tax rate is over three times higher, although the total transfer to the low-ability child is almost 25 percent smaller. This comparison indicates that implicit marginal taxation through parental bequests and intervivo transfers can be quite large, even though total transfers are small.

The different parameter combinations considered in the second two columns of table 9.1 suggest that children's labor earnings can be quite sensitive to the extent of altruism (the level of β). Columns 5 and 6 of this table consider a lower value of the probability q of having a low-ability child. In the case of imperfect information the smaller value of q leads to smaller transfers to both the high- and low-ability children, but to a higher implicit tax on the low-ability child.

9.3 Summary

The inability of parents to know or to monitor perfectly their children's work efforts can significantly alter parental transfers to children. Parents are likely to respond to their information problem by making larger bequests to higher-earning children and by using their transfers implicitly to tax at the margin lower-earning children. This implicit tax rate may be quite large, even though total transfers are small; hence labor supply studies should take into account potential implicit family taxation as well as official government taxation. In addition, that the family may play an implicit role in taxation means that there may be less need for the government to play such a role.

IV

Income Distribution and
Social Security

10

The Intergenerational Role of Social Security

Bequest constraints have played a major role in discussions of various issues pertaining to intergenerational transfers. For example, in his famous article on debt neutrality Barro (1974) showed that if finite-lived parents left their descendants positive bequests in the absence of government debt, the introduction of public debt would not affect those parents' optimal consumption plans and would not create new opportunities to transfer resources from parents to children. Barro's proposition thus requires an interior solution to the intergenerational transfer problem (or the absence of non-negativity constraints on bequests). Subsequent developments of this subject have focused on the implications of such nonnegativity constraints and the possiblity of boundary solutions; see Drazen (1978), Kimball (1987), Weil (1987), and Abel (1988). This literature focused mainly on the positive economics aspects of institutional constraints on bequests and their implications for government debt neutrality.

In this chapter we follow Becker and Murphy (1988) in focusing on the welfare implications of bequest constraints. We extend the analysis of chapter 8, in which we studied the implications of institutional nonnegativity constraints on bequests implying the inability of parents to force transfers among their children, who have different abilities to make use of human capital. When children have different abilities, so that investments in their human capital are not equally productive, and parents cannot enforce transfers among them, an egalitarian parental attitude may lead to inefficient investment in human and nonhuman capital. For example, the parents may be led to invest too much in the human capital of the low-ability children so that these children will be equal (in the productivity of their human capital) to their more able siblings.

In this chapter we treat the diseconomies associated with institutional constraints on the family by focusing on the implications of bequest constraints for the intergenerational distribution of welfare when no differences exist among children. We examine several potential welfare-improving policies designed to correct institutional constraints to negative bequests and the implications of such policies for population growth. Among such policies, we consider a social security scheme. It is worth noting that *inter*generational transfers in our context are within the family and are therefore also termed *intra*family transfers.

10.1   Bequest-Constrained Laissez-Faire

To highlight the economic mechanism underlying the problem at hand we use the simple stylized model developed in chapter 8, except that we ignore differences among siblings. There are only two periods, two generations, and a single all-purpose composite good. The first generation consists of identical individuals (parents) who live for one period. Each parent is endowed with k units of the composite good. She consumes c_1 units of the composite good in the first period and bears n identical children, each of whom possesses one unit of adult labor in the second period.

Investing e units of the single good in the first period in the education of a child augments the parent's labor supply, as measured in efficiency units, to $g(e)$. The marginal product of human capital is positive but diminishing, that is,

$$g' > 0, g'' < 0. \tag{10.1}$$

The child then earns $g(e)$ in the second period, where the wage rate per efficiency unit is set equal to one. The parent can also bequeath b units of the composite good to each child in the first period. This bequest grows to be bR units in the second period, where $R - 1 > 0$ is the (fixed) rate of interest.

The parent's budget constraint is

$$c_1 + n(e + b) = k. \tag{10.2}$$

We assume that bequests cannot be negative. Accordingly:

$$b \geq 0. \tag{10.3}$$

The consumption (c_2) of each child in the second period is constrained by

$$c_2 \leq g(e) + bR. \tag{10.4}$$

We assume that the nonnegativity constraint on bequest is only institutional, namely, that parents cannot obligate their children to repay debts the parents accumulate before they die. The economy lasts for two periods, however, and is not constrained in its ability to transfer resources from the future back to the present. For instance, the economy (via the government) can borrow in the present from abroad at the rate of interest $R - 1$ and repay the loan in the second period. One can also maintain a similar distinction between the intertemporal constraint faced by the individual and by the economy in a closed economy when generations overlap (see appendix 10A.1). Thus constraint 10.3 is binding for the individual but not for the economy. Therefore, there may be a market failure in the intertemporal allocation of resources.

Caring about the number and the well-being of her children, the parent in the first period chooses c_1, n, e, b, and a planned c_2 so as to maximize her utility function

$$u(c_1, n, c_2), \tag{10.5}$$

subject to the resource constraints, (10.2) and (10.4), and the institutional nonnegativity constraint on bequests, (10.3). We call the solution to this optimization problem, denoted by $(c_1^*, n^*, c_2^*, b^*, e^*)$, the laissez-faire equilibrium. Recall that when the institutional constraint is not binding, that is, when the parent wishes to bequeath a positive amount to her children, the parent invests in the human capital of each child up to the point where the marginal productivity of human capital is equal to the rate of interest:

$$g'(e^*) = R. \tag{10.6}$$

The rate-of-return equalization ensures efficiency in the choice between investment in human capital (education) and physical capital (bequests) as a means of transferring resources from the present to the future. Notice that this efficiency rule is obtained independently of the optimal choice of c_1, n, b, and c_2.

This efficiency rule no longer holds, however, when the non-negativity bequest constraint is binding. Then $b^* = 0$, and (10.6) becomes

$$g'(e^*) > R. \tag{10.6a}$$

This implies, by (10.1), that investment in human capital is insufficient. The parent would have liked to invest more in the human capital of her children if she could keep some of the return to this investment to herself by borrowing from her children. But this would have required b to be negative, which is institutionally impossible. In this chapter we focus on this bequest-constrained equilibrium ($b^* = 0$).

There are several key factors that determine whether the bequest constraint is binding or not; see also Abel (1988). First, the magnitude of the parent's altruism towards her children, that is, the marginal rate of substitution of children's consumption for parent's consumption ($\partial c_2 / \partial c_1$ along the parent's indifference curve), affects the size of the total transfer (i.e., $e + b$) to each child. The smaller the magnitude of the parent's altruism, the smaller the transfer and the larger the likelihood that the nonnegativity bequest constraint be binding. Second, the magnitude of the marginal productivity of human capital investment (i.e., the schedule g'), relative to the return on physical capital (i.e., R), determines the composition of the total transfer $b + e$ between b and e. The larger is g', relative to R, the more that the parent would like to invest in the human capital of her children, and even borrow for this purpose, in which case the non-negativity constraint becomes binding.

In contrast to the parent, the economy is not constrained by (10.3). The optimum for the economy is obtained by maximizing the utility function (10.5), subject only to the resource constraints, (10.2) and (10.4). The optimal allocation is denoted by $(c_1^{**}, n^{**}, c_2^{**}, e^{**}, b^{**})$. In this case $b^{**} < 0$, and investment in human capital is efficient:

$$g'(e^{**}) = R. \tag{10.7}$$

(Hence $e^{**} > e^*$). Obviously, not only investment in human capital is distorted in the laissez-faire equilibrium because of the institutional constraint on bequests, but also all other choice variables (c_1, n, and c_2) are distorted.

Notice that this concept of optimality is considered from the parent's point of view, namely, the optimal allocation maximizes the parent's utility function (subject to the economy's resource constraints). Because the parent is altruistic towards her children, the optimal allocation may plausibly lead to a higher utility for children, compared to the laissez-faire allocation. In this case the optimal allocation Pareto-dominates the laissez-faire allocation. However, this is not always true. It may well happen that the optimal allocation renders a lower utility (consumption) for children than the laissez-faire allocation. In this case the optimal allocation does not bring about a Pareto improvement over the laissez-faire allocation.

10.2 Optimum versus Laissez-Faire: A Pareto Comparison

As indicated in the preceding section, parental altruism toward children does not necessarily imply that the optimal allocation dominates the laissez-faire allocation in the Pareto sense. That is to say, although the parent's utility is, by definition, greater at the optimum than at the laissez-faire allocation, the children's utility (consumption) may be smaller. To see the factors at play in the movement from the laissez-faire to the optimal allocation, and in particular their effect on the children's consumption, let us consider a simplified version of this model, in which the number of children n is exogenous, but their quality (c_2) remains endogenous.

Notice that b is equal to zero at the laissez-faire allocation and becomes negative at the optimal allocation. Therefore, to analyze the difference between the laissez-faire and the optimal consumption per child, let us parameterize b and consider the effect on c_2 of lowering b from zero to its optimal level. That is, we first solve the problem

$$\max_{\{c_1, c_2, e\}} u(c_1, n, c_2),$$

subject to

$$c_1 + n(e + b) \le k,$$

$$c_2 \le g(e) + bR,$$

where b is treated as a parameter. We then consider the effect of changing b on the solution for c_2, denoted by $\bar{c}_2(b)$.

A straightforward comparative statics analysis yields

$$\frac{d\bar{c}_2}{db} = \frac{1}{D}[(R - g')n^2(u_{11} - u_{13}u_1/u_3)] + \frac{1}{D}[Ru_3 g''],$$

where

$$D = n^2 u_{11} - 2ng' u_{13} + u_{33}(g')^2 + u_3 g''$$

is negative by the second-under conditions for utility maximization.

Notice that the expression for $d\bar{c}_2/db$ is composed of two terms. The first represents the real income (welfare) effect of relaxing the bequest constraint. Because the constraint is binding along the path from the laissez-faire to the optimum allocation, $g' > R$ along this path, and the expression $u_{11} - u_{13}u_1/u_3$ is negative when c_2 is a normal good, which is a plausible assumption. Hence the first term is negative, working in the direction of increasing c_2 as the bequest constraint is relaxed. That is to say, the real income effect works in the direction of increasing c_2—hence, by itself, enhances Pareto improvement—as one moves from the laissez-faire to the optimum allocation.

The second term in the expression for $d\bar{c}_2/db$ is unambiguously positive; relaxing the bequest constraint allows the parent to provide less consumption for each of her children. Thus the second term tends, by itself, to lower the children's utility in the optimal allocation, making the laissez-faire and the optimal allocations Pareto-noncomparable. If the income effect on c_2 is relatively strong, then it dominates the second effect and the children's utility is higher in the optimal allocation than in the laissez-faire allocation. The optimal allocation Pareto-dominates the laissez-faire allocation in this case; on the other hand, if the real income effect is relatively small, the two allocations are Pareto-noncomparable.

The above analysis was carried out under the assumption that the number of children is exogenous; however, it should be clear that the same factors are at work when n is endogenous. Indeed, the children's utility may also well be lower in the optimum than in the laissez-faire allocation when n is endogenous. Appendix 10.A2 provides such an example.

10.3 The Effect of the Bequest Constraint on Population Growth

As mentioned earlier, a binding bequest constraint forces parents to underinvest in the human capital of their children. It may seem that this distortion will induce parents to have an inadequate number of children (i.e., $n^* < n^{**}$) because they face a binding limit on the "financing" of children.

This may indeed be the case. The loss of utility due to the institutional constraint on bequests may lead to a smaller number of children in the laissez-faire solution relative to the optimum solution. To gain some insight into the effects determining the difference between the number of children in the two allocations, observe that the laissez-faire allocation with a binding bequest constraint can be represented as a solution to the following problems:

$$\max_{\{c_1, n\}} u^*(c_1, n), \tag{10.8}$$

subject to

$$c_1 + ne^* = k,$$

where $u^*(c_1, n) = u(c_1, n, g(e^*))$. The optimal allocation can be represented as a solution to the following problem:

$$\max_{\{c_1, n\}} u^{**}(c_1, n), \tag{10.9}$$

subject to

$$c_1 + n(e^{**} + b^{**}) = k,$$

where $u^{**}(c_1, n) = u(c_1, n, g(e^{**}) + b^{**}R)$.

In both (10.8) and (10.9), only c_1 and n are the choice variables, while investment in human capital (e) and bequest (b) are set at their predetermined solution levels (e^* and $b^* = 0$ for the laissez-faire allocation; e^{**} and $b^{**} < 0$ for the optimal allocation). A comparison between the above two consumer optimization problems suggests two differences. First, the objective (utility) function is different. Second, the "price" of n in the budget constraint is different (see chapter 3). The laissez-faire solution is suboptimal because the transfer of resources from parents to children cannot be efficiently channeled via physical and human capital investments. If the removal of the constraint on the efficient allocation of investment between human and physical capital leads to a larger total yield (i.e., $c_2^* = g(e^*) < g(e^{**}) + b^{**}R = c_2^{**}$) with a smaller total investment (i.e., $e^* > e^{**} + b^{**}$), then it is plausible that the laissez-faire rate of population growth is too slow (i.e., $n^* < n^{**}$). To see this, refer to figure 10.1. The laissez-faire budget constraint AB is steeper than the optimal budget constraint AB', because the laissez-faire price of children is larger than the optimal price of children ($e^* > e^{**} + b^{**}$). If an increase in the quality of children (i.e., $c_2 = g(e) + bR$) changes preferences in (c_1, n)-space in favor of the number of children (which is plausible), then the indifference curves corresponding to u^{**} are steeper than those corresponding to u^*. If, furthermore, u^{**} implies that the number of children is not a Giffen good, then the optimal allocation must yield a larger number of children than the laissez-faire allocation.

This is not always true, however. Indeed, the existence of the nonnegativity constraint on bequests may force the parent to allow

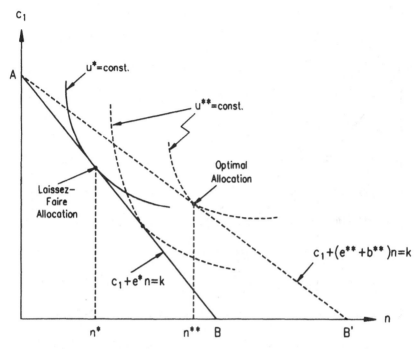

Figure 10.1
Laissez-faire and optimal numbers of children

more consumption per child than otherwise desired. Hence the removal of the constraint will, in this case, lower the consumption per child, that is, $c_2^{**} = g(e^{**}) + b^{**}R < g(e^*) = c_2^*$ (see the preceding section). Because investment is more efficiently channeled in the optimum allocation, this will require a smaller total investment in the optimum: $e^{**} + b^{**} < e^*$. If, as before, the decline in the quality of children changes preferences in (c_1, n)-space against the number of children, then the indifference curves corresponding to u^{**} are flatter than those corresponding to u^* (see figure 10.2). In this case, the optimal allocation can be either to the right or to the left of point D, showing that the optimal number of children can be either smaller or larger than the laissez-faire number of children. Appendix 10.A2 presents an example in which the optimal number of children is indeed smaller than the laissez-faire number of children.

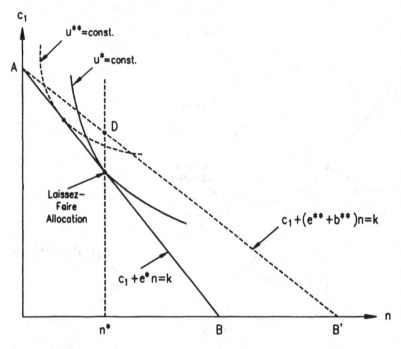

Figure 10.2
Laissez-faire and optimal numbers of children

10.4   Corrective Policies

The source of the market failure in the presence of an institutional constraint on negative bequests is the inability of the parent to transfer resources from their heirs to herself. Such a transfer enables the parent to have an efficient number of children, to invest efficiently in their human capital, and makes the parent, and possibly, each one of their children, better off. As shown in section 10.2, maximizing the altruistic parent's utility will lead also to a higher children's utility if the real income effect on c_2, arising from the effective relaxation of the bequest constraint, is relatively strong.

A first-best remedy to this market failure may seem to be a per-parent subsidy in the first period, debt-financed by a head tax on children in the second period. Notice, however, that when fertility is endogenous (as is the case here), a head tax on children is not neutral, because it affects the "price" of children and thereby distorts the parent's behavior. In the absence of genuine second-period lump-sum taxes, we therefore examine second-best corrective policies. Such policies are aimed at raising the parent's utility beyond the laissez-faire level, but they cannot attain the first-best level.

Consider then a consumption tax at the rate t_c (in the two periods), an education subsidy at the rate s', a child allowance of β', an income tax at the rate t' in the second period, and a lump-sum tax T' in the first period. (Notice that because first-period income is exogenous, an income tax in the first period is essentially a nondistortionary lump-sum tax.) Observe that this menu of policy tools includes, as a special case, a social security scheme. Such a scheme obtains when $t' > 0$ and $T' < 0$, that is, when children are taxed in order to provide a lump-sum transfer to parents. The taxes modify the budget constraints, (10.2) and (10.4), faced by the parent to

$$(1 + t_c)c_1 + n(1 - s')e - \beta'n \leq k - T' \tag{10.10}$$

and

$$(1 + t_c)c_2 \leq (1 - t')g(e). \tag{10.11}$$

Dividing (10.10) and (10.11) by $(1 + t_c)$, we see that the consumption tax t_c is redundant. We therefore rewrite (10.10) and (10.11) as

$$c_1 + n(1 - s)e - \beta n \leq k - T \tag{10.10a}$$

and

$$c_2 \leq (1 - t)g(e), \tag{10.11a}$$

where

$$1 - s = (1 - s')/(1 + t_c),$$

$$\beta = \beta'/(1 + t_c),$$

$$1 - t = (1 - t')/(1 + t_c),$$

and

$I - T = (I - T')/(1 + t_c)$.

In what follows we examine the effects of sufficiently small taxes at the neighborhood of the laissez-faire allocation ($t_c^* = s^* = t^* = T^* = 0$).

The parent maximizes the utility function (10.5), subject to the budget constraints, (10.10a) and (10.11a). The first-order conditions are given in appendix 10.A.3. Denote the solution to this problem by

$$c_1 = C_1(s, \beta, t, T), \tag{10.12a}$$

$$n = N(s, \beta, t, T), \tag{10.12b}$$

$$e = E(s, \beta, t, T), \tag{10.12c}$$

$$c_2 = C_2(s, \beta, t, T), \tag{10.12d}$$

and the indirect utility function by

$$v(s, \beta, t, T) = u(C_1(s, \beta, t, T), N(s, \beta, t, T), C_2(s, \beta, t, T)). \tag{10.13}$$

The government, which can lend and borrow also over periods in which parents and children do not overlap, faces the following present-value budget constraint:

$$[\beta N(s, \beta, t, T) + sE(s, \beta, t, T)N(s, \beta, t, T) - T]R$$

$$- tN(s, \beta, t, T)g[E(s, \beta, t, T)] \le 0. \tag{10.14}$$

As mentioned before, we examine small changes in s, β, t, and T around the laissez-faire allocation ($s^* = \beta^* = t^* = T^*$). Totally differentiating v with respect to s, β, t, and T yields

$$dv = v_s\,ds + v_\beta\,d_\beta + v_t\,dt + v_T\,dT$$

$$= \lambda_1 NE\,ds + \lambda_1 N\,d\beta - \lambda_2 g(E)\,dt - \lambda_1\,dT \tag{10.15}$$

(see appendix 10A.3, equation 10A3.6). Totally differentiating the government's budget constraint (10.14) with respect to s, β, t, and T yields, at $s^* = \beta^* = t^* = T^* = 0$,

$$(N\,d\beta + NE\,ds - dT)R - Ng(E)\,dt = 0. \tag{10.16}$$

We now examine the welfare effects of changes in each one of the distortionary taxes s, β, and t, offset by a change in the first-period lump-sum tax, T. These revenue-neutral welfare effects are derived from (10.15) and (10.16):

$$dv/ds = v_s + v_T \, dT/ds$$

$$= \lambda_1(NE - dT/ds) = 0, \tag{10.17}$$

$$dv/d\beta = \lambda_1(N - dT/d\beta) = 0, \tag{10.18}$$

and

$$dv/dt = -\lambda_2 g(E) - \lambda_1 \, dT/dt$$

$$= -(\lambda_2 R - \lambda_1 N)g(E)/R$$

$$= \lambda_3 g(E)/R \geq 0. \tag{10.19}$$

Thus, (10.19) implies, a small income tax (in the second period) that finances a first-period lump-sum subsidy (a negative T) is welfare-improving. This is a sort of an old age social security scheme. The rationale for this result is as follows. On the one hand, such a policy transfers resources from the children to the parent and thereby both alleviates the nonnegativity constraint on bequests and raises welfare. On the other hand, an income tax is distortionary because it discourages investment in human capital. This distortionary effect is of a second-order magnitude, however; in general, a small tax has only a second-order effect on welfare around the laissez-faire equilibrium. Therefore, a second-period income tax with a first-period lump-sum subsidy increases welfare. Interestingly, here, as in chapter 8, an income tax is justified purely on grounds of efficiency rather than on the more conventional redistribution grounds.

Equations 10.17 and 10.18 imply that a small education subsidy and a child allowance have no first-order effects on welfare. This follows since they do not play any role in intertemporal redistributions (being financed by a lump-sum tax in the same period) and because their distortionary effect on welfare is, in general, only of a second-order magnitude. Furthermore, in the absence of any intertemporal distribution role, one can show that a *finite* education subsidy/tax or a *finite* child allowance/tax reduces welfare. To see this, observe that the parent's choices of c_1, n, c_2, and e in the presence of s, β and T satisfy the budget constraints

$$C_1(s, \beta, 0, T) + N(s, \beta, 0, T)(1 - s)E(s, \beta, 0, T),$$

$$- \beta N(s, \beta, 0, T) \leq k - T, \tag{10.20}$$

and

$$C_2(s, \beta, 0, T) \leq g[E(s, \beta, 0, T)]. \tag{10.21}$$

Because the government's budget constraint in this case is

$$\beta N(s, \beta, 0, T) + sE(s, \beta, 0, T)N(s, \beta, 0, T) - T = 0, \tag{10.22}$$

it follows from (10.20) and (10.22) that

$$C_1(s, \beta, 0, T) + N(s, \beta, 0, T)E(s, \beta, 0, T) \leq k. \tag{10.23}$$

Thus the bundle chosen in the presence of s, β, and T is affordable under the laissez-faire budget constraints (compare (10.23) and (10.21) with (10.2) and (10.4) respectively). Therefore, as in chapter 8, an education tax or subsidy and a child allowance or tax, budget-balanced by a first-period lump-sum tax or subsidy cannot possibly increase welfare. Such taxes or subsidies will usually reduce welfare. We remain therefore only with the old age social security scheme as a corrective policy.

10.5   Conclusions

When institutional constraints to the transfer of resources from children to their parent exist, welfare of the parent's generation may be improved by some sort of old age social security scheme: a lump-sum subsidy to the parent, financed by debt creation to be paid by the revenues from an income tax on children. Such an income tax is justified not by income redistribution considerations, as is typically the case, but rather on grounds of pure efficiency. Due to its *inter*generational, *intra*family transfer role, this social security scheme is Pareto-improving with the altruistic parent, provided the real income effect, which tends to raise children's consumption, is relatively strong. If the model is extended to an infinite overlapping-generations model, the social security scheme will not only tax children when they are young, but will also subsidize them when they are old. In such a setup, social security is more likely to be Pareto-improving.

In order to explore the implications of such a corrective policy for children's welfare and for the rate of population growth, we identified a feature that can make this policy improve the welfare of children and that has a strong real income effect on the children's consumption. Intuition suggests that population growth will be greater when bequest constraints are lessened or eliminated; however, this is not necessarily the case because of income effects and because the trade-offs between the number and the welfare (quality) of children may vary.

Appendix 10A.1

In this appendix we describe a simple closed economy with overlapping generations in which a parent is constrained in her ability to transfer resources from the future back to the present, while society is not. Suppose an individual, whom we call Eve, lives for three periods. Eve is born in the first period, in which she receives an education from her parents and at the end of which she inherits $b \geq 0$ from them. In the second period she works, consumes, and saves for the third period. In the third and last period of her life Eve has children, invests in their human capital, and bequeaths $b' \geq 0$ to each of them.

Now consider the third period of Eve's life. In this period a person from another generation, Adam, who was born in the previous period, is also alive. Adam is in the second period of his life, in which he works and can save. Thus society can transfer resources in the third period of Eve's life from Adam to her. In the next period Eve's children will be in the second (working/saving) period of their lives, and society can transfer resources from them back to Adam. In this way, society is able to transfer resources indirectly from Eve's children to herself (via Adam). Eve, herself, cannot make such a transfer because of the nonnegativity constraint on bequests.

Appendix 10A.2

In this appendix we provide an example in which the number of children is smaller in the (parent's) optimum allocation than in the laissez-faire allocation, and the welfare (quality) of children is also lower.

Let the utility function be

$$u(c_1, n, c_2) = c_1 + an - hn^2/2 + n \log c_2, \tag{10A2.1}$$

and let g take the form

$$g(e) = 2e^{1/2}. \tag{10A2.2}$$

The optimal allocation is obtained by maximizing (10A2.1) subject to (10A2.2), (10.2), and (10.4). The solution to e is given by $g'(e) = R$, implying that

$$e^{**} = 1/R^2, g(e^{**}) = 2/R. \tag{10A2.3}$$

Upon substitution, the optimal allocation can be found by solving

$$\max_{\{b,n\}} [k - (1/R^2 + b)n + an - hn^2/2 + n \log(2/R + bR)]. \tag{10A2.4}$$

The first-order conditions are

$$-1/R^2 - b + a - hn + \log(2/R + bR) = 0 \tag{10A2.5}$$

and

$$-1 + R/(2/R + bR) = 0. \tag{10A.6}$$

From (10A2.6) we can find the optimal bequest:

$$b^{**} = (R^2 - 2)/R^2. \tag{10A2.7}$$

Assuming that $R < 2^{1/2}$ ensures that $b^{**} < 0$. Substituting (10A2.7) into (10A2.5), we can solve for the optimal number of children:

$$n^{**} = [\log R + 1/R^2 + a - 1]/h. \tag{10A2.8}$$

Substituting (10A2.7) and (10A2.3) into (10.4) yields the optimal level of c_2:

$$c_2^{**} = R. \tag{10A2.9}$$

The laissez-faire allocation, $b^* = 0$ in this case, can be found by solving the following optimization problem:

$$\max_{\{e,n\}} [k - en + an - hn^2/2 + n \log 2e^{1/2}]. \tag{10A2.10}$$

The first-order conditions are

$$-e + a - hn + \log 2e^{1/2} = 0 \tag{10A2.11}$$

and

$$-1 + 1/2e = 0. \tag{10A2.12}$$

From (10A2.12) we can solve for the laissez-faire quantity of investment in human capital:

$$e^* = 1/2. \tag{10A2.13}$$

Substituting (10A2.13) into (10A2.11), we can find the laissez-faire number of children:

$$n^* = (-1/2 + \alpha + \log 2^{1/2})/h. \tag{10A2.14}$$

Substituting (10A2.13) into (10.4) yields the laissez-faire level of c_2:

$$c_2^* = 2^{1/2}. \tag{10A2.15}$$

Comparing (10A2.8) with (10A2.14), we can see that if R is sufficiently small so that $2(\log R + 1/R^2) < 1 + \log 2$, then n^* will be larger than n^{**}. Thus there is no presumption that a binding bequest constraint causes the parent to have fewer than an optimal number of children.

Comparing (10A2.9) with (10A2.15), we can see that since, by assumption, $R < 2^{1/2}$, then $c_2^* > c_2^{**}$. This result is in line with the analysis of section 10.2, which suggests that when the real income effect on c_2 is relatively small, then c_2 is lower in the optimum than in the laissez-faire allocation. Indeed, in this example c_2 is a neutral good, so that the real income effect is zero.

Appendix 10A.3

In this appendix we derive the first-order conditions for the corrective policy and equation 10.16. The parent maximizes $u(c_1, n, c_2)$ subject to the following budget constraints:

$$c_1 + n(1 - s)e + nb - \beta n \le k - T, \tag{10A3.1}$$

$$c_2 \le (1 - t)g(e) + br, \tag{10A3.2}$$

$$b \ge 0. \tag{10A3.3}$$

The Lagrangian is

$$L = u(c_1, n, c_2) + \lambda_1 [k - T - c_1 - n(1 - s)e - nb + \beta n]$$

$$+ \lambda_2 [(1 - t)g(e) + bR - c_2] + \lambda_3 b, \tag{A103.4}$$

where λ_1, λ_2, $\lambda_3 \ge 0$. The first-order conditions when constraint 10A3.3 is binding (i.e., $b = 0$) are

$$u_1 - \lambda_1 = 0, \tag{10A3.5a}$$

$$u_2 - \lambda_1 (1 - s)e + \lambda_1 \beta = 0, \tag{10A3.5b}$$

$$u_3 - \lambda_2 = 0, \tag{10A3.5c}$$

$$-\lambda_1 n(1 - s) + \lambda_2 (1 - t)g' = 0, \tag{10A3.5d}$$

and

$$-\lambda_1 n + \lambda_2 R + \lambda_3 = 0. \tag{10A3.5e}$$

Notice that, at the laissez-faire allocation, (10A3.5d) and (10A3.5e) imply that $g' = R + \lambda_3/\lambda_2 \ge R$, which is (10.6a).

Differentiating (10A3.4) with respect to s, β, t, and T, and employing the envelope theorem yields

$$v_s = \lambda_1 NE, \qquad\qquad (10A3.6a)$$

$$v_\beta = \lambda_1 N, \qquad\qquad (10A3.6b)$$

$$v_t = -\lambda_2 g(E), \qquad\qquad (10A3.6c)$$

and

$$v_T = \lambda_1, \qquad\qquad (10A3.6d)$$

which proves (10.16).

11

Intragenerational Income Distribution Policies

We have dealt so far only with intrafamily issues of efficiency and equity. Because the parent of a family is conceived in this book as the decision-making agent who cares about her offspring, *intra*family issues are necessarily also *inter*generational. Similarly, *inter*family issues are also *intra*generational. In this chapter we consider familiar distribution tools (such as an income tax) in order to analyze *inter*family, *intra*generational income distribution policies. In the next chapter we combine both *inter*family, *intra*generational and *intra*family, *inter*generational features in order to explore the role of an income-tested social security scheme.

Demographic variables in general and number of children or family size in particular were recognized as determinants of household demand patterns. For instance, Pollak and Wales (1980, 1981) follow the method of "equivalence scale" or "standard adults" in explaining the differences in demand patterns caused by household size differences. According to this method, the preferences (U) of a family of i members over bundles of commodities [$c = (c_1, \ldots, c_m)$] is given by

$$U(c) = u(c/n(i)),$$

where u describes the preferences of a family of a normalized size (say, one member; that is, $n_1 = 1$). The function $n(i)$ is then interpreted as the number of standard adults in a family of i members. Of course, this approach assumes that fertility is exogenous. Therefore it is not adequate for studying normative issues related to intragenerational income distribution policies. For that purpose, it is more appropriate to assume that parents care about the number of their children, so that having more children does not necessarily mean being worse off as implied by the above specification of preferences.

Since Schultz (1974), it has been widely recognized that fertility and labor supply interact in an important way. It is not possible to analyze female labor force participation rates taking the number and age distribution of children in the family as exogenous, nor is it possible to model parents' choices adequately with respect to the number and spacing of their children when the mother's participation decision is taken as given. That endogenous fertility has important implications for other topics, such as the determination of family equivalence scales in demand analysis or optimal taxation policy in public finance, is less widely appreciated. More recently, Deaton and Muelbauer (1983) considered the implications of endogenous fertility on the measurement of child costs, recognizing that parents' welfare is determined by both goods and children, so that variations in children can be compensated by goods and vice versa. For the most part, the literature on optimal taxation policy ignores family size and composition entirely (e.g. Mirrlees (1971)); Those studies taking family size into account treat it as exogenous (e.g. Mirrlees 1972; Bruno and Habib 1976; Balcer and Sadka (1986))[1] the descriptive literature on tax policy deals extensively with the treatment of family size in taxation systems (e.g., Musgrave (1959), Pechman 1966).

In this chapter we analyze alternative *intra*generational income distribution policies, focusing on income taxation and child allowances, where the parent is altruistic and fertility to be endogenous.[2] Tax and family policies designed to affect the distribution of income or welfare that do not take into account their effects on fertility, may have unintended consequences. For example, if poverty, in the sense of low family income per capita, tends to be associated with large family size, a system of child allowances and tax exemptions designed to alleviate poverty and reduce inequality may actually worsen the situation.

The distributive role of income taxation is now quite familiar; child allowances, though not common in all countries, nevertheless play a

Table 11.1
Child allowances and income tax credits for children (Israel, 1990, in U.S. dollars)

Number of children	Annual income tax credits for working mothers	Annual family child allowances
1	415	415
2	415	830
3	830	1,660
4	830	3,320
5	1,245	4,565
6	1,245	6,018
7	1,660	7,470
8	1,660	8,923
9	2,075	10,375
10	2,075	11,828

Source: Razin and Sadka (1993).

major role in income distribution policies in quite a few countries. To name just one, Israel has a universal system of child allowances and income tax credits for working mothers with a significant order of magnitude (see table 11.1). In Israel a family of four children, for example, receives an annual allowance of $3,320 (approximately 20% of the average wage, which amounted to $16,320 per annum in 1990); if the mother is working, she qualifies for an additional income tax credit of $830 (approximately 5% of the average wage).

11.1   Fixed Labor Supply

Consider an economy with families who have identical tastes but different (exogenous) incomes. For the sake of simplicity, suppose that there are only two income levels (k^1 and k^2, where $k^1 < k^2$). The common utility function of each household is, as before, of the Becker-Lewis (1973) type (see also chapter 3):

$$\bar{u}(c, z, n),$$

where

c = the parent's consumption,

z = child's quality as measured by the expenditure per child, and

n = number of children.

The parent cares not only about herself but also about the quality and the number of her children, so that $\bar{u}$ is increasing in c, z, and n, that is, $\bar{u}_i > 0$, $i = 1, 2, 3$.

We find it convenient to work with a transformed version of the above utility function:

$$u(c, q, n) = \bar{u}(c, q/n, n),\tag{11.1}$$

where $q = zn$ is the total expenditure on children. Observe that while u is increasing in c and q, it need not be increasing in n, because $u_3 = \bar{u}_3 - \bar{u}_2 q/n^2$, which may be of any sign. While the parent still enjoys having more children ($\bar{u}_3 > 0$), nevertheless, increasing the number of children reduces the expenditure on (the quality of) each child, given total expenditure ($-\bar{u}_2 q/n^2 < 0$).

The government employs a very simple income tax: a child allowance, β, which may be either positive or negative, budget-balanced by a uniform lump-sum tax, T, on each family (parent). Note that because income is exogenous, a nonlinear tax on income may be used to achieve any Pareto-optimal allocation. Similarly, if the government can impose a proportional tax on income in addition to T, it can achieve perfect equality between the two families by taxing away all the exogenous income (a 100% marginal tax rate), redistributing the proceeds equally (using T). We analyze these more general tax systems in the next section, where labor supply and therefore incomes are variable. When labor supply is fixed, these more general tax systems can circumvent the problem at hand altogether. For this reason we restrict the analysis in this section to the simple system described above.

The budget constraint of a family with income k^i ($i = 1, 2$) is therefore

$$c + q - \beta n \leq k^i - T.\tag{11.2}$$

The parent chooses c, q, and n so as to maximize (11.1), subject to (11.2). This yields an indirect utility function, $V(k^i - T, \beta)$, as well as demand functions, $C(k^i - T, \beta)$, $Q(k^i - T, \beta)$, and $N(k^i - T, \beta)$, for consumption, total child expenditure, and number of children, respectively. The arguments of these functions are disposable income $(k^i - T)$ and child allowance (β). Observe that because the tastes are the same for all families, these functions are the same, except that their arguments can of course take different values for different families.

Employing the envelope theorem, we can conclude that

$$V_2 = NV_i. \tag{11.3}$$

In order to simplify the notation, we write v^i, c^i, q^i, and n^i for $V(k - T, \beta)$, $C(k^i - T, \beta)$, $Q(k^i - T, \beta)$, and $N(k^i - T, \beta)$, respectively. Similar notation is used for the partial derivatives of these functions; we write v_1^i for $V_1(k^i - T, \beta)$ and so on.

We assume that poverty goes together with large families, that is,

$$N_1 < 0. \tag{11.4}$$

Note that (11.4) refers to the reduced form demand function for the number of children and does not assume that the number of children is an inferior good in the usual sense. Specifically, if we write the budget constraint as $c + zn = k$ (ignoring the government's instruments, T and β), it is clear that z is the "price" of n and vice versa, as in chapter 3. Assumption 11.4 is perfectly consistent with the assumption that n is a normal good in the usual sense, that is, an increase in income increases n if z is kept constant. But z does not stay constant; indeed, chapter 3, in reviewing Becker and Lewis (1973), shows that if z is sufficiently income-elastic in the usual sense (i.e., when keeping n constant) and substitutable to n, then z rises and n falls when income is increased, which leads to our assumption (11.4).

The government budget constraint is given by

$$2T - \beta[N(k^1 - T, \beta) + N(k^2 - T, \beta)] \geq 0. \tag{11.5}$$

The government wishes to maximize a social welfare function, $W(V(k^1 - T, \beta), V(k^2 - T, \beta))$, which depends positively on the parent's utilities (i.e., $W_1 > 0$ and $W_2 > 0$). In general, W may be written as a weighted average of the two utility functions. Here we analyze only the two polar cases in which all the weight is assigned to either the first or the second kind of household. The government does not employ individual-specific taxes or subsidies, but this does not mean that the government is not engaged in redistributing income from the small rich families to the large poor families or vice versa. A positive child allowance, for example, redistributes income from small rich families to large poor families; because each family can choose whether to be large or small in size, the poor household (i.e., the household with a pretax income k^1) will always be worse off than the rich household (i.e., the household with a pretax income k^2). Thus our two polar cases correspond to the Rawlsian max-min social welfare criterion and to the max-max social welfare criterion. All the other cases and the results corresponding to them are intermediate between these two polar cases.

11.1.1   Rawls's Extreme Egalitarianism: Max-Min

The social objective is to choose T and β so as to maximize the welfare of the poor family, $V(k^1 - T, \beta)$, subject to the government's revenue constraint. The first-order conditions are

$$-v_1^1 + 2\lambda + \lambda\beta(n_1^1 + n_1^2) = 0 \tag{11.6}$$

and

$$v_2^1 - \lambda(n^1 + n^2) - \lambda\beta(n_2^1 + n_2^2) = 0, \tag{11.7}$$

where $\lambda > 0$ is the Lagrange multiplier associated with (11.5). Multiplying (11.6) by n^1 and adding it to (11.7) yields

$$(1 + \beta n_1^2)(n^1 - n^2) - \beta(n_2^1 - n^1 n_1^1) - \beta(n_2^2 - n^2 n_1^2) = 0, \tag{11.8}$$

where (11.3), which states that $v_2^1 = n^1 v_1^1$, is employed.

Observe that, by (11.4), $n_1^2 < 0$. Hence it follows that $n^1 - n^2 > 0$ because the exogenous difference between the two families is in income alone. Note that, again by the envelope theorem, an increase in β changes the real income of family i by n^i. Thus the term $(n_2^i - n^i n_1^i)$ is the Hicks-compensated derivative of n^i with respect to β. Because β is a subsidy to the number of children, it follows from consumer theory that $n_2^i - n^i n_1^i > 0$. Rewriting the family budget constraint as $c + q = k - T + \beta n$, it follows that $\partial(C + Q)/\partial(k - T) \equiv C_1 + Q_1 = 1 + \beta N_1$. Assuming that the family's total consumption, $(C + Q)$, is a normal good, it follows that $1 + \beta N_1 > 0$. Hence, by (11.2), $\beta > 0$. Thus a max-min optimal policy results in a positive child allowance. To finance these allowances, a positive lump-sum tax must be employed as well (i.e., $T > 0$).

11.1.2   Extreme Inequality: Max-Max

Replacing the objective function $V(k^1 - T, \beta)$ of the preceding subsection by $V(k^2 - T, \beta)$, the analog of (11.8) now becomes

$$(1 + \beta n_1^1)(n^2 - n^1) - \beta(n_2^1 - n^1 n_1^1) - \beta(n_2^2 - n^2 n_1^2) = 0. \qquad (11.9)$$

Since $n^2 - n^1 < 0$ by (11.4), and since $1 + \beta n_1^1 > 0$ by the normality assumption, it follows from (11.9) that $\beta < 0$. Thus a max-max optimal policy results in a tax on children redistributed back to the two families by a uniform lump-sum subsidy ($T < 0$).

When $N_1 > 0$, as when z and n are not highly substitutable and both are normal, β is *negative* for the max-min welfare function and *positive* for the max-max welfare function.

Here we have assumed that labor supply is perfectly inelastic. For this reason we did not introduce a wage tax because it is nondistortionary and its superiority over other redistributive tools (such as child allowances) is trivial. In the next section we consider variable labor supplies, in which case a wage tax becomes distortionary and a balance must be then found between a wage tax and child allowances in any optimal redistribution policy.

11.2   Variable Labor Supply

Let utility also depend on leisure, which varies inversely with labor services (l). The utility function (11.1) becomes

$$u(c, q, n, l), \tag{11.10}$$

where $\mu_4 < 0$, that is, there is disutility of labor. In addition to assuming identical tastes, we assume different abilities that are reflected in the wage rates. Income is now no longer exogenous. Specifically, the poor family can earn a wage rate of w^1, and the rich family can earn a wage rate of w^2, where $w^1 < w^2$. In addition to the child allowance, β, the government imposes a linear income tax with a marginal rate, t, and a lump-sum tax, T (per family, not per capita). The budget constraint of family i is now

$$c + q - \beta n \leq w^i(1 - t)l - T, \qquad i = 1, 2. \tag{11.11}$$

A maximization of the utility function (11.10), subject to the budget constraint (11.11), gives rise to the indirect utility function $V(-T, \beta, w^i(1 - t))$ and the demand functions for consumption, quantity of children, total child expenditures, and labor supply, $C(\cdot, \cdot, \cdot)$, $N(\cdot, \cdot, \cdot)$, $Q(\cdot, \cdot, \cdot)$ and $L(\cdot, \cdot, \cdot)$, respectively, of the same arguments. It follows again from the envelope theorem that

$$V_2 = NV_1; V_3 = LV_1. \tag{11.12}$$

Again we simplify the notation by writing l^i for $L(-T, \beta, w^i(1 - t))$ and so on.

The government's budget constraint now becomes

$$t[w^1 L(-T, \beta, w^1(1 - t)) + w^2 L(-T, \beta, w^2(1 - t))]$$

$$+ 2T - \beta[N(-T, \beta, w^1(1 - t)) + N(-T, \beta, w^2(1 - t))] \geq 0. \tag{11.13}$$

The government chooses t, T, and β so as to maximize the social welfare function $W(V(-T, \beta, w^1(1 - t)), V(-T, \beta, w^2(1 - t))$, subject to the budget constraint (11.13). As before, we consider the two polar cases of max-min and max-max.

11.2.1   Max-Min

The government in this case maximizes $V(-T, \beta, w^1(1 - t))$, subject to (11.13). The first-order conditions are

$$-v_1^1 + 2\lambda + \lambda\beta(n_1^1 + n_1^2) - \lambda t(w^1 l_1^1 + w^2 l_1^2) = 0, \qquad (11.14)$$

$$v_2^1 - \lambda(n^1 + n^2) - \lambda\beta(n_2^1 + n_2^2) + \lambda t(w^1 l_2^1 + w^2 l_2^2) = 0, \qquad (11.15)$$

and

$$-v_3^1 w^1 + \lambda\beta(n_3^1 w^1 + n_3^2 w^2) + \lambda(w^1 l^1 + w^2 l^2)$$
$$- \lambda t[(w^1)^2 l_3^1 + (w^2)^2 l_3^2] = 0. \qquad (11.16)$$

Multiply (11.14) by n^1 and add the product to (11.15) to get

$$[(n_2^1 - n^1 n_1^1) + (n_2^2 - n^2 n_1^2)]\beta - [w^1(l_2^1 - n^1 l_1^1) + w^2(l_2^2 - n^2 l_1^2)]t$$
$$= (1 + \beta n_1^2 - w^2 l_1^2)(n^1 - n^2), \qquad (11.17)$$

where use is made of (11.12).

Also, multiply (11.14) by $-w^1 l^1$ and add the product to (11.16) to get

$$-[w^1(n_3^1 - l^1 n_1^1) + w^2(n_3^2 - l^2 n_1^2)]\beta$$
$$+ [(w^1)^2(l_3^1 - l^1 l_1^1) + (w^2)^2(l_3^2 - l^2 l_1^2)]t$$
$$= (1 + \beta n_1^2 - tw^2 l_1^2)(w^2 l^2 - w^1 l^1), \qquad (11.18)$$

where, again, use is made of (11.12).

Under suitable assumptions we can sign the terms of the system (11.17) and (11.18). Consider first the term $(n^1 - n^2)$; as in the preceding section, we can show that it is positive. To see this, let us write N_3 as $N_3 = (N_3 - LN_1) + LN_1$. Observe that $N_3 - LN_1$ is the Hicks-compensated derivative of N with respect to the net wage $(1 - t)w$. Because a compensated increase in the net wage reduces leisure and because it is plausible to assume that children are time-intensive (i.e., children and leisure are complements), we assume that $N_3 - LN_1 < 0$.[3] Continuing to assume as before that $N_1 < 0$

(condition 11.4), it follows that $N_3 < 0$. Since $(1 - t)w^1 < (1 - t)w^2$, we conclude that $n^1 - n^2 > 0$.

Second, consider the term $1 + \beta n_1^2 - tw^2 l_1^2$; again, the normality of $C + Q$ implies that it is positive. Third, we assume that the labor supply curve is not backward-bending so that

$$w^2 l^2 - w^1 l^1 > 0. \tag{11.19}$$

Fourth, observe that $(L_2 - NL_1)$ is the Hicks-compensated derivative of the labor supply function with respect to β and, by symmetry of the Hicks-Slutsky substitution effects, $L_2 - NL_1 = N_3 - LN_1$, which was assumed to be negative:

$$L_2 - NL_1 = N_3 - LN_1 < 0. \tag{11.20}$$

Finally, as before, the term $(N_2 - NN_1)$ is the Hicks-compensated derivative of N with respect to β, which is positive; similarly, the term $(L_3 - LL_1)$ is positive because it is the Hicks-compensated derivative of the labor supply function with respect to the wage rate. Thus the right-hand sides of the system (11.17) and (11.18) are both positive. Also, the terms multiplying β and t in this sytem are all positive, which proves

PROPOSITION 1   In the Rawlsian extreme egalitarian max-min case, either the child allowance (β) is positive or the marginal wage tax rate (t) is positive or both are positive.

The rationale of this result is quite intuitive: both the child allowance and the wage tax redistribute from the rich to the poor; if both are negative, the government will be doing the opposite, namely, redistributing from the poor to the rich, which is inconsistent with the egalitarian objective of max-min.

The above proposition does not of course rule out the possibility that either β or t will be negative. Of particular interest is the case where t is negative (and where β must be positive) because it is in contrast to the common result in the optimal income tax literature that a wage subsidy is not desirable. To get some intuition of when the various possibilities about the signs of β and t may emerge, apply Cramer's rule to the system (11.17) and (11.18) in order to get

$$\beta = \frac{1 + \beta n_1^2 - tw^2 l_1^2}{D} \{(n^1 - n^2)[(w^1)^2(l_3^1 - l^1 l_1^1)$$

$$+ (w^2)^2(l_3^2 - l^2 l_1^2)] + (w^2 l^2 - w^1 l^1)[w^1(l_2^1 - n^1 l_1^1)$$

$$+ w^2(l_2^2 - n^2 l_1^2)]\} \tag{11.21}$$

and

$$t = \frac{1 + \beta n_1^2 - tw^2 l_1^2}{D} \{(n^1 - n^2)[w^1(n_3^1 - l n_1^1) + w^2(n_3^2 - l^2 n_1^2)]$$

$$+ (w^2 l^2 - w^1 l^1)[(n_2^1 - n^1 n_1^1) + (n_2^2 - n^2 n_1^2)]\}, \tag{11.22}$$

where D is the determinant of the system (11.17) and (11.18), that is,

$$D = \det \sum_{i=1}^{2} \begin{bmatrix} n_2^i - n^i n_i^i & w^i(l_2^i - n^i l_1^i) \\ w^i(n_3^i - l^i n_1^i) & (w^i)^2(l_3^i - l^i l_1^i) \end{bmatrix}. \tag{11.23}$$

Observe that the matrices in (11.23) are nothing else but principal minors of the Hicks-Slutsky substitution matrices, except that the second row and the second column are each multiplied by the scalar $w^i > 0$. Hence $D > 0$.

It is clear from (11.21) and (11.22) that the own-substitution and the cross-substitution effects work in opposite directions; the own-substitution effects tend to make β and t positive, while the cross-substitution effects tend to make them negative. Several possibilities are discussed below.

(1) If the cross-substitution effect between leisure and number of children vanishes (i.e., $n_3^i - l^i n_1^i = l_2^i - n^i l_1^i = 0$) or is very small, then the own-substitution effect dominates, and both β and t are positive.

(2) Now consider the case where the cross-substitution effect is large. Suppose also that $w^2 l^2 - w^1 l^1$ is relatively small, while $n^1 - n^2$ is relatively large. In this case, a positive β is more effective than a positive t in redistributing income from the rich to the poor. If, in addition, the own-substitution effect of the child allowance on the number of children (i.e., $n_2^i - n^i n_1^i$) is small relative to the own-substitution effect of the wage on the labor supply (i.e., $l_3^i - l^i l_1^i$),

then β is also less distortionary than t. (Note that the distortions created by β on L and by t on N are the same, by the symmetry of the cross-substitution effects.) In this case, β will be positive, while t is negative.

(3) Similarly, under opposite assumptions regarding the relative sizes of $w^2l^2 - w^1l^1$, $n^1 - n^2$ and the own-substitution effects, β will be negative and t will be positive.

11.2.2   Max-Max

In a similar way, we have here

PROPOSITION 2   In the max-max case, at least one of the pair (β, t) must be negative.

Also, in complete analogy to possibilities 1–3 of the preceding subsection, both β and t are negative when the cross-substitution effects vanish, while one of them could be positive otherwise.

11.3   Conclusions

The main purpose of this chapter has been to investigate the implications of endogenous fertility for optimal *inter*family, *intra*generational redistributive taxation. In particular, the interaction between leisure, labor choice, and fertility has been shown to be crucial for the determination of both the signs and the magnitudes of the optimal child allowances and income tax rates. A notable deviation from the standard optimal tax literature is the possibility of a negative marginal tax rate under an egalitarian social welfare function. Another significant result is the possibility of a negative child allowance, again under an egalitarian social welfare function.

Finally, it should be emphasized that we have assumed that children enter the social welfare function only insofar as they generate utility to their parents. Both the sign and the magnitude of the child allowance may change if children's utilities are inserted directly into the social welfare function.

12

Inter- and Intragenerational Distribution: The Extended Role of Social Security

The redistributive role of a social security system is widely recognized. Current discussions in the United States regarding treatment of the so-called social security trust fund as an offset to the federal deficit are a reflection of this view. Recent shifts in the population age structure in many industrialized countries point to another redistributive concern. To confine the social security system to a purely redistributive role, however, ignores the possibility that the system may also mitigate inefficiencies arising from institutional constraints to individual *intra*family, *inter*generational transfers.

In chapter 10 we dealt with *intra*family, *inter*generational transfers (social security scheme) that aimed at enhancing the efficiency of resource allocation. More specifically, the role of social security was seen to correct a market failure associated with the institutional constraint that prevented the parent from obligating her children to pay her net debt after her death. In chapter 11 we examined the role of income taxation in making *inter*family, *intra*generational redistributions. In this chapter we combine *intra*family, *inter*generational with *inter*family, *intra*generational issues to examine the role of an extended social security scheme where contributions made by the young are income-related and benefits to the aged are uniform. Such redistributions improve the social welfare both by reducing income inequality and by mitigating the effects of bequest constraints. For a neat account of the role of the extended social security system, see Rosen (1988). This chapter provides a calibrated example of an extended social security scheme.

12.1   An Analytical Framework

It is convenient to combine here the main features of the models employed in the two preceding chapters, that is, we specify a two-family, two-generation model in which the parents' incomes are unequal. Parents' utility functions are assumed to be identical and to include their children's consumption and the number of offspring the parents have, in addition to their own consumption. Parents are assumed to provide for their children's consumption in the second period by investing in their human capital when they are young. When the children grow up, this human capital is translated into earnings capacity, part of which the parents may wish to tap to provide for their own consumption when they are old. Parents, however, are constrained from doing so by their inability to enforce "negative" bequests.

Let k^1 be the income of the poor family and k^2 the income of the wealthy family in the first generation. Then

$$k^1 < k^2.$$

Let c_1^i represent the parent's consumption for family $i = 1, 2$ (the poor and the wealthy family, respectively) and c_2^i, $i = 1, 2$ represent the respective per capita consumption of each of their children. Let n^i be the number of children and e^i the per capita investment in each child, $i = 1, 2$. We allow a nonnegative bequest, $b^i \geq 0$, which may be invested to become bR for each child, where R is the interest factor.[1] Let $w \equiv 1$ be the wage rate per efficiency unit of labor in the second generation. We assume that the number of efficiency units a child has depends on what the parent has invested in that child, e, according to an increasing and concave function, $g(e)$, with $g' > 0$ and $g'' < 0$. That is, there is a positive but diminishing return to investment in human capital.

Finally, let t be a proportional tax levied on the incomes of parents and children alike and S an equal lump-sum transfer granted to each family in the first generation (the demogrant).[2] As before, the utility of a first-generation family is assumed to be an increasing function of its own consumption, the number of children which it has, and the consumption of each child. Suppressing the superscript i where it is unnecessary, we write family i's maximization problem as

$$\underset{(c_1, n, e, b, c_2)}{\text{Max}} \quad u(c_1, n, c_2), \tag{12.1}$$

subject to

$$c_1 + n(e + b) \leq (1 - t)k^i + S,$$

$$c_2 \leq (1 - t)g(e) + bR,$$

and

$$b \geq 0.$$

The first-order conditions are

$$u_1 - \lambda_1 = 0,$$

$$u_2 - \lambda_1(e + b) = 0,$$

$$-\lambda_1 n + \lambda_2(1 - t)g'(e) = 0, \tag{12.2}$$

$$-\lambda_1 n + \lambda_2 R + \lambda_3 = 0,$$

and

$$u_3 - \lambda_2 = 0.$$

These conditions may be solved for the optimum values of c_1, n, c_2, b, and e for the ith family, which we denote by capital letters, C_1, N, C_2, B, and E, as functions of k^i, t, and S:

$$c_1^i \equiv C_1(k^i, t, S),$$

$$n^i = N(k^i, t, S),$$

$$e^i = E(k^i, t, S), \tag{12.3}$$

$$c_2^i = C_2(k^i, t, S),$$

and

$$b^i = B(k^i, t, S).$$

If the bequest constraint is binding, we must have

$$b^i = 0. \tag{12.4}$$

Substituting the maximizing values from (12.3) in the common parent's utility function yields the indirect utility function

$$V(k^i, t, S) = u[C_1(k^i, t, S), N(k^i, t, S), C_2(k^i, t, S)]. \tag{12.5}$$

We assume that the government must maintain a balanced budget over the whole time horizon but not necessarily at each point in time. The present-value budget constraint is therefore

$$2S - t\{k^1 + k^2 + \frac{1}{R}[n^1 g(e^1) + n^2 g(e^2)]\} = 0. \tag{12.6}$$

The specification of a social welfare function permits determination of the optimal levels of t and S that maximize welfare, subject to (12.6). Discussion of the optimum tax/transfer social security system is undertaken in section 12.3. In the next section we take the question of whether some social security scheme is warranted (i.e., better than nothing), when the bequest constraint is binding and provided a Rawlsian, max-min egalitarian criterion is adopted.

12.2   Is Social Security Warranted?

In the laissez-faire case $t = 0 = S$, that is, there is no government intervention. Suppose that in this case the functions u and g and the values of the parameters R, k^1, and k^2 are such that both families would like to bequeath negative amounts to their children and, correspondingly, to invest more in the human capital of each child. In this case, they are prevented from driving down the marginal product of human capital to the rate of return on bequests in the form of physical or financial capital by their inability to recoup anything from their children.

Suppose that the extreme egalitarian social criterion of maximizing the welfare of the poorest family is adopted, that is, the social objective is

$$\text{Max } V(k^1, t, S), \tag{12.7}$$
$$\underset{(t, S)}{}$$

subject to (12.6). Notice that from $k^1 < k^2$ it must follow that $V(k^1, t, S) < V(k^2, t, S))$.

In this section we show that a small shift from the laissez-faire regime of $t = 0 = S$ to one in which $t, S > 0$ is welfare-improving because it helps to achieve egalitarian social goals and also because it promotes efficiency by mitigating the institutional constraint against negative bequests.

The balanced-budget change in social welfare with respect to changes in t and S from zero is

$$\{\lambda_1 R(k^2 - k^1) + (\lambda_1 n^1 - \lambda_2 R)g(e^1) + \lambda_1 n^2 g(e^2) - \lambda_2 Rg(e^1)\}/(2R) \tag{12.8}$$

(see appendix 12A.1).

Since $k^2 > k^1$, the first term in (12.8) is positive. From (12.2)

$$\lambda_1 n^i - \lambda_2 R = \lambda_3 \geq 0, \qquad i = 1, 2,$$

so that the second term is positive. To sign the third term in (12.8), we need the additional plausible assumption that children's consumption (i.e., $c_2 = (1 - t)g(e)$) is a normal good. Hence $g(e^2) \geq g(e^1)$; by (12.2), the last term is also positive. Because an increase in S, financed by an appropriate increase in t, improves social welfare, we conclude that a social security scheme with income-based contributions (t) and universal benefits (S) is warranted.

We can see that income inequality provides an additional rationale for a social security (tax/transfer) scheme over and above that stemming from the desirability of reducing the inefficiency caused by the institutional constraint of non-negative bequests. The combined scheme of inequality-reducing contributions and universal benefits is justified, even though income-based contributions distort decisions with respect to human capital investment.

It is noteworthy that the *inter*family, *intra*generation differences add the term $\lambda_1 R(k^2 - k^1)/(2R)$ to the welfare-improving effect of social security. When *inter*family differences vanish (i.e., $k^2 = k^1$, $n^1 = n^2 \equiv n$, and $e^1 = e^2 \equiv e$), then (12.8) reduces to

$$(\lambda_1 n - \lambda_2 R)g(e)/R = \lambda_3 g(e)/R, \tag{12.8'}$$

which is identical to (10.19) in chapter 10, where there was no *inter*family income inequality.

12.3   An Optimal Social Security System: A Calibrated Example

In the preceding section we have seen that a "small" social security is welfare-improving. In this section we deal with how "big" the social security system should be. We present results based on numerical maximization of social welfare in a particular case in which the utility function is linear in the logs of c_1 and c_2, and the human capital/earnings function is also logarithmically linear. For the sake of simplicity, we also consider the number of children as exogenous.

Even in this simple case, specification of the appropriate maximand and appropriate constraint for the government is no simple matter. Essentially, the problem is that the maximand and the constraint depend on whether, at the particular chosen tax rate (t), with the benefit (S) then determined by the constraint, both families are bequest-constrained, one family is bequest-constrained (it must be the poorer of the two if children's consumption, c_2, is a normal good) and the other not, or neither family is bequest-constrained. Moreover, as t and S are varied, the regime will in general change.

The details of how the maximization problem is set up are contained in appendix 12A.2. For the results reported here, we choose $n = 1$, $\alpha = 0.7$ in

$$u = \alpha \log c_1 + (1 - \alpha) \log c_2$$

and $\beta = 0.2$ in

$$g(e) = \frac{1}{\beta} e^{\beta}.$$

A real rate of interest of 20 percent was assumed, so $R = 1.2$ in the calculation because of our assumption that a period is approximately one-half generation in length.

Table 12.1

k^2/k^1	1	2	5
t^*	0.62	0.60	0.74
S^*	2.57	2.79	4.32
$V^*(k^1, t^*, S^*)$	0.799	0.882	1.088
$V^*(k^2, t^*, S^*)$	0.799	0.973	1.271
b^{1*}	0.000	0.000	0.81
b^{2*}	0.00	0.12	1.13
e^{1*}	0.23	0.252	0.15
e^{2*}	0.23	0.252	0.15
c_1^{1*}	2.71	2.95	3.62
c_1^{2*}	2.71	3.23	4.35
c_2^{1*}	1.40	1.52	1.86
c_2^{2*}	1.40	1.66	2.24

Parameter specification: $\alpha = 0.7$, $\beta = 0.2$, $R = 1.2$.

Since we have assumed an extremely egalitarian social welfare function, it is of interest to see how the results are affected by variations in income inequality among the first-generation families. Setting the income of the poorer first-generation family to $k^1 = 1$, we examined three cases: $k^2 = 1$, 2, and 5, that is, equality, moderate inequality, and extreme inequality.

The parameter values were chosen so that in the laissez-faire case ($t = S = 0$) both families are bequest-constrained; t and S were chosen optimally ($t = t^*$ and $S = S^*$). The results of our calculations are presented in table 12.1.

For each of the three alternative predetermined income distributions, we present the optimal values of the contribution rate, t^*, the lump-sum benefit, S^*, and the corresponding values of all the endogenous variables of the model, where

$V^*(k^i, t^*, S^*)$	=	the utility level of family i,
b^{i*}	=	the bequest of the family i,
e^{i*}	=	investment of family i in its child's human capital,

c_1^i $=$ the consumption level of family i, and

c_2^{i*} $=$ the consumption level of the child of family i,

and where $i = 1, 2$.

(Recall that family 1 is the poor family, while family 2 is the wealthy one.)

It can be seen from the first column that, in the case of equal incomes, the welfare of both families is the same, both families are bequest-constrained (i.e., both would like to bequeath negative amounts to their children), and all consumption and investment variables are also identical. With moderate income inequality, the more well-to-do family is no longer bequest-constrained at the optimum level of social security, but the poor family remains so. The leveling effects of the redistribution aspects of the program are more pronounced in the second generation, in which consumption of the two children is nearly the same. Interestingly, the difference, such as it is, is due almost entirely to the wealthier family's positive bequest, for the two families invest almost identical amounts in their respective child's human capital. Finally, with extreme income inequality in the first generation, the reverse is true: most of the reduction in inequality of consumption is in the first generation, both families bequeath different amounts, but each invests the same amount in the human capital of its child. The three different degrees of income inequality illustrate the three different regimes: (1) both families are bequest-constrained; (2) only the poor family is bequest-constrained; and (3) neither family is bequest-constrained.[3]

In order to examine more carefully the issue of how the bequest constraint operates, we computed, for various nonoptimal contribution rates what each family would like to bequeath if it were not constrained. That is, we computed t and S for the appropriate constraint, corresponding to $b^1 = 0$, $b^2 = 0$ (when $k^2/k^1 = 1$); $b^1 = 0$, $b^2 > 0$ (when $k^2/k^1 = 2$); or $b^1 > 0$, $b^2 > 0$ (when $k^2/k^1 = 5$), but then we went back and solved each family's maximization problem as though bequests were not constrained. This solution frequently gave a negative bequest for the first two cases.

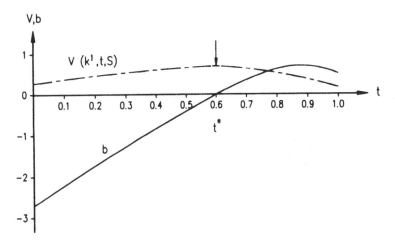

Figure 12.1
$k^2/k^1 = 1$

Our results are presented in figures 12.1–12.3. Also presented in the graph is the correctly calculated (when the bequest constraints are taken into account) value of the function being maximized, that is, the welfare of the poor family. One can see from figure 12.1 that both families are bequest-constrained until the contribution rate is just equal $t^* = 0.60$, the optimum rate. The magnitude of the constraint is very large at $t = 0$, indicating that with no social security system, both families would like to bequeath a large negative amount. When there is moderate income inequality, the optimal contribution rate, $t^* \cong 0.60$, is almost the same as before, as is the magnitude of the effect of the bequest constraint on the poor family. But now the burden of the constraint is somewhat lighter for the wealthier family. When inequality is extreme, the optimal contribution rate jumps to $t^* = 0.74$, but the effect of the constraint is much lighter for the wealthy family.

The results presented in these figures also suggest how the regime is determined by the contribution rate: as t increases from zero, at first both families are bequest-constrained, then only the poor family, and finally neither family. In the case of extreme income inequality, bequests of both families become positive long before the optimum contribution rate is reached.

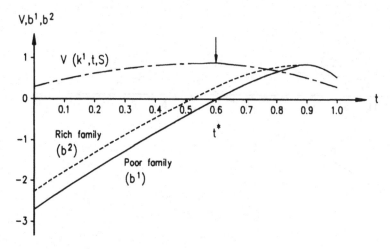

Figure 12.2
$k^2/k^1 = 2$

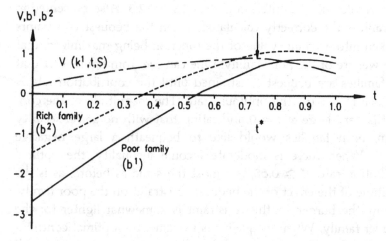

Figure 12.3
$k^2/k^1 = 5$

12.4   Conclusions

Our findings suggest that, given an egalitarian max-min social welfare function, there are two motives for introducing a social security tax/transfer scheme: first, the reduction in *inter*family inequality and, second, the improvement of the loss of economic efficiency resulting from institutional constraints to negative bequests (i.e., direct transfers from children to their parents). When parents are altruistic and fertility is endogenous, we find that government intervention to introduce a social security tax/transfer system is always socially welfare-improving. More specific results in a calibrated example suggest very large effects of the bequest constraint as well as important differences in these effects and in socially optimal policies when *inter*family inequality is more marked than when it is slight.

Appendix 12A.1   Derivation of the Welfare Gain from Social Security

In this appendix we derive (12.8).

The balanced-budget change in social welfare with respect to changes in t and S from zero is

$$dV(k^1, t, S) = v_2^1 \, dt + v_3^1 \, dS. \tag{12A1.1}$$

Employing the envelope theorem, we obtain

$$v_2^1 = -\lambda_1 k^1 - \lambda_2 g(e^1),$$
$$v_3^1 = \lambda_1, \tag{12A1.2}$$

which implies

$$dV(k^1, t, s) = -\lambda_1 k^1 \, dt - \lambda_2 g(e^1) \, dt + \lambda_1 \, dS. \tag{12A1.3}$$

From (12.6), the government's budget constraint, we obtain for variations dt and dS from zero:

$$2 \, dS - \left\{ k^1 + k^2 + \frac{1}{R} [n^1 g(e^1) + n^2 g(e^2)] \right\} dt = 0. \tag{12A1.4}$$

So to maintain the balanced budget, we have from (12A1.3) and (12A1.4) that the change in social welfare due to a variation, dt, in the tax rate is

$$\frac{dv(k^1, t, s)}{dt} = v_2^1 + v_3^1 \frac{dS}{dt}$$

$$= -\lambda_1 k^1 - \lambda_2 \dot{g}(e^1)$$

$$+ \frac{\lambda_1}{2} \{k^1 + k^2 + \frac{1}{R}[n^1 g(e^1) + n^2 g(e^2)]\}$$

$$= \{\lambda_1 R(k^2 - k^1) + (\lambda_1 n^1 - \lambda_2 R)g(e^1)$$

$$+ \lambda_1 n^2 g(e^2) - \lambda_2 R g(e^1)\}/(2R), \qquad (12A1.5)$$

which proves (12.8).

Appendix 12A.2   Derivation of the Calibrated Example of Social Security

In this appendix we derive analytical results for specific forms of the utility function and the human capital/earnings function that appear in section 12.3. In these derivations we assume, for simplicity, that fertility is exogenous.

The specification of the example is as follows:

$n = 1$, exogenous; $\qquad\qquad\qquad\qquad\qquad\qquad\qquad$ (12A2.1)

$u = \alpha \log c_1 + (1 - \alpha) \log c_2, \qquad 0 < \alpha < 1;$ $\qquad$ (12A2.2)

and

$g(e) = e^\beta / \beta, \qquad \beta > 0.$ $\qquad\qquad\qquad\qquad\qquad$ (12A2.3)

There are three possible regimes that have to be considered as the contribution rate, t, and the lump-sum benefit, S, are increased from 0. These regimes concern both the maximand and the government budget constraint. Note that the relation between t and S also changes. One possibility is that both families' bequests are constrained. A second possibility is that only one family's bequest is constrained but that the other family will make a positive bequest to its child. If investment in human capital is a normal good (i.e., if c_2 is normal) and is subject to diminishing returns, then this case will occur only when the wealthier family is unconstrained, since only this family will push e to the point at which $(1 - t)g = R$ and at that point will begin to make positive financial bequests. A final possibility is that both families will be unconstrained, that is, both will both make positive bequests.

Which of these three regimes will prevail is endogenous, that is, depends on the contribution rate, t. We will distinguish regimes by two dichotomous variables, δ_1 and δ_2, which are a function of t, such that

$\delta_1 = 1, \delta_2 = 0$ if both families are constrained,

$\delta_1 = 0, \delta_2 = 1$ if the poor family is constrained,

$\hspace{9cm}$ (12A2.4)

and

$\delta_1 = 0, \delta_2 = 0$ if both families are unconstrained.

We derive the relation between (t, S) and e_1, c_1, c_2 and b in each of these three cases and use the results to set up the government's objective function and constraint in each case. The results may then be combined using the function $\delta(t)$ to set up the overall maximization problem in terms of a combined maximand and a combined constraint that includes the regime, δ, as one of the endogenous variables.

CASE 1 Both families are constrained, $\delta_1 = 1, \delta_2 = 0$.

The ith family's problem is

$$\text{Max}_{(c_1, c_2, e)} \ u = \alpha \log c_1 + (1 - \alpha) \log c_2, \hspace{2cm} (12A2.5)$$

subject to

$$c_1 + e \leq (1 - t)k^i + S,$$

$$c_2 \leq (1 - t)\frac{1}{\beta}e^\beta,$$

and

$$b = 0.$$

The solution to this problem yields the optimal values C_1^i, C_2^i, and E^i as functions of t and S, with

$$b^i = 0,$$

$$C_1^i = (1 - \gamma)[(1 - t)k^i + S],$$

$$C_2^i = \frac{(1 - t)}{\beta}\gamma^\beta[(1 - t)k^i + S]^\beta = (1 - t)g(E^i), \qquad (12A2.6)$$

and

$$E^i = \gamma[(1 - t)k^i + S],$$

where

$$\gamma = \frac{\beta(1 - \alpha)}{\alpha + \beta(1 - \alpha)}$$

and

$$i = 1, 2.$$

In this case, the indirect utility of the poorer family, which is the social maximand, is given by

$$V(k^1, t, S) = u[C_1(k^1, t, S), C_2(k^1, t, S)]$$

$$= \alpha \log C_1^1 + (1 - \alpha) \log C_2^1$$

$$= (1 - \alpha) \log(1 - t) + \sigma$$

$$+ [\alpha + \beta(1 - \alpha)] \log[(1 - t)k^1 + S], \qquad (12A2.7)$$

where

$$\sigma = \alpha \log(1 - \gamma) + (1 - \alpha)(\beta \log \gamma - \log \beta).$$

The government's constraint is

$$2S - t \left\{ k^1 + k^2 + \frac{\gamma^\beta}{R\beta} \left[[(1 - t)k^1 + S]^\beta \right. \right.$$

$$\left. \left. + [(1 - t)k^2 + S]^\beta \right] \right\} \leq 0. \tag{12A2.8}$$

CASE 2   The poorer family is constrained, $\delta_1 = 0$, $\delta_2 = 1$.

In this case the poor family will solve the maximization problem (12A2.5) and the social maximand will be (12A2.7); however, the government's budget constraint changes because the wealthier family, $i = 2$, now solves

$$\underset{(c_1, c_2, e, b)}{\text{Max}} \quad u = \alpha \log c_1 + (1 - \alpha) \log c_2, \tag{12A2.9}$$

subject to

$$c_1 + e + b \leq (1 - t)k^i + S,$$

$$c_2 \leq (1 - t)\frac{1}{\beta}e^\beta + bR,$$

and

$$b \geq 0.$$

This problem is solved by

$$C_1^i = \frac{\alpha}{1 - \alpha}\left[\frac{1}{\beta}\left(\frac{1 - t}{R}\right)^{\frac{1}{1-\beta}} + B^i\right],$$

$$C_2^i = \left(\frac{1 - t}{\beta}\right)\left(\frac{1 - t}{R}\right)^{\frac{\beta}{1-\beta}} + B^i R, \tag{12A2.10}$$

and

$$E^i = \left(\frac{1 - t}{R}\right)^{\frac{1}{1-\beta}},$$

where the bequest function B^i is given by

$$B^i = (1 - \alpha)k^i - \left(1 - \alpha + \frac{\alpha}{\beta}\right)\left(\frac{1}{R}\right)^{\frac{1}{1-\beta}}, \text{ for } t, S > 0, i = 2.$$

In this case, the government's constraint is not (12A2.8) but rather

$$2S - t\left\{k^1 + k^2 + \frac{\gamma^\beta}{R\beta}[(1 - t)k^1 + S]^\beta + \frac{1}{R\beta}\left(\frac{1 - t}{R}\right)^{\frac{\beta}{1-\beta}}\right\} \le 0.$$

$$(12A2.11)$$

CASE 3   Both families are unconstrained, $\delta_1 = 0$, $\delta_2 = 0$.

In this case the social maximand is

$$V(k^1, t, S) = \alpha \log C_1^1 + (1 - \alpha) \log C_2^1,\qquad (12A2.12)$$

where C_1^1 and C_2^1 are given in (12A2.10). Note that B^1 and B^2, while both are positive in this case, differ in value depending on whether $t = 0 = S$ or $t, S > 0$.

The government's budget constraint in this case is

$$S - t\left[\frac{k^1 + k^2}{2} + \frac{1}{R\beta}\left(\frac{1 - t}{R}\right)^{\frac{\beta}{1-\beta}}\right] \le 0.\qquad (12A2.13)$$

The Overall Maximization Problem

Observe that from (12A2.4):

Case 1: $\delta_1 = 1, \delta_2 = 0, 1 - \delta_1 - \delta_2 = 0$;

Case 2: $\delta_1 = 0, \delta_2 = 1, 1 - \delta_1 - \delta_2 = 0$;

Case 3: $\delta_1 = 0, \delta_2 = 0, 1 - \delta_1 - \delta_2 = 1$.

Thus the overall maximand for the government is

$$\underset{(t, S)}{\text{Max}} \left\{\begin{array}{l} \delta_1 \times \text{expression in (12A2.7)} + \delta_2 \times \text{expression in (12A2.7)} \\ + (1 - \delta_1 - \delta_2) \times \text{expression in (12A2.12)} \end{array}\right\}.$$

$$(12A2.14)$$

Maximization is carried out subject to the following constraint:

$\delta_1 \times$ expression in (12A2.8) $+ \delta_2 \times$ expression in (12A2.11)

$+ (1 - \delta_1 - \delta_2) \times$ expression in (12A2.13) $\leq 0.$ (12A2.15)

The results, presented in table 12.1 of the text, are based on a numerical calculation of the above maximization problem for

$\alpha = 0.7, \beta = 0.2, R = 1.2, k^1 = 1,$ and $k^2 = 1, 2, 5.$

V

Growth and Development

13

Engines of Growth

Long-run economic growth has been a subject of major interest in economics for theorists, empiricists, and policy designers. Pioneering works on the theory of economic growth were written by Ramsey (1928), Harrod (1939), von Neumann (1945), Domar (1947), and others. Stylized facts were compiled by Abramovitz (1956), Denison (1962), Kuznets (1966), and others. The rate of capital accumulation (through savings) and the rate of growth of the labor force (commonly considered as identical to the rate of population growth) were the major determinants of economic growth. Balanced (or steady-state) growth was characterized by equal rates of growth of both total output and population. Thus output per capita was constant at the balanced-growth path. The savings rate, while determining the *level* of this constant output per capita, has no effect on the rate of growth of total output (which is equal to the population growth rate) and on the rate of growth of per capita output (which is equal to zero).

Solow (1956, 1957) recognized the role of technical change (or productivity growth) in generating a positive rate of growth of per capita output on the balanced growth path. Still, neither the saving rate nor the population growth rate had any effect on the growth rate of output per capita (which was solely determined by the exogenously determined rate of technical change). Thus the balanced growth rate was exogenously a priori determined. More recent works (e.g., Romer 1986; Lucas 1988; and Rebelo 1992) reexamined the determinants of economic growth and endogenized them. That is, the balanced growth rate of per capita output becomes a function of the saving rate and the population growth.

A key feature of this book is the endogeneity of fertility. That is, the population growth rate is determined by utility-maximizing parents and is therefore affected by economic conditions. On the other hand, as the aforementioned recent works suggest, the population growth rate itself affects long-run economic growth; thus fertility and long-run economic growth interact with each other and can be influenced by economic policy. This interaction is studied in this chapter. We begin with a simple exposition of how (exogenous) fertility can affect long-run growth. In a subsequent section, we endogenize fertility in the way followed throughout this book and examine the interaction between endogenous fertility and the balanced growth rate of per capita output.

13.1   Exogenous Fertility and Long-Run Growth

We follow the model and analysis developed by Rebelo (1992) in order to illustrate the role of exogenous fertility in explaining balanced growth. Let there be N_0 identical founding parents in period 0. In order to analyze long-run (steady-state or balanced) growth, we have to assume an infinite horizon economy. It is most convenient to consider dynasties. Each parent in period zero is the founder of a dynasty and designs a plan for the whole infinite horizon of her dynasty. A period is the lifetime of a generation. Each dynasty (and the population) grows at a constant rate of g_n. The preferences of the founding parent of a dynasty are given by

$$U_0 = \sum_{t=0}^{\infty} \beta^t a(n_t) u(c_t), \tag{13.1}$$

where β is the subjective discount factor; n_t is the number of members of the dynasty in period t (and hence the population size is $N_0 n_t$); c_t is the consumption of each member of the dynasty in period t; $u(\cdot)$ is the instantaneous utility function; and $a(\cdot)$ is a monotonically increasing function that represents parental altruism towards their children. Note that $a(\cdot)$ multiplies $u(\cdot)$, so that the weight attached in the dynastic preferences, U_0, to a generation is increasing with the size of the generation.[1]

There is a single composite good which serves for all purposes: as a capital good and as a consumption good. We denote by k the stock of capital per capita. (Henceforth, all stock and flow variables are measured in per capita terms.) For simplicity and without loss of the main theme, we assume that gross output per capita (y) is linear in the per capita stock of capital, that is,

$$y_t = Ak_t, \qquad A > 0, \tag{13.2}$$

where the subscript t denotes period t. Given this linearity, it is straightforward to see that the rate of interest (r) is constant over time and is equal to the net (after-depreciation) marginal productivity of capital:

$$r = A - \delta, \tag{13.3}$$

where δ is the depreciation rate.

Gross output is allocated for consumption (c) and gross investment (i):

$$y_t = c_t + i_t. \tag{13.4}$$

Because we assumed that capital depreciates at a rate of δ, the stock of capital evolves over time according to the following equation:

$$k_{t+1}(1 + g_n) = i_t + (1 - \delta)k_t. \tag{13.5}$$

Each parent in period 0 chooses the stream of consumption $\{c_t\}_0^\infty$, so as to maximize the objective function (13.1), subject to the dynasty present-value budget constraint:

$$\sum_{t=0}^{\infty} c_t(1 + r)^{-t} n_t = \text{Initial endowment}. \tag{13.6}$$

The left-hand side of (13.6) is the present-value of consumption expenditure of the dynasty. First-order conditions for this optimization problem are given by

$$\frac{u'(c_t)a(n_t)}{\beta u'(c_{t+1})a(n_{t+1})} = \frac{1 + r}{1 + g_n} \quad t = 0, 1, \ldots, \infty. \tag{13.7}$$

y

The saving rate (denoted by s_t) is defined as the ratio of net investment $(i_t - \delta k_t)$ to net output $(y_t - \delta_t)$, that is,

$$s_t = (i_t - \delta k_t)/(y_t - \delta k_t) = [(1 + g_n)k_{t+1}/k_t - 1]/r, \quad (13.8)$$

where use is made of equations 13.2, 13.3, and 13.5.

For tractability, we specify the altruism function, $a(\cdot)$, and the instantaneous utility function, $u(\cdot)$, as follows:

$$a(n_t) = n_t^\alpha, \quad \alpha > 0 \quad (13.9)$$

and

$$u(c) = c^\sigma/\sigma, \quad 0 < \sigma < 1. \quad (13.10)$$

Note that α is some measure of the degree of parental altruism. For instance, when $\alpha = 1$, then the founding parent and each parent thereafter cares about the total utility of all subsequent generations (discounted by β). Under these specifications, the first-order conditions (13.6) become

$$(c_{t+1}/c_t)^{1-\sigma}(1 + g_n)^{\alpha-1} = \beta(1 + r). \quad (13.7a)$$

Equation 13.7a suggests that a balanced (steady-state) growth is achieved instantaneously: c_{t+1}/c_t is constant for all t. We denote this constant growth rate of consumption per capita by g_c, that is, $c_{t+1}/c_t = 1 + g_c$. Along this balanced growth path, per capita (net and gross) output grows at the rate g_y, which is given by

$$g_y = g_c = \frac{(sr + 1)}{1 + g_n} - 1, \quad (13.11)$$

where the saving rate, s, is given by

$$s = \{(1 + g_n)^{(\alpha-\sigma)/(1-\sigma)}[\beta(1 + r)]^{1/(1-\sigma)} - 1\}/r.^2 \quad (13.12)$$

The last two equations clearly indicate the role of the population growth rate (g_n) in determining the balanced-growth rate of per-capita output; here, too, the productivity of capital (r) and the subjective discount factor (β) have the usual effects on long-term growth.

Observe that total output (Y) and total consumption (C) grow at equal rates (denoted by g_Y and g_C, respectively), which are given by

$$g_C = g_Y = (1 + g_y)(1 + g_n) - 1 = sr$$

$$= (1 + g_n)^{(\alpha-\sigma)/(1-\sigma)}[\beta(1 + r)]^{1(1-\sigma)} - 1, \qquad (13.13)$$

where use is made of equations 13.11 and 13.12. Thus the population growth rate affects positively or negatively the rate of growth of total output and total consumption as α is larger or smaller than σ. Note that when α just equals σ, then the growth rates of total output and consumption do not depend on the population growth rate. The rationale for this result is straightforward. When $\alpha = \sigma$ (the benchmark case), then total utility at each point of time is equal (except for multiplicative and additive terms, which are exogenously given) to $(n_t c_t)^\sigma = C_t^\sigma$. Thus parents care about total consumption and not its decomposition between the number of children and per capita consumption. Because technology exhibits constant returns to scale, so that the founding parent's resource constraint is also expressible only in terms of total output and total consumption of her dynasty, the founding parent chooses the growth path of total consumption irrespective of the (exogenous) population growth rate. If $\alpha > \sigma$ (i.e., the degree of parental altruism is greater than in the benchmark case), then total output and consumption grow at a higher rate when population grows faster. If $\alpha < \sigma$ (i.e., the degree of parental altruism is smaller than in the benchmark case), total output and consumption grow at a slower pace when population grows faster.

Upon substitution of (13.12) into (13.11), we obtain a direct formula for the per capita growth rate of output and consumption:

$$g_y = g_c = \{\beta(1 + g_n)^{\alpha-1} r\}^{1/(1-\sigma)} - 1. \qquad (13.14)$$

Now, in the benchmark case when $\alpha = 1$, the rate of growth of population does not affect the growth rates of per capita output and consumption. The rationale for this result is straightforward. The marginal rate of transformation between two consecutive generations' per capita consumption is seen from the resource constraint, (13.6), to be $(1 + g_n)/(1 + r)$. The corresponding marginal rate of substitution is seen from (13.1), (13.9), and (13.10) to be $(1 + g_n)^\alpha \beta$ $c_{t+1}^{\sigma-1}/c_t^{\sigma-1}$. Now, when $\alpha = 1$, the population growth rate affects equally both the marginal rate of transformation and substitution. Thus g_n has no effect on g_c and g_y. When $\alpha > 1$ (i.e., the degree of parental altruism is larger than in the benchmark case), then the effect of the population growth rate is larger on the marginal rate of substitution than on the marginal rate of transformation. As a result, the growth rate of per capita consumption rises with the population growth rate. When $\alpha < 1$ (i.e., the degree of parental altruism is smaller than in the benchmark case), the growth rates of per capita output and consumption are negatively related to the population growth rate.

13.2 Endogenous Fertility and Long-Run Growth

So far we have assumed that the population growth rate was exogenously given. In this section we endogenize the population growth rate and study its interactions with the growth rate of output and consumption per capita along the balanced growth path.

Let us assume that at each period t, the parent is endowed with one unit of time that can be divided between work (l_t) and child rearing (v_t for virility):

$$l_t + v_t = 1. \tag{13.15}$$

Following Razin and Yuen (1993), we specify the evolution of population as follows:

$$(n_{t+1}/n_t) = v_t^\theta, \qquad 0 < \theta \leq 1, \tag{13.16}$$

or

$$1 + g_n = v_t^\theta.$$

Note that the left-hand side of (13.16) denotes the number of children of a parent in period t. Equation 13.16 then states that this number is an increasing function of the time allocated for child rearing, with nonincreasing returns (because $\theta \leq 1$). In other words, each additional child costs more in time allocated for child rearing.

For the sake of simplicity we follow the literature (e.g., Saint-Paul 1992; Bertola 1993) in continuing to assume a linear production function as in (13.2), with the shares of labor (γ) and capital ($1 - \gamma$) being constant over time and institutionally (and exogenously) determined:

$$\gamma = w_t l_t / (y_t - \delta k_t), \qquad 1 - \gamma = \frac{r_t k_t}{y_t - \delta k_t}, \tag{13.17}$$

where w_t is the wage rate at period t. Thus, it follows immediately from (13.2) and (13.17) that

$$r_t \equiv r = (1 - \gamma)(A - \delta). \tag{13.3a}$$

The dynasty's budget constraint (13.6) now becomes

$$\sum_{t=0}^{\infty} c_t (1 + r)^{-t} n_t = \text{Initial endowment}$$

$$+ \sum_{t=0}^{\infty} w_t (1 - v_t)(1 + r)^{-t} n_t, \tag{13.6a}$$

with n_t evolving according to (13.16).

The balanced growth path (which is achieved instantaneously in our specification of the model) is characterized by the following two equations (see appendix):

$$\frac{(\alpha - \sigma)[(1 + g_n)^{1/\theta}]}{\sigma \gamma (A - \delta)}[1 + A - \delta - (1 + g_y)(1 + g_n)]$$

$$+ 1 - (1 + g_n)^{1/\theta}\left(\frac{\theta - 1}{\theta}\right)$$

$$- \frac{1 + (1 - \gamma)(A - \delta)(1 + g_n)^{(1-\theta)/\theta}}{\theta(1 + g_y)} = 0 \tag{13.18}$$

and

$$(1 + g_y) = [\beta(1 + g_n)^{\alpha-1}(1 - \gamma)(A - \delta)]^{1/(1-\sigma)}. \tag{13.19}$$

the last two equations determine g_y and g_n. We thus observe that long-run economic growth and fertility interact with each other.

It is interesting to see how changes in the productivity parameter A and the factor share parameter γ affect long-run growth and fertility. This can be done analytically for some parameter configuration. For instance, suppose that $\alpha = \sigma$ (i.e., parents care about total consumption and not its decomposition between number of children and per capita consumption) and that $\theta = 1$ (i.e., a linear child-rearing function). In this case, (13.18) and (13.19) reduce to

$$1 - \frac{1 + (1 - \gamma)(A - \delta)}{1 + g_y} = 0 \tag{13.18a}$$

and

$$1 + g_y = \frac{[\beta(1 - \gamma)(A - \delta)]^{1/(1-\sigma)}}{1 + g_n}, \tag{13.19a}$$

respectively. Hence we conclude that

$$g_y = r = (1 - \gamma)(A - \delta)$$

and

$$g_n = \frac{[\beta(1 - \gamma)(A - \delta)]^{1/(1-\sigma)}}{1 + (1 - \gamma)(A - \delta)} - 1 = \frac{(\beta r)^{1/(1-\sigma)}}{1 + r} - 1.$$

Note that g_y is positive but that g_n is likely to be negative (since an empirically plausible value of $\beta(1 + r)$ would be roughly one, where $\beta r < 1$).[2] As expected, an increase in r, that is, a rise in productivity (A) or a rise in the capital share $(1 - \gamma)$ or both, raises the rate of growth of per capita output (g_y). On the other hand, an increase in r lowers fertility (g_n) when $(1 + r)\beta r < 1 - \sigma$, which is empirically plausible.

For other values of the parameters α, σ, and θ, we resort below to numerical simulation in order to study the effects of changes in the parameter values on long-run economic growth and fertility. The qualitative results are summarized in table 13.1. An increase in the capital share $(1 - \gamma)$ increases economic growth and fertility. The driving force for this result is an increase in the interest rate, which

Table 13.1
The effects of capital share, intertemporal elasticity of substitution, and parental altruism on long-term per capita output growth and fertility

Rate of growth	Capital share $(1 - \gamma)$	Intertemporal elasticity of substitution $(1/(1 - \sigma))$	Parental altruism (α)
Per capita output (g_y)	+	+	−
Population (g_n)	+	−	?

Note: Based on equations 13.8–13.9.

stimulates savings. An increase in the intertemporal elasticity of substitution (thus an increase in σ since the elasticity is $1/(1 - \sigma)$) lowers fertility and raises economic growth. Finally, increasing the degree of parental altruism (α) lowers economic growth, but its effect on fertility is ambiguous.

13.3 The Benthamite Criterion Revisited[3]

One of the criticisms leveled at the Benthamite (sum-of-utilities) criterion is the so-called repugnant conclusion which claims that this criterion may lead to an excessively high population size at the cost of embarassingly low standards of living of future generations. We have already analyzed this conclusion in a static framework (see chapter 5), but it is evident that a more appropriate framework for analyzing this conclusion, which refers to a long-run phenomenon, is a dynamic context such as the one considered in this chapter.

Notice that when $\alpha = 1$ in equation (13.9), then equation (13.1) becomes a Benthamite social welfare function. In this case, equations (13.3a) and (13.19) imply that

$$g_y = (\beta r)^{1/1 - \sigma} - 1, \tag{13.19b}$$

which is typically negative. In this case, the "repugnant conclusion" indeed holds: output and consumption per capita shrink eventually to zero.

However, a typical vehicle for altruistic parental transfers to offsprings is parental investment in their children's human capital. Also, in many endogenous growth models (e.g., Lucas 1988), investment in human capital generates the mechanism for sustainable growth. Indeed when the model of the preceding section is modified to include human capital, the "repugnant conclusion" is much less likely to be supported.

Specifically, imagine a dynastic world with a representative dynasty that has n_t identical agents in each period ($t = 1, 2, \ldots$) and two engines of growth (human capital and population). The head of a dynasty cares about her own consumption (c_0) and the future stream of consumption of each member of the dynasty (c_t) and the number of members in the dynasty (n_t). As before, preferences of the dynastic head are given by

$$\sum_{t=0}^{\infty} \beta^t n_t^\alpha c_t^\sigma. \tag{13.20}$$

(Note that $n_0 = 1$).

In this altruistic framework, the utility function of the dynastic head coincides with the social welfare function. As usual, in the absence of externalities and market failures, the optimal allocations can be decentralized as a competitive equilibrium.

Each household member is endowed with one unit of time (net of the leisure and working time, assumed to be perfectly inelastic) and possesses h_t units of human capital (given h_0 at $t = 0$) in each period t. She can split the unit time between learning in school (e_t for education) and child rearing (v_t for virility). Newly acquired human capital (h_t) accumulated from the previous period is supplied to the labor market in each period t at the prevailing competitive wage (w_t).

The dynamics of the two growth engines are determined as follows. The child-rearing activity gives rise to population growth similar to equation (13.16), that is,

$$n_{t+1} = D v_t^\theta n_t, \tag{13.21}$$

when D is a fertility efficiency coefficient. Recall that since the child-rearing cost (v) is increasing with the number of children, v^θ is the inverse function of this cost-quantity relation. The schooling activity contributes to human capital growth as follows:

$$h_{t+1} = Be_t^{\eta}h_t, \tag{13.22}$$

where B is the knowledge efficiency coefficient and η the productivity parameter. For simplicity, full depreciation is assumed for n_t and h_t in each period.

Final output is produced by competitive firms using total effective labor ($H_t = n_t h_t$) via, as before, a linear technology: $Y_t = AH_t$, where A is the production coefficient. Goods produced are the total consumed by the private sector ($n_t c_t$). The economywide resource constraint is thus given by

$$n_t c_t = Y_t = AH_t. \tag{13.23}$$

That is, in such a closed economy, aggregate consumption must equal aggregate output.

In the absence of a (physical) capital and in a closed economy, the (effective) dynastic budget constraint is $n_t c_t \leq w_t n_t h_t$. The optimization problem facing the dynastic head is to choose $\{c_t, e_t, n_{t+1}, h_{t+1}\}_{t=0}^{\infty}$ so as to maximize (13.20), subject to (13.21)–(13.22), and the temporal budget constraints, given $\{w_t\}_{t=0}^{\infty}$. The firm's problem is to choose the amount of effective labor, H_t^d, in each period t, so as to maximize profit, $Y_t - w_t H_t^d$, given w_t. The equilibrium wage rate (w_t) is determined in the labor market under market clearing: $n_t h_t = H_t^d$.

The consumer's first-order conditions with respect to c_t, e_t, n_{t+1} and h_{t+1} are given by

$$n_t^{\alpha-1}c_t^{\sigma-1} = \mu_t, \tag{13.24}$$

$$\mu_{h_t}\theta Be_t^{\eta-1}h_t = \mu_{n_t}\theta D(1 - e_t)^{\theta-1}n_t, \tag{13.25}$$

$$\mu_{n_t} = \beta\left(\mu_{n_{t+1}}D(1 - e_{t+1})^{\theta} + \mu_{t+1}(w_{t+1}h_{t+1} - c_{t+1}) + \left(\frac{\alpha}{\sigma}\right)n_{t+1}^{\alpha-1}c_{t+1}^{\sigma}\right), \tag{13.26}$$

and

$$\mu_{h_t} = \beta(\mu_{h_{t+1}} Be^n_{t+1} + \mu_{t+1} w_{t+1} n_{t+1}).$$ (13.27)

The Lagrange multipliers at time t associated with the consumer budget constraint and the laws of motion of population and human capital are denoted by μ_t, μ_{n_t}, and μ_{h_t} respectively. The equilibrium wage rate is given by

$$w_t = A.$$ (13.28)

The equilibrium condition derived from (13.23) is

$$c_t = Ah_t.$$ (13.29)

Substituting (13.21) and (13.22) into (13.25), we get

$$\frac{\eta \mu_{h_t} h_{t+1}}{e_t} = \frac{\theta \mu_{n_t} n_{t+1}}{1 - e_t}.$$ (13.30)

Substituting (13.21), (13.24), (13.28), and (13.29) into (13.26) and multiplying it by n_{t+1}, we have

$$\mu_{n_t} \frac{n_{t+1}}{\beta \mu_{n_{t+1}} n_{t+2}} = \left[1 - \frac{\beta \left(\dfrac{\alpha}{\sigma} \right) n^\alpha_{t+1} c^\sigma_{t+1}}{\mu_{n_t} n_{t+1}} \right]^{-1}.$$ (13.31)

Substituting (13.22), (13.24), (13.28), and (13.29) into (13.27) and multiplying it by h_{t+1}, we have

$$\frac{\mu_{h_t} h_{t+1}}{\beta \mu_{h_{t+1}} h_{t+2}} = \left(1 - \frac{\beta n^\alpha_{t+1} c^\sigma_{t+1}}{\mu_{h_t} h_{t+1}} \right)^{-1}.$$ (13.32)

Along the balanced growth path—the special path along which the time allocations as well as the rates of growth of population, human capital, and output are all constant—$e_t = e_{t+1}$. Equation (13.30) therefore implies that the left-hand expressions of (13.31) and (13.32) are equal. Divide equation (13.30) for time t throughout by the same equation for time $t + 1$ and using equations (13.31) and (13.32), we obtain one equation in one unknown, e. The time allocations (e and v) can be solved from this equation as

$$e = \left[1 + \left(\frac{\alpha}{\sigma}\right)\left(\frac{\theta}{\eta}\right) \right]^{-1}$$

and   (13.33)

$$v = \left(\frac{\alpha}{\sigma}\right)\left(\frac{\theta}{\eta}\right) e.$$

The growth rates are given by $g_h = Be^\eta - 1$ and $g_n = D(1 - e)^\theta -$ 1, with $g_c = g_y = g_h$ and $g_Y = (1 + g_n)(1 + g_h) - 1$. (Recall that y is per capita income and Y gross income.) Note that since $e + v = 1$, the competing use of time for the two growth activities implies a negative relation between $g_y = g_h$ and g_n. Note also the dependence of the time allocations and the growth rates on the preference of the agent toward child quantity relative to quality (reflected by α/σ) and on the effectiveness of time in producing quantity relative to quality (reflected by θ/η). In fact, one can show that, in this specific model, there do not exist any transitional dynamics. So the above solution indeed characterizes the entire dynamic path.

Note that in the Benthamite case, when $\alpha = 1$,

$$g_y = Be^\eta - 1 = B\left[1 + \left(\frac{1}{\sigma}\right)\left(\frac{\theta}{\eta}\right) \right]^{-\eta} - 1.$$

For a sufficiently high knowledge efficiency coefficient B, g_y is positive, so that the standards of living increase indefinitely and therefore are certainly not "embarassingly low."

Appendix 13A.1   Long-Run Growth with Endogenous Fertility: Derivation of the Balanced-Growth Equations

The balanced-growth equations can be derived from the first-order conditions for the founding parent's optimization problem together with the resource constraint and the factor share institutional specification.

The founding parent chooses c_t, v_t, and n_t for $t = 0, \ldots, \infty$ as so to maximize the utility function (13.1) subject to the dynasty-long budget constraint (13.6a) and the child-rearing function (13.16). The Lagrangian expression for this optimization problem is

$$L = \sum_{t=0}^{\infty} \beta^t n_t^{\alpha} c_t^{\sigma}$$

$$+ \lambda \{\text{Initial endowment} + \sum_{t=0}^{\infty} [w_t(1 - v_t) - c_t]n_t(1 + r)^{-t}\}$$

$$+ \sum_{t=0}^{\infty} \varphi_t(v_t^{\theta} n_t - n_{t+1}), \tag{13A.1}$$

where $\lambda \geq 0$ and φ_t $(t = 0, \ldots, \infty)$ are Lagrange multipliers. The first-order conditions are

$$\beta^t n_t^{\alpha-1} c_t^{\sigma-1} - \lambda(1 + r)^{-t} = 0, \tag{13A.2}$$

$$- \lambda w_t(1 + r)^{-t} + \varphi_t \theta v_t^{\theta-1} = 0, \tag{13A.3}$$

and

$$\alpha \beta^t n_t^{\alpha-1} c_t^{\sigma}/\sigma + \lambda[w_t(1 - v_t) - c_t](1 + r)^{-t} + \varphi_t v_t^{\theta} - \varphi_{t-1} = 0. \tag{13A.4}$$

Substituting $\beta^t n_t^{\alpha-1} c_t^{\sigma-1}$ from (13A.2) for the first term in (13A.4) and substituting φ_t and φ_{t-1} from (13A.3) for the last two terms in 13A.4 and rearranging terms yields

$$\frac{\alpha - \sigma}{\sigma} c_t + w_t \left[1 - v_t\left(\frac{\theta - 1}{\theta}\right)\right] - \frac{(1 + r)w_{t-1}}{\theta v_{t-1}^{\theta-1}} = 0. \tag{13A.5}$$

Along the balanced-growth path, v_t is constant (denoted by v) and $w_t = (1 + g_w)w_{t-1}$, where g_w denotes the growth rate of the wage. Thus dividing (13.A.5) by w_t and rearranging terms yields

$$\frac{\alpha - \sigma}{\sigma} \frac{c_t}{w_t} + 1 - v\left(\frac{\theta - 1}{\theta}\right) - \frac{(1 + r)}{\theta v^{\theta-1}(1 + g_w)} = 0. \tag{13A.6}$$

Substituting $l_t = 1 - v_t$ and $y_t = Ak_t$ into (13.17) yields

$$w_t = \frac{\gamma(A - \delta)y_t}{(1 - v)A}. \tag{13A.7}$$

Substituting (13A.7) into (13A.6) yields

$$\frac{(\alpha - \sigma)(1 - v)Ac_t}{\sigma\gamma(A - \delta)y_t} + 1 - v\left(\frac{\theta - 1}{\theta}\right) - \frac{(1 + r)}{\theta v^{\theta-1}(1 + g_w)} = 0. \tag{13A.8}$$

It follows from (13.2), (13.4), and (13.5) that

$$\frac{c_t}{k_t} = 1 + A - \delta - (1 + g_y)(1 + g_n).$$ (13A.9)

Substituting $(1 + g_n)^{1/\theta} = v$ (from equation 13.16) and (13A.9) into (13A.8) yields

$$\frac{(\alpha - \sigma)[1 - (1 + g_n)^{1/\theta}]}{\sigma\gamma(A - \delta)}[1 + A - \delta - (1 + g_y)(1 + g_n)]$$

$$+ 1 - (1 - g_n)^{1/\theta}\left(\frac{\theta - 1}{\theta}\right) - \frac{1 + r}{\theta}(1 + g_n)^{(1-\theta)/\theta}(1 + g_y)^{-1} = 0,$$

(13A.10)

where use is made of (13A.7) to conclude that $g_y = g_w$. Recalling that $r = (1 - \gamma)(A - \delta)$ completes the derivation of equation 13A.18.

Equation 13A.2 implies that

$$1 + g_y = [\beta(1 + g_n)^{\alpha-1}(1 - \gamma)(A - \delta)]^{1/(1-\sigma)},$$ (13A.11)

which is equation 13.19. (This equation is identical to (13.14) in the exogenous fertility case, recalling that $\gamma = 0$ there.)

14

Development and Population:
A Survey

Whether rapid population growth influences the pace of economic development positively or negatively, or indeed whether the relationship is the other way round, that is, the pace of economic development influences the rate of population growth, are issues that continue to attract scholarly and popular attention. Concern about the possible adverse consequences of population growth on the environment has stimulated renewed interest in population policies. A number of surveys of the issues by individual scholars and reports by national and international agencies are also available.[1] It is not easy to add much to the analyses and insights contained in these surveys and reports, let alone resolve the substantial differences among some of them on the crucial issue whether population growth is central or merely peripheral to the process of development. Instead of attempting this virtually impossible task, I propose to view some of the more important analytical and empirical findings in light of recent research in order to assess the implications for the process of development of rapid population growth. In keeping with most of the literature, I also do not carefully distinguish the effect of a large *size* of population per se from that of a rapid *growth* in the size of population, although this distinction is important.

14.1 Two-Way Linkages between Population Growth and Economic Development

Kelley (1988) points out that "it took over one million years for population to reach one billion—and that was 200 years ago. But the pace quickened, and in a relatively short span of 120 years the population doubled to two billion. The third billion took only thirty-five years to arrive, and the fourth fifteen." Few demographers anticipate that a stationary global population will be attained any earlier than the end of the twenty-first century, by which time global population is likely to exceed ten billion. The World Bank (1992, pp. 25–26) projects in its base case scenario of fertility decline that world population will stabilize at about 12.5 billion around the middle of the twenty-second century. If, on the other hand, the decline in fertility is slower than in the base case, population will stabilize at a level of 23 billion only towards the end of the twenty-second century. A more rapid decline, however, would lead to a stable population of 10.1 billion, to be reached early in the twenty-second century. Keyfitz and Flieger (1990) project a level between 7.6 billion (low variant) and 9.4 billion (high variant) for the year 2025, at which time they expect the global population to be still growing at an average annual rate of about 1 percent.

Even though global population is likely to continue to grow in the next century, available data suggest that the rate of growth of population in the developing countries as a group has ceased to increase and in fact has been declining, and that the total fertility rate has begun to decline as well. Indeed, Keyfitz and Flieger report that from an annual average rate of natural increase of 23.83 per thousand and an average total fertility rate of 5.4 for the period 1970–1975, a decade later the figures had declined to 21.07 and 4.2, respectively, in the less developed regions. They project these figures to be 11.37 and 2.3, respectively, by the period 2020–2025. While even a 1 percent rate of growth is rapid from the perspective of the broad sweep of history, if these trends are generally correct, in the long run, the issue becomes not so much the promotion of economic development in a context of rapid population *growth* in less developed regions as a group but, rather, whether some poor countries in Asia and Africa which are still experiencing rapid population growth will be able to achieve the transition to a regime of declining population growth. In attempting to analyze this issue, it is useful to recapitulate the main channels of interaction between population growth and economic development so well exposited by Kelley (1988).

The earliest identified channel, and one that continues to haunt popular imagination, is the Malthusian (I mean Malthus of the first edition of the *Essay*) specter of diminishing marginal returns to labor (and hence diminishing output per worker as population and the labor force increase) because of the fixity of other inputs to production such as land and other resources (renewable and nonrenewable). A more recent, considerably more complex but nonetheless purely mechanical reformulation of this channel, is found in several studies following Forrester (1971) and Meadow et al. (1972). As is by now well known, these studies incorporated virtually no economic reasoning and ignored several processes that tend to offset the diminishing returns; nor did they incorporate the possible slowing of population growth itself through modification of fertility behavior by individuals on their own and in response to incentives provided by the state. Although the early popular excitement induced by these studies deservedly died down, they spawned attempts to estimate the earth's "carrying capacity" in terms of the size of population that it could support. The environmental movement has also revived interest in some of the issues raised in these studies. I return to these themes in the next section.

The second channel (Kelley 1988) is the effect of a more rapid population growth on the time path of output arising from (1) its lowering the capital-labor ratio from what it would otherwise have been; (2) its increasing the proportion of children, thus diverting family resources towards raising children that would otherwise have been saved and invested; and (3) its accelerating rural-urban migration and growth of cities, thereby diverting public resources away from investment into larger expenditures on such publicly provided services as education, transportation, and other urban infrastructure. Kelley points out that while most scholars viewed the effect of rapid population growth on output growth as negative, empirical research showed that effect to be weak quantitatively or negative. Further, a small minority of scholars saw positive effects of a large population arising primarily from scale economies and agglomeration effects induced by the large market size associated with it, and secondarily from a somewhat less certain favorable effect of a large population on the rate of innovation and technical progress.

Several analytical models incorporating many of these negative and positive effects are available in the literature. Empirical studies intended to assess the significance of these effects vary substantially in the attention given to econometric problems. For example, Kelley (1988) reports that there is virtually no correlation between the average annual rate of growth of income per capita and population growth during 1970–1981 in developing countries. But, as he points out, it cannot obviously be concluded that the processes of development and population growth do not interact with each other: neither the existence of a significant nonzero correlation does not imply a causal relationship between the two variables nor does the absence of such a correlation imply the absence of an influence of one variable on the other. Indeed, because in such simplistic correlation exercises the possible differences among countries in other variables that might influence either or both income growth and population growth are not taken into account, it is impossible to interpret the correlation coefficient.

Studies that attempt a multivariate analysis often do not clearly distinguish between *exogenous* variables (i.e., variables that influence other variables without being influenced by them) and *endogenous* variables (i.e., variables that influence each other and are influenced by exogenous variables as well). Estimating a single equation from a system of equations (that together explain the set of jointly determined endogenous variables) by treating all explanatory variables (including endogenous variables) in that equation as exogenous would lead to biased estimates of parameters. For example, if a relationship between, say, income growth and population growth, as well as other exogenous variables is estimated through ordinary least squares, the estimated coefficient of population growth would be biased if population growth and income growth are jointly determined endogenous variables. Johnson and Lee (1987, p. xi) describe the situation thus: "Studies completed to date are frequently based on limited samples and data of poor quality, as well as on only partial and occasionally inappropriate conceptual models and statistical techniques. Simply put, the scientific literature contains few adequate studies of the effects of slower population growth in developing countries."

Before briefly summarizing the empirical findings, it is worth recalling that the short- and long-run effects of rapid population growth on development could not only be different quantitatively but also be in opposite directions. For this reason, even those who do not foresee rapid population growth as a development problem in the long run would still recognize that, in the short and medium run, difficulties of adjustment to accelerating population growth might be severe, indeed, severe enough to make its long-run neutrality moot. Few empirical studies address the dynamics of adjustment.

The empirical findings on the effect of population size and growth on various aspects of economic development were surveyed and evaluated by the contributors to Johnson and Lee (1987). Let me briefly summarize their conclusions on the effect on population growth of the following (the page numbers refer to Johnson and Lee 1987):

1 DIMINISHING RETURNS TO LABOR AND ENVIRONMENTAL DEGRADATION Pingali and Binswanger (p. 51) conclude:

The potential problems of declining labor productivity and environmental degredation are not problems of *levels of population densities*. Given sufficient time, it is likely that a combination of farmer inventions, savings, and the development of research institutions and institutions for dealing with soil degradation issues will be able to accommodate much more than the current population in most countries, especially in many of the low-density ones. However, if all these changes are required quickly and simultaneously because of rapid population growth rates, they may emerge at too slow a pace to prevent a decline in human welfare.

2 AGRICULTURAL PRODUCTIVITY Hayami and Ruttan (p. 93) find:

The question is frequently raised as to whether advances in indigenous technology induced by population density, along the lines outlined by Boserup (1965), would be sufficient to sustain rising levels of per capita income and consumption. Such advances, however, have rarely been rapid enough to do more than slow the rate of decline in labor productivity.

The association between more intensive cultivation and declining levels of labor productivity under conditions of rapid population growth has, at times, been reversed by a combination of technology transfer and institutionalization of the domestic capacity to adapt and invent biological and chemical technologies. This view is consistent with the green revolution experience in East, Southeast, and South Asia. If rapid population growth continues indefinitely, however, these gains will be difficult to maintain. For example, we have no experience in agricultural output in the range of 4 percent per annum or above over a sustained period.

3 LABOR SUPPLY AND EMPLOYMENT Bloom and Freeman (p. 138) point out that

developing countries have faced an enormous increase in population in the past two decades. Fertility and mortality patterns guarantee a similar large increase in the future. The experience of the past indicates, however, that despite inefficient dualistic labor markets due potentially to government-induced and other imperfections, developing countries were, on the whole, relatively successful in improving their economic positions over the period.... Overall, the experiences of the 1960–80 period tend to be more supportive of an optimistic than a pessimistic view of the ability of developing economies to adjust to population growth.

They conclude (p. 139):

if modern technology is applied to less developed countries at the same rate as in the past two decades—which presumably will require both human and physical capital investments of enormous absolute magnitudes, but of relative magnitudes comparable to those of the past—Malthusian disasters will not necessarily be the result of forecasted population growth.

4 URBAN GROWTH Montgomery (p. 150) finds that

although definitive statements are premature ... it would appear that the direct impact of population growth ... (on urban share of total population and on the structure of urban labor force) ... is either weak or ambiguous. Both theory and limited empirical evidence suggest that the economic consequences of urban population growth will vary depending on the nature of market imperfections in an economy and on the special constraints that face the public sector.

5 TECHNICAL CHANGE IN THE MANUFACTURING SECTOR James (p. 249) examined four mechanisms through which population variables

transmit an influence on technical change. Two mechanisms operated through the influence of rapid population growth or larger population size on labor supply and induced innovation and on economies of scale from larger market size. A third was the influence of higher population density on economies of scale in infrastructural investment. The last was the influence of larger population size on the enhanced capability to produce domestic capital goods and scientific knowledge for innovations. He did not find a simple relationship between population variables and technical change in any of them.[2]

6   EXHAUSTIBLE NATURAL RESOURCE SCARCITY   McKellan and Vining, Jr. (p. 317) reviewed trends at the global level in scarcity for a spectrum of natural resources and found that no sweeping general answers are possible for the critical questions: "Are natural resources becoming more scarce? Are conservation and population-control policies called for?" The primary reasons for this are that "all scarcity indices are deeply flawed: the analytical tools at our disposal are very blunt." This led them to arrive at a mixed set of conclusions: some resources were becoming scarcer while others were not, and as such, selective policy responses and no broad reordering of priorities were required.

Slade (p. 364) focused on the question whether natural resources could (and eventually would) constrain the growth of population and economic well-being and concluded that all attempts to give positive answers to the question at the macro level failed. This failure did not preclude her from drawing some tentative conclusions. She believes that problems associated with common-property resources will be more constraining than those associated with nonrenewable resources. Among the exhaustible resources she expects petroleum as likely to be most constraining in the sense of being in short supply and posing serious problems in adjusting to its increasing scarcity. She suggests that developing countries attempting a rapid program of industrialization will be most affected by exhaustible resource constraints and are most apt to suffer from common-property problems.

7   WELFARE OF CHILDREN AND PARENTS   Elizabeth King (p. 397) reviewed the literature on the influence of family size on the welfare of

children and their parents. She points out that past studies presumed that rapid population growth, and hence large family size, adversely affected the welfare of children and their parents. But once it is recognized that the number of children and the investments made in each child's health and education are the decisions of parents who presumably maximize family welfare, any negative association between family size and investments in a child's human capital will be seen as simply a reflection of the trade-off at the family welfare optimum between "quantity" and "quality" of children, given the family's budget (time and resources) constraints.[3] Of course, the trade-off is influenced also by factors exogenous to (i.e., beyond the control of) the family. For example, improvements of the quality of publicly provided goods and services (e.g., drinking water, sewage, health and educational facilities) would affect the trade-off. According to King, available studies do not provide reliable quantitative estimates of these influences. This is unfortunate since a priori reasoning suggests that the direction of influence might be ambiguous. For example, a reduction in overall child mortality rates, if perceived by the family and incorporated in its fertility decisions, improves the rate of return to investment in child quality. If family welfare depends on the expected number of surviving children and the cost of having children as in Heckman and Willis (1976), the effect on fertility of the improvement in mortality is ambiguous. On the other hand, if parents maximize expected utility, where utility depends on the number of surviving children, Sah (1991) shows that fertility is a declining function of mortality.

8   PUBLIC EXPENDITURES ON SCHOOLING   Schultz (p. 450) finds that income (i.e., real income per adult) and price (i.e., relative price of teachers) contribute to determining the equilibrium level of expenditures within a country:

The working hypothesis that private demands for educational services explain public expenditures is not rejected. Holding constant for these dominant income and price constraints on the public educational system, urbanization is found to be associated with lower expenditures per school-aged child, and this reduction in outlays on education in more urbanized countries is associated with a lower price of teachers relative to other goods.

9 NATIONAL SAVING RATES Mason (pp. 549–550) summarizes the evidence based on aggregate data as follows:

Available evidence from the international cross-section supports the proposition that a higher dependency ratio leads to lower saving, particularly among countries with moderate to high rates of income growth.

10 ON ECONOMIC GROWTH Ahlburg (p. 479) reviewed

several economic-demographic models of developing countries, focusing on the predicted impact of population change on economic development. Early models found a very large negative impact of population growth on economic development. More recent models have found this negative impact to be smaller than previously thought, and a few have found the impact to be positive in the long run. Other models have shown the impact of population change to vary widely across countries and to have little impact on the degree of urbanization.

On the basis of his review, Ahlburg (p. 514) found himself concurring with Preston (1982) that

population growth is not so overwhelmingly negative a factor for economic advance as to swamp the impact of all other influences. That is a worthwhile lesson that bears repeating, but it is no argument for faster demographic growth.

11 INCOME DISTRIBUTION Rapid population growth could, but need not, have a deleterious effect on interhousehold distribution of income and intrahousehold distribution of economic well-being by age and sex. David Lam (p. 619) finds the existing evidence on this issue to be ambiguous. Empirical and theoretical analyses examined by him did not provide strong support for the deleterious distributional effects. Lam, like Elizabeth King, correctly emphasizes the point that

population growth cannot be independently controlled as a policy instrument, but rather results from the behavior of individual couples. It is misleading to attempt to analyze the distributional effects of population growth in the same way that we might examine the distributional effects of a direct policy instrument such as income tax.

12   EXTERNALITIES TO CHILDBEARING AND FERTILITY   Lee and Miller (1991, p. 295) identified[4]

four broad categories of externalities: dilution of the per capita value of collective wealth; dilution of costs of collective projects with public good aspects; incentive reduction due to proportional taxes; and the effect of population age distribution on the tax rate necessary to support public sector activities such as health, education, pensions, social infrastructure, and other services ... A rough evaluation of many kinds of externalities in each of these four categories for a variety of countries [suggests the following]: For some of the countries widely viewed as having serious population problems, the net total of these quantifiable externalities was close to zero. For others, the value of collectively held mineral rights dominated the calculation, leading to a large negative externality, but one that may seem unconvincing to many as a basis for fertility policy.

They conclude that

externalities to childbearing, although apparently somewhat negative in most developing nations, do not typically provide a strong rationale for fertility policies going beyond pure family planning (the point estimates of the negative externalities are often large enough to warrant interventionist policies).

14.2   Population Growth, Resources, and the Environment

It was already noted that no generalization is possible on the effects of population growth on the scarcity of exhaustible resources. Excessive use of resources that are regenerative, that is, renewable, could cause severe environmental problems. Population pressures could lead to extended periods of overuse. Attempts to define and arrive at what constitutes a "sustainable" use have led to calculations of population carrying capacity of the earth's land, water, and atmospheric resources. For example, a study undertaken jointly by the Food and Agriculture Organization (FAO), the United Nations Fund for Population Activities and the International Institute for Applied Systems Analysis (IIASA) compared projected population with the potential for feeding this population in developing countries (Higgins et al. 1983). The study combined a climate map providing spatial information on temperature and moisture conditions with a soil map providing spatial data on soil texture, slope, and ph value, and then divided the study area into grids of 100 km^2 each. In all, 14 major climates were distinguished during the growing period and the 15 most widely grown food crops were considered, including wheat, rice, maize, barley, sorghum, pearl millet, white potato, sweet potato, cassava, phaselous bean, soy bean, groundnut, sugar cane, banana plantain, and oil palm. Three alternative levels of farm technology were postulated, varying from no change in existing cropping patterns, no use of fertilizers and pesticides, and no mechanization to optimum use of plant genetic potential along with needed fertilizers and pesticides and full mechanization.

The soil characteristics, climate, length of growing season, technology, and cropping pattern together with the requirement that production be sustainable (using appropriate fallowing requirements and soil conservation measures) determined the production potential in each soil-climate grid. These were aggregated to yield production potential for each country. Deduction of seed, feed, and wastage provided an estimate of the potential output available for human consumption for each crop. Livestock production potential was also assessed under the assumption that only grassland would be used to support herds and also under the assumption that crop residues and by-products would be used in addition (Shah et al. 1984). Given average calorie and protein requirements based on the 1973 recommendations of the expert committee of the FAO and the World Health Organization (WHO), the projected age and sex distribution of the population of a country, and the food production available for human consumption in terms of energy and protein, the maximum population which could be supported was estimated. Countries were defined as critical if they could not meet the basic food needs of their population even if all their arable land were devoted to growing food crops. Limited countries were the ones that could not meet these needs if part of their arable land had to be diverted to produce other food and nonfood crops.

The study found that the aggregate population carrying capacity was as low as 5.6 billion at a low level of farming technology and as

high as 33 billion at a high level of farming technology as against a
then-projected population of 3.6 billion in the year 2000. At a low
level of technology, however, nearly a billion of the projected population in year 2000 lived in critical countries with a carrying capacity
of 600 million, and another 1.5 billion in limited countries with a
capacity of 1.8 billion. As is to be expected with a high level of
technology, the projected population living in limited and critical
countries together amounted to 425 million against a carrying capacity in the aggregate of 441 million.

Not too much should be made of the results of the studies of this
type for several reasons. There is virtually no economic analysis
underlying these projections. Because farming is done by millions of
individual peasants, unless it is in their private economic interest,
given the prices for inputs and outputs they face and the constraints
to which they are subject, they will not produce a particular set and
level of crop outputs merely because it is agro-climatically and technologically feasible to produce it. In particular, the investments in
land, capital equipment, livestock, technical skills, and knowledge
needed to attain the potential output will not be forthcoming unless
the returns are adequate.

Asking whether each country or region within a country has the
potential to sustain its projected year-2000 population or its even-
tual stationary population, ignores the economic cost of such
autarkic development, even if it were feasible to sustain such a
population. Furthermore, fundamental ideas of comparative advantage and gains from trade between regions within a country and
between countries are absent in such analyses. At best, these studies
are useful in pinpointing countries where, with a technology that
raises the output per unit of land to the fullest extent, even the
current level of population cannot be sustained relying solely on
home production. This may be taken as indicating the need for
out-migration of a part of its population or for investment in production for exports to pay for food imports or some combination of
both.[5]

Going beyond the limited but vital question of capacity to meet
the food requirements of future populations, it is easy enough to

describe the general mechanisms of the environment-population growth interactions. World Bank (1992, p. 26) puts the issues as follows:

Population growth increases demand for goods and services, and, if practices remain unchanged, implies increased environmental damage. Population growth also increases the need for employment and livelihoods which —especially in crowded rural areas—exerts additional direct pressure on natural resources. More people also produce more waste, threatening local health conditions and implying additional stress on the earth's assimilative capacity.

The same report also recognizes the dependence of the poor countries (and the poor in each country) on natural resources, such as soil, forest cover, water, fisheries, and so on and points out that "the poor are both victims and agents of environmental damage." To the extent that rapid population growth is a reflection of poverty, the link between environmental degradation and population growth through poverty is established as well. As should be self-evident, and the report explicitly recognizes it, alleviating poverty is a moral imperative and, indeed, should be the overarching objective of economic development.

International discussions on the impact of the development process on the environment has led to a popular phrase called "sustainable development" by which presumably all the "right-minded," "morally upright" individuals and organizations swear. Indeed, World Bank (1992, p. 34) approvingly quotes and strongly supports the principle of sustainable development as enunciated by the World Commission on Environment Development (the Brundtland Commission, as it is popularly known), namely, a development process that ensures that the present generations "meet their needs without compromising the ability of future generations to meet their own needs." Some have gone further:

We can summarize the necessary conditions for sustainable development as constancy of natural capital stock: more strictly, the requirement for non-negative changes in the stock of natural resources, such as soil and soil quality, ground and surface water and their quality, land biomass, water biomass, and waste-assimilation capacity of the receiving environments.

(Pearce, Barlier, and Makandya 1988 as quoted in Dasgupta and Maeler 1991)

Neither the principle enunciated by the Brundtland Commission nor the necessary conditions described by Pearce et al. make much sense. The former does not define "needs" of present or future generations, and the latter does not justify why natural resource stocks inherited from the past have to be maintained at the same level into the future. Indeed, as Dasgupta and Maeler (1991, p. 105) correctly point out, the time path of future changes (positive, negative, or zero) in natural resource stocks has to be *deduced* "from considerations of population change, intergenerational well-being, technological possibilities, environmental regeneration rates, and the existing resource base. The answer cannot be pulled from the air."

There is another important consideration to which Dasgupta and Maeler draw attention, namely, that it is not enough to confine environmental analysis to the aggregate concerns such as, for example, the greenhouse effect that is sweeping across regions, nations, and continents. One has also to take into consideration the needs and concerns specific to poor people of as small a group as a village community. The reason is that in the given socioeconomic-political context of developing countries with ill-defined property rights, imperfect and nonexistent markets, and weak fiscal systems, the poor cannot be compensated for the losses imposed on them by policies meant to protect the environment. Since for poor people some environmental resources are complementary to other goods and services and others supplement their income in times of acute economic stress, in the absence of alternative insurance arrangement and fiscal transfers, the poor might end up bearing the cost of providing environmental protection for the community as a whole.

This is not the occasion to discuss in detail and depth various channels of environment-population or growth-poverty-development interactions. A useful reference is Asian Development Bank (1990). One particular channel, however, is worth noting, namely, that in poor subsistence economies children add to household income as workers. Children are also essential in household production activities such as cultivation and animal husbandry and, above all, in fetching potable water, collecting "free" fuel, such as animal waste and wood from forests. Under these circumstances, high fertility and rapid population growth degrade environmental resources to which access is free. Degredation of resources increases the time cost of their use, which, in turn, means a household needs more child-hours to collect the same quantity of water, animal waste, and fuel wood. Needless to say, this creates private incentives to have more children, which means a further degredation of the environment until eventually the process of increasing fertility and environmental degradation is halted, either by positive checks à la Malthus or by social action. Some suggest that these fertility-environment dynamics can be seen in operation in Sub-Saharan Africa. A formal model of this is provided by Nerlove and Meyer (1992). Raut and Srinivasan (1991) also exhibit similar dynamics for some combination of parameter values and functional forms.

It should be emphasized that the unpleasant dynamics mentioned above are not inevitable but simply reflect the unequal distribution of income and wealth; more importantly, they reflect an institutional failure in the sense of creating free private access to socially costly resources and of the absence of social safety nets and transfers to the poor. As such, while population growth contributes directly and indirectly to environmental problems, it is not the primary and exogenous driving force but merely a response to institutional failures. Thus the long-term solution to resource degradation lies in the creation of a suitable institutional framework including rules of access to common-property resources. In the short run, until the institutional change is accomplished, providing incentives or reducing fertility and population growth would be an appropriate form of an environmental perspective.

14.3 Conclusions and Policy Implications

The findings reviewed in the previous sections do not lead to any firm and unambiguous conclusion about the direction and magnitude of the consequences of rapid population growth for the process of economic development or, for that matter, the consequences for population growth of a slow pace of economic development. There is enough in them, however, to support the cautious conclusion of the Working Group on Population Growth and Economic Development of the National Academy of Science of the United States, that "on balance, ... slower population growth would be beneficial to economic development for most developing countries" (National Research Council 1986, p. 90). There is also clear evidence that in some of the poorest countries there is a "population problem" in the sense of a seemingly perpetual cycle of poverty and high fertility rates (Dasgupta 1993). However, this cycle is a reflection of policy failures such as policy-induced distortions in markets (for agricultural commodities, labor, credit, and capital), inadequate definition and enforcement of access rights to common property and anti-poor bias in the provision of infrastructure and public goods. The evidence also points to the fertility-lowering and child-health-improving effects of public expenditures on education (particularly female education) and health infrastructure. And as the National Research Council points out, government support for family planning programs can have an economic and social rationale quite apart from the effect of programs on population growth. Indeed, poverty alleviation policies that include improvement in the functioning of markets for those goods and services produced and consumed by the poor, improvement of employment opportunities outside of the family farm, and improvement in the availability of basic household needs such as safe water and fuel would have a favorable side effect on the fertility and welfare of mothers and children. Whether or not governments should pursue an active population policy beyond policies that, introduced for achieving other objectives, also influence population growth involves difficult ethical questions (Dasgupta 1987).[6] But one does not need to resolve the ethical dilemmas to rule out coercive population policies such as those pursued in China.

VI

Migration and Trade

15

Empirical Regularities and Trends

In the last two centuries, natural changes in population due to births and deaths were themselves partly siphoned off in emigration. No study of population growth would therefore be complete without some discussion of international migration.

A multitude of factors—social, political, religious, ethnic, and economic—push people to migrate from their country of origin (e.g., religious persecution) and attract the migrants to their country of destination (as the "land of unlimited opportunities"). Occasionally, countries may impose strict restrictions on the exodus of people (e.g., the former Communist bloc). And very often, potential destination countries impose strict entry quotas (e.g., the United States and Canada). The observed patterns of international migration reflect a combination of these factors and barriers. We now briefly describe these patterns over the last two centuries.

15.1 International Migration

Evidently, the flows of people from the Old World of Europe to the New World of the Americas and Australia in the second half of the nineteenth century and early twentieth century stand out as the major international migration waves that accelerated over time. Great Britain has been a primary source of the registered out-migration from Europe throughout this period, although its share gradually petered out (see table 15.1). Germany supplied a sizable share of the migrants early in this period, but its share dropped to almost zero at the end. One explanation for the decline in emigration from

Table 15.1
The distribution of registered migrants from Europe by country of origin, 1846–1910 (percent)

Country of origin	1846–50	1851–60	1861–70	1871–80	1881–90	1891–1900	1901–10
Austria and Hungary	—	2	2	3	6	10	18
Germany	43	29	24	19	17	7	2
Great Britain	47	62	59	51	32	24	22
Ireland	—	—	—	5	9	6	2
Italy	—	—	1	5	1	22	29
Portugal and Spain	—	2	3	4	9	15	12
Russia	—	—	—	2	4	7	7
Scandinavian countries	3	3	9	7	7	6	6
Others[a]	7	2	2	4	15	3	2
Total (thousands)	422	2,122	2,660	3,304	7,977	7,150	12,704

Source: Koerner (1990), based on Woytinski and Woytinski (1953).
a. Belgium, France, Netherlands, Poland, and Switzerland.

Table 15.2
The distribution of registered migrants from Europe by country of destination, 1846–1910 (percent)

Country of destination	1846–50	1851–60	1861–70	1871–80	1881–90	1891–1900	1901–10
African colonies	2	5	2	1	1	1	3
Argentina and Uruguay	—	2	7	10	13	11	12
Australia and New Zealand	—	1	6	6	4	7	11
Brazil	—	4	3	6	7	18	5
Canada	16	9	9	5	5	4	8
United States	79	77	71	71	70	57	59
Others	3	2	2	1	—	2	2
Total (thousands)	1,588	3,394	3,273	3,987	7,518	6,423	14,939

Source: Koerner (1990), based on Woytinski and Woytinski (1953).

Germany might be that country's unification in 1871, which brought about for the first time in the whole world the now-familiar elements of the welfare state, such as national health insurance (*Krankenversicherung*) in 1883 and the old age benefits (*Pensionsversicherung*) in 1889. Interestingly enough, the Italian unification marked an opposite trend, namely the acceleration of emigration.

Portugal, Spain, and Italy started out as very minor suppliers of emigrants, but then rose to become major suppliers at the end of the period. Ireland, despite its small population, supplied 5–9 percent of the overall emigration from Europe at the end of the nineteenth century.

Table 15.2 presents the distribution of registered migrants from Europe among the most important people-receiving countries. Clearly, the United States stands out as the largest destination country throughout the period, absorbing between about 60 to 80 percent of the registered migrants.[1] In fact, as indicated by table 15.3,

Table 15.3
The composition of growth of the white population in the United States, 1800–1930 (percent)

Period	The share of natural growth in total growth	The share of net migration in total growth
1800–1810	96.0	4.0
1810–1820	96.5	3.5
1820–1830	95.4	4.6
1830–1840	86.5	13.5
1840–1850	73.5	26.5
1850–1860	65.3	34.7
1860–1870	72.0	28.0
1870–1880	71.5	28.5
1880–1890	57.1	42.9
1890–1900	68.5	31.5
1900–1910	58.2	41.8
1910–1920	83.0	17.0
1920–1930	78.4	21.6

Source: Koerner (1990), based on Rostow (1978).

Table 15.4
Migration to the United States by continent of origin, 1950–1985 (percent)

Continent of origin	1950–54	1955–59	1960–64	1965–69	1970–74	1975–79	1980–85
Asia	3	7	8	14	29	35	47
Europe	65	49	39	33	24	18	12
Central and South America	16	28	36	41	40	42	36
Others	16	16	17	12	7	5	5
Total (thousands)	1,099	1,400	1,419	1,795	1,923	2,291	3,395

Source: Koerner (1990, table 20).

net migration contributed a significant portion of the total growth of the white population in the United States. For instance, net migration accounted for as much as 32 to 43 percent of the total increase in the white population during the period 1880–1910; nevertheless, the immigration share of the United States even when combined with Canada, another significant destination country, sharply declined, while that of the South American and Australian continents rose.

After World War II both the magnitude and composition of immigration to the United States changed significantly. Table 15.4 emphasizes the sharp decline in total immigration to the United States, compared with the pre–World War I period,[2] and the marked decline in the share of Europe as an origin of the immigrants. In Europe's stead, Latin America and Asia became major sources of immigrants.

Also in the period after World War II, one can detect a clear increase both in inter-European migration (especially, from the relatively poor South to the relatively rich North) and in migration from North African and Mediteranean countries to Europe.

Table 15.5 illustrates the volume of emigration from the Mediteranean countries in Europe[3] and North Africa to the countries of Western and Northern Europe. Notice that the 1950s and 1960s are marked by high economic growth and low unemployment in Western and Northern Europe. Table 15.5 also indicates the tendency to remigrate back to the country of origin, which may be due to absorption hardships in the host country or changes in political regimes and the patterns of economic prosperity in the country of origin, or both. Occasionally, emigrants tend to remigrate to their country of origin, either after acquiring some professional skill and expertise and accumulating enough nonhuman wealth (so that they can start their own small businesses in their home country) or upon retirement. In some of the population-sending countries the effect of emigration on the working age population is much more pronounced than on the total population (see table 15.6). Portugal, for example, lost as much as a one-half of the potential increase in the working age population because of emigration.[4]

Table 15.5
Migration in the post–World War II period by country of origin, selected countries (in thousands)

Country	Emigration[a] 1950–1959	1960–1984	Remigration[a] 1950–1959	1960–1984
Greece	40	730	—	138
Italy	1,512	3,490	877	3,026
North African countries	1,161	7,429	425	6,673
Portugal	23	1,129	—	—
Spain	—	2,288	—	1,595
Turkey	—	955	—	—
Yugoslavia	—	1,276	—	1,011

Source: Koerner (1990, table 7).
a. Figures refer only to emigration and remigration to and from Northern and Western European countries.

Table 15.6
Growth of working age population in South European countries with and without migration, 1950–1975 (percent)

Country	Annual rate of growth of working age population			
	Actual (with migration) 1950–1960	1960–1975	Without migration 1950–1960	1960–1975
Greece	1.0	0.6	1.2	0.9
Italy	0.6	0.7	0.8	0.8
Portugal	0.5	0.6	1.2	1.0
Spain	0.8	1.0	1.1	1.1

Source: Koerner (1990, table 12).

Table 15.7
Share and number of foreigners in population and in employment in major European destination countries, selected years

| | Share of foreigners | | | |
| Country | In population | | In employment | |
	1950	1982	1962	1982
Belgium				
Total (thousands)	323	886	170	332
Percentage	4.3	9.0	—	9.1
Federal Republic of Germany				
Total (thousands)	568	4,667	549	2,038
Percentage	1.1	7.6	1.7	8.1
France				
Total (thousands)	1,760	4,459	1,093	1,503
Percentage	4.1	8.2	5.6	7.2
Luxembourg				
Total (thousands)	29	96	20	52
Percentage	10.0	26.0	—	33.0
The Netherlands				
Total (thousands)	104	543	47	185
Percentage	1.1	3.8	—	3.7
Switzerland				
Total (thousands)	285	926	424	526
Percentage	6.1	14.3	—	17.3

Source: Koerner (1990, table 13).

On the population receiving side, the developed countries of Northern and Western Europe stand out (see table 15.7). In 1950 France had the largest absolute number of foreigners (1.76 million). In 1983, when the Federal Republic of Germany was already established as an economic superpower, most of the foreigners were attracted there. Luxembourg had always had an exceptionally high percentage of foreigners.[5] It is worth noting that in all countries (except for France and the Netherlands), the percentage of foreigners in employment is higher than in population. This indicates that foreigners have, on average, fewer dependents than the veterans (in 1982).

With the new world order that followed the collapse of communism, one can expect the major flows of migrants to take place from the former Eastern Bloc to Western countries willing to absorb migrants (some European countries, Israel, etc.). This kind of migration very much resembles the South-North (and West) migration in post–world War II Europe.

A review of recent developments in international migration conducted by Stanton-Russell and Teitelbaum (1992) states: "The magnitude of human flows across national boundaries has become very large over the past three decades. Estimates are necessarily crude, but as of the late 1980s, some 80 million persons were residents outside their nations of citizenship. Conservatively, these numbers are likely to have reached 100 million since the dissolution of the former Soviet Union and are expected to increase further in the coming decades. The international financial flows that follow such human movements are substantial. The total value of official remittance inflows (credits) worldwide was U.S.$ 65.6 billion in 1989—second in value only to trade in crude oil and larger than official development assistance."

International migration is closely intertwined with international trade. The international migration of people can often substitute for both international movements of capital and international trade in goods and services. In many other cases international migration is a complement to international flows of capital or commodities. We turn our attention now to the international flows of goods and capital.

15.2 International Trade in Goods and Services

Over the years, one can detect a clear trend of growth in the volume of international trade. This may be due to three main factors that facilitated trade: (1) technological improvements lowered both the money and time costs of transportation; (2) output growth reinforced international trade (especially, via intra-industry trade); and (3) the public at large and policymakers in particular became more and more aware of the mutual gains from trade and have gradually been pushing for removal of tariff and nontariff trade barriers.

The surplus in the current account of the balance of payments, which is equal to net trade flows (i.e., exports minus imports), cannot properly measure the volume of trade. For instance, when trade is balanced and the surplus is nil, it obviously does not mean that there is no trade. For this reason, it is customary to measure the volume of trade by gross trade flows, that is, by the *sum* of exports *and* imports. Alternatively, one can look just at exports *or* imports in order to infer trends over time or to compare among different countries.

Figure 15.1 depicts the growth rates of exports, and of gross domestic products (GDPs) for the six major industrialized countries, from the eighteenth century until now. Exports grew much faster than GDP throughout this period, except for the period covering the two world wars, which was governed by political conflicts and

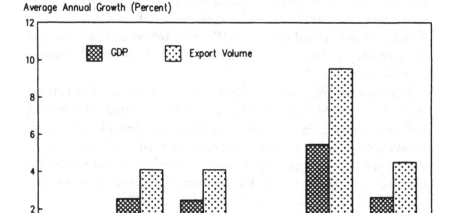

Figure 15.1
GDP and export growth trends, 1720–1990
Note: The figure for first-period GDP uses 1700–1820 data. Data are for France, Germany, Italy, Japan, the United Kingdom, and the United States. Not all countires are represented in the first two periods. The figure is reproduced from the *Economic Report of the President*, U.S. Government Printing Office, February 1992.
Source: U.S. Department of Labor, International Monetary Fund, World Bank, and Maddison, *Phases of Capitalist Development*

resultant protectionist attitudes. Note also that high growth rates of exports are accompanied also by high growth rates of GDP. For instance, the exceptionally high growth rate of GDP in the fifties and sixties (about 6% annually) is matched by an even higher growth rate in exports (about 10% annually). In contrast, the inter–world war period is marked by a very low growth rate of both exports and GDP. This casual observation may suggest the existence of a positive interaction between trade liberalization and economic growth.

Similarly, table 15.8 shows the sharp increase in the volume of trade, in recent years, of the major economic power in the world, the United States. In this table the volume of trade is measured by the sum of exports *and* imports, as a percentage of GNP. The volume of trade stayed about constant from 1929 until the end of the 1950s, around 9–11 percent of GNP (except for a deep dip during the Second World War period), and then took off in the 1960s and reached a level of 31 percent of GNP in 1991. In absolute terms and in 1982 dollars, the volume of trade increased from $79.5 billion in 1929 to $1.3 trillion in 1991 (almost a twentyfold increase); by comparison, GNP rose from $709.6 billion in 1979 to $4.1 trillion in 1991 (or only about a sixfold increase).

15.3   International Capital Flows

The historical developments of international capital flows show ups and downs until the last two decades. Early on, there were quite sizable flows during the gold standard period. International flows of capital shrank during both the period of the two world wars and the Bretton-Woods era of fixed exchange rates and capital controls (1944–1973). More recently, with the liberalization of the international capital markets, international capital movements picked up considerably.

In economies open to international flows of capital, *net* capital flows are accounted for by the difference between national saving and investment. Measured by the current account deficits or surpluses in the balance of payments. Net exports by surpluses and net imports by deficits), these net capital flows (or typically understate

Table 15.8
U.S. GNP and volume of trade, 1929–1991 (selected years)

Year	GNP (in billions of 1982 dollars)	Volume of trade[a] (in billions of 1982 dollars)	Volume of trade[a] (percent of GNP)
1929	709.6	79.5	11.0
1933	498.5	46.9	9.4
1939	716.6	66.3	9.2
1944	1,380.6	78.4	5.7
1946	1,096.9	111.0	10.1
1950	1,203.7	113.8	9.5
1955	1,494.9	153.8	10.3
1960	1,665.3	200.8	12.1
1965	2,087.6	266.7	12.8
1970	2,416.2	386.6	16.0
1975	2,695.0	500.5	18.6
1980	3,187.1	720.9	22.6
1985	3,618.7	838.6	23.2
1986	3,717.9	924.0	24.9
1987	3,845.3	1,022.1	26.6
1988	4,016.9	1,145.3	28.5
1989	4,117.7	1,240.7	30.1
1990	4,155.8	1,298.1	31.2
1991	4,126.2	1,279.0	31.0

Source: *Economic Report of the President*, U.S. Government Printing Office, February 1992.

a. Volume of trade is measured in this table by the *sum* of exports and imports.

Table 15.9
Gross international capital movements of the seven major industrial countries, 1970–1989 (percent of GNP/GDP)

Country	1970–1974	1975–1979	1980–1984	1985–1989
Canada	5.9	5.9	7.9	5.6
France	7.0	9.0	8.6	11.2
Germany (FRG)	6.0	9.2	9.9	14.2
Italy	9.4	4.9	5.2	3.7
Japan	3.3	2.4	5.4	19.5
United Kingdom	6.4	11.4	26.6	32.6
United States	2.5	3.4	4.8	5.8

Source: International Monetary Fund.
Note: This table is reproduced from Frenkel, Razin, and Sadka, *International Taxation in an Integrated World* (MIT Press, 1991).

flows of capital into and out of a country. Removal of barriers to international capital movements tends to be followed by a *two-way* increase in *gross* capital flows, which are not necessarily reflected in the net exports or imports of capital.

Table 15.9 shows the developments in the measure of *gross* international capital movements of the seven major industrial countries (the G-7) during the 1970s and 1980s. The volume of international capital movements is measured in this table by the *sum* of capital exports and capital imports. To normalize the units of measurement and facilitate intercountry comparisons, the volume of capital movements is expressed as a percentage of gross national product or gross domestic product (GNP/GDP). The table reveals the dramatic increase in capital movements from the early 1970s through the late 1980s. In this regard, both the United Kingdom and Japan stand out: gross capital flows (as percentage of GNP) rose about fivefold during the two decades (from 6.4% 32.6% in the United Kingdom, and from 3.3% to 19.5% in Japan). In the United States and Germany, the share of gross capital flows in GDP more than doubled during the same period. Indeed, in recent years the degree of integration of capital markets (as measured by gross capital movements) has grown more rapidly than the degree of integration of goods markets (as measured by the *gross* volume of trade in goods and services, i.e., exports *plus* imports).

The stylized facts and trends reported in this chapter motivate the choice of topics and issues examined in the two subsequent chapters. Although the various real-world developments provide a stimulus for the analysis, the orientation of these chapters is analytical. The purpose is to identify key channels and pertinent mechanisms through which international migration affects international trade, in terms of both positive and normative economic analysis. In particular, special attention is paid to the question of whether and to what extent trade in goods and capital mobility relieve the pressure for international migration.

16

Factor and Goods Mobility and International Migration

In an autarkic situation, different countries typically have different commodity prices and factor prices. Such a situation may have been characteristic of protectionist pre–World War II Western Europe vis-à-vis the American market or may be characteristic of the former Eastern European bloc, vis-à-vis the industrialized countries. For instance, Table 16.1 highlights the wage gap between Eastern Europe (with wages below U.S.$ 1/hour) and the industrialized countries (with wages typically above U.S.$ 10/hour). Obviously, if barriers to labor mobility are lowered or removed, then labor tends to migrate from low-wage countries (e.g., Eastern Europe) to high-wage countries (e.g., Western Europe).

A crucial question for migration policy is whether trade in goods can narrow the wage gap, thereby reducing the pressure for labor migration, or whether such a trade widens the wage gap and further exacerbates the incentive to migrate. Put differently: Is trade in goods a substitute or a complement to labor mobility? And is capital mobility a substitute for labor mobility? These two questions are dealt with in this chapter.

16.1 Substitution and Complementarity between Labor Mobility and Goods Mobility

To analyze the interaction between trade in goods and labor mobility, we shall employ a standard international trade model with two factors (labor and capital), two goods, and possibly different technologies in the two countries.[1]

Table 16.1
Wage gaps and population (1990)

	Wage per hour (U.S. dollars)	Population (millions)
Eastern Europe		
Poland	0.7	38
Hungary	0.7	11
Czechoslovakia	0.8	16
Bulgaria	0.2	9
Rumania	0.6	23
Yugoslavia	1.1	24
Soviet Union (European)	0.9	222
Eastern Europe (total)	0.9	343
Industrialized countries		
Germany (West)	11	61
France	8	56
Italy	11	57
United Kingdom	8	57
EC (total)	9	340
EFTA (total)	13	25
Western Europe (total)	10	365
United States	13	250
Canada	13	27
Australia	14	17

Source: Layard et al. (1992).

Our starting point will be a set of assumptions that nullify all forces that can generate either commodity trade or labor mobility. By relaxing these assumptions, one at a time, we create room for commodity trade and incentive for labor mobility, and we can then study their interaction. Following Markusen (1983), we at first assume that

1. The two countries have the same relative endowments of capital and labor;

2. The two countries have the same technologies.

We further assume that there are constant returns to scale and that the two countries have the same homothetic preferences. Under these assumptions, there will be no commodity trade between the two countries and no cross-country factor price differentials that can lead to international factor mobility.

16.1.1   Substitution

Now let us relax assumption 1 and assume that the two countries differ in their relative factor endowments. Suppose that labor and capital are initially locked within the national boundaries.

Let there be two goods, x and y; two factors, labor (L) and capital (K); and two countries, home (H) and foreign (F). This is the familiar Heckscher-Ohlin-Samuelson model of international trade. Suppose, for concreteness, that good x is more labor-intensive than good y (in the two countries that have identical technologies), that is,

$$\frac{a_{Lx}}{a_{Kx}} > \frac{a_{Ly}}{a_{Ky}} \tag{16.1}$$

for all factor price ratios, where a_{ij} is the unit input requirement of factor i in the production of good j, and where $i = L, K$ and $j = x, y$. Of course, these unit input requirements depend on the factor price ratio.

Suppose that country H is more abundant in labor (relative to capital) than country F, that is,

$$\frac{\bar{L}^H}{\bar{K}^H} > \frac{\bar{L}^F}{\bar{K}^F}, \tag{16.2}$$

where $\bar{L}^i$ and $\bar{K}^i$ are the endowments of labor and capital, respectively, in country i, where $i = H, F$.

Suppose that good y is the numéraire with its price set to unity in both countries, and denote by p^i, r^i, and w^i the price of good x, the rental price of capital, and the wage rate in country i, respectively, where $i = H, F$.

First observe the quite intuitive result due to Stolper and Samuelson (1947): an increase in the wage-rental ratio (w/r) raises

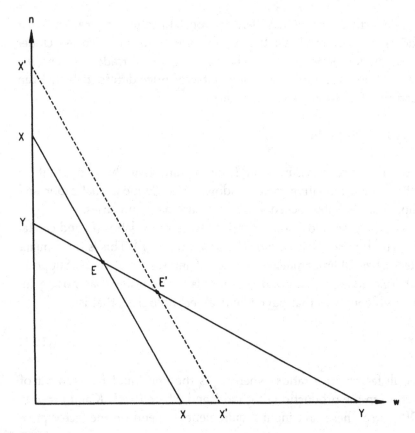

Figure 16.1
The Stoper-Samuelson theorem

the unit cost of the labor-intensive good (x) relative to the unit cost of the capital-intensive good (y) and must therefore raise the relative price (p) of the labor-intensive good.

To demonstrate this result graphically, refer to figure 16.1.[2] For a fixed p, the line XX represents the zero-profit locus for industry x, given by $p = ra_{Kx} + wa_{Lx}$. The slope of this line is a_{Lx}/a_{Kx}. The line YY is the analogous locus for industry y, given by $1 = ra_{Ky} + wa_{Ly}$. Its slope is a_{Ly}/a_{Ky}. The point of intersection between these two loci (point E) yields the equilibrium factor prices for the given p. Now, if p rises, the zero-profit locus for industry x shifts outward from XX to

$X'X'$. The new factor price equilibrium is a point E', in which the wage rate (w) is higher and the rental price of capital (r) is lower. Conversely, an increase in w/r raises p.

Now, consider the autarky equilibrium in the two countries. Since country H has a higher relative endowment of labor than country F, it is natural and straightforward to show (see below) that, under autarky, labor will be relatively less expensive in country H, that is,

$$\frac{\bar{w}^H}{\bar{r}^H} < \frac{\bar{w}^F}{\bar{r}^F}, \tag{16.3}$$

where $\bar{w}^i$ and $\bar{r}^i$ are the autarky prices of labor and capital, respectively, in country i and where $i = H, F$. Hence, by the Stolper-Samuelson theorem, the autarkic price of good x is lower in country H than in country F. Thus, when trade is allowed, good x will be exported from country H to country F until commodity prices are equalized across countries. Of course, good y will be exported from country F to country H. The common equilibrium price of x in both countries will be higher than the autarkic price of x in country H and lower than the autarkic price of x in country F. This is the essence of the Heckscher-Ohlin-Samuelson proposition. (With more than two commodities, various complementarity-substitution configuration may, however, determine an equilibrium price that is outside the autarkic-price range.)

To complete the proof of the Heckscher-Ohlin-Samuelson proposition, it remains to show that (16.2) implies (16.3), namely, that the country with the higher initial labor-capital ratio will, under autarky, have a lower wage-rental ratio. This result follows from the Rybczynski proposition, which asserts that at a given factor price ratio, a higher labor-capital endowment ratio results in a higher output ratio of x to y (where good x is more labor-intensive than good y). To see this refer to figure 16.2. The line LL describes the locus of output pairs (x, y) that yield full employment of labor, given by $\bar{L} = xa_{Lx} + ya_{Ly}$. The slope of this line is a_{Lx}/a_{Ly}. Similarly, the line KK represents full employment of capital, given by $\bar{K} = xa_{Kx} + ya_{Ky}$. Its slope is a_{Kx}/a_{Ky}. The equilibrium pair of outputs is at point E. Now suppose $\bar{L}$ rises. This shifts the full-employment-of-labor line

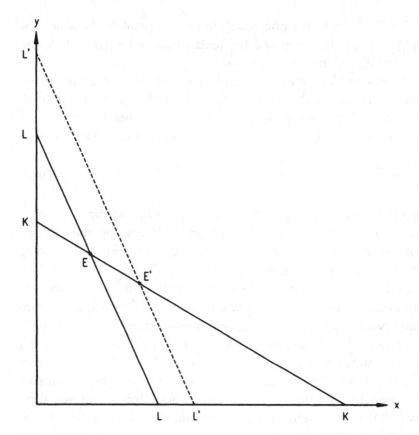

Figure 16.2
The Rybczynski theorem

outward from LL to $L'L'$. The new pair of equilibrium outputs is
point E' with a higher x/y ratio. Hence, at the autarky price ratios of
country F (i.e., $\bar{w}^F/\bar{r}^F$ and $\bar{p}^F$), country H has an excess supply of
good x and an excess demand for good y (because the two countries
have the same homothetic preferences). This implies that at an autarky
equilibrium in country H we must have

$$\bar{p}^H < \bar{p}^F \text{ and } \bar{w}^H/\bar{r}^H < \bar{w}^F/\bar{r}^F.$$

Thus we have shown that (16.2) implies (16.3).[3]

One can also calculate the factor content of the trade in goods.
Denoting by Q_i^j and C_i^j, respectively, the output and the consump-

tion of good $i = x, y$ in country $j = H, F$, we can calculate the net import vector of country H by

$$M^H \equiv \begin{pmatrix} M_x^H \\ M_y^H \end{pmatrix} = \begin{pmatrix} C_x^H - Q_x^H \\ C_y^H - Q_y^H \end{pmatrix} \equiv C^H - Q^H.$$

Full employment in country $i = H, F$ requires that

$$AQ^i = \begin{pmatrix} \bar{L}^i \\ \bar{K}^i \end{pmatrix} \equiv \bar{V}^i,$$

where

$$A = \begin{pmatrix} a_{Lx} & a_{Ly} \\ a_{Kx} & a_{Ky} \end{pmatrix}$$

is the unit-input-requirement matrix.

From the assumption of identical homothetic preferences it follows that

$$C^H = s^H(Q^H + Q^F) = s^H(A^{-1}\bar{V}^H + A^{-1}\bar{V}^F) \equiv s^H A^{-1}\bar{V},$$

where s^H is the share of country H in worldwide income and $\bar{V} \equiv \bar{V}^H + \bar{V}^F$ is the world factor endowment vector.

Hence

$$M^H = C^H - Q^H = s^H(A^{-1}\bar{V}^H + A^{-1}\bar{V}^F) - A^{-1}\bar{V}^H.$$

Therefore, the factor content of the net import flows, AM^H, can be expressed as

$$AM^H = s^H \bar{V} - \bar{V}^H = s^H \begin{pmatrix} \bar{L}^H + \bar{L}^F \\ \bar{K}^H + \bar{K}^F \end{pmatrix} - \begin{pmatrix} \bar{L}^H \\ \bar{K}^H \end{pmatrix}. \tag{16.4}$$

Equation 16.4 gives a simple measure of the factor content of trade that depends only on initial factor endowments and the cross-country distribution of world income. This measure can be empirically computed. Since country H exports good x, which is labor-intensive, and imports good y, which is capital-intensive, the factor content of its net imports follows a similar pattern: the labor component is negative, while the capital component is positive. That is, country H implicitly exports labor and imports capital via its net imports of goods.

The conclusion of this model, known as the Heckscher-Ohlin-Samuelson proposition, is that in the absence of international factor mobility, each country exports the good intensive in that country's abundant factor; and goods mobility equalizes not only commodity prices but also factor prices across countries. Thus, when free commodity trade takes place, it nullifies the incentives for factors to move from one country to another.

Now suppose that commodity trade is not allowed. In this case, factor (say, labor) mobility can fully substitute for commodity trade. In the model above, labor from the labor-abundant country (country H) will be employed in country F or capital will move in the opposite direction until factor prices are equalized, or both. It then follows, from the Stolper-Samuelson proposition, that commodity prices will also be equalized across countries. In this case, commodity trade becomes redundant (see Mundell 1957); indeed, we can easily calculate the magnitude of factor mobility needed to substitute for trade in goods. The magnitude of this mobility is given by equation 16.4, which describes the factor content of the trade in goods.

In both cases, with either commodity trade and no labor mobility or labor mobility and no commodity trade, the same international allocation of consumption obtains (even though patterns of production and trade differ). Thus, if the only difference between the two countries lies in their relative abundance of labor, then commodity trade and labor (or capital) mobility are perfect substitutes. When both free commodity trade and factor mobility are possible, there is a complete indeterminancy between the two modes of international flows.

16.1.2 Complementarity

Let us now reinstate assumption 1 about identical relative endowments across countries, but relax assumption 2. That is, suppose that technologies are *not* identical. For simplicity and concreteness, suppose that country H has a more productive technology for producing good x than country F, in a Hicks-neutral sense, that is,

$$G_x^H(K_x, L_x) = \alpha G_x^F(K_x, L_x), \qquad \alpha > 1 \tag{16.5}$$

and that the technologies for producing y are identical, that is,

$$G_y^H(K_y, L_y) = G_y^F(K_y, L_y), \tag{16.6}$$

where G_j^i is the production function of good j in country i, and where $j = x, y$ and $i = H, F$.

In this case we show that trade in goods does not suffice to equalize factor prices. Indeed, under free trade the wage in the home country, which is technologically superior in the labor-intensive market, is higher than in the foreign country; and the opposite holds true with respect to the rental price of capital:

$$w^H > w^F \text{ and } r^H < r^F. \tag{16.7}$$

To see this, plot the production possibility frontiers for the two countries in figure 16.3. Note that the frontier for H is achieved by pulling the frontier for F to the right by the multiplicative factor α. Thus the slope at B, for instance, is $1/\alpha$ times the slope at F_1. It is important to note that F_1 and B represent the same point (say, point F_2) on the identical contract curve in the identical Edgeworth box of the two countries (figure 16.4). (The two countries have the same Edgeworth box because they have the same factor endowments; and the same contract curve because their technologies differ only by a Hicks-neutral multiplicative coefficient.) Thus, if both countries produce at the same point in the Edgeworth box (say, point F_2 in figure 16.4, corresponding to F_1 and B in figure 16.3), then they cannot have the same commodity price ratio required under free trade (recall that the commodity price ratio is equal to the slope of the production possibility frontier). Hence, with the equal commodity prices required under free trade, country H must produce less y (and obviously more x) than country F. Thus, suppose that country H is at H_1 and H_2 in figures 16.3 and 16.4, respectively, while country F is at F_1 and F_2 in figures 16.3 and 16.4, respectively.

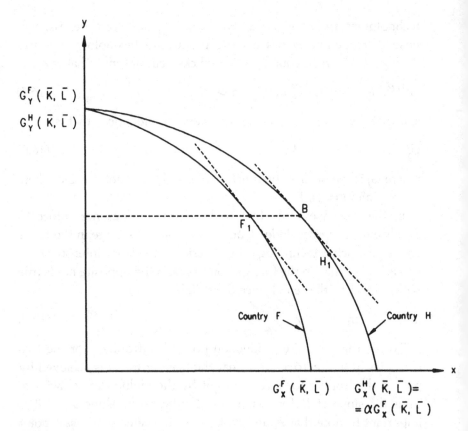

Figure 16.3
Production possibility frontiers

Because the two countries have the same (homothetic) demand patterns, while country H produces a higher x/y ratio than country F, it follows that, under free trade, country H exports good x (in which H enjoys a superior technology) and imports good y. Given the convex shape of the contract curve, it follows that the factor price ratio w/r is higher in country H than in country F. Since both produce good y with the same technologies and for the same price (i.e., unity), it follows that (16.7) holds. Thus, commodity trade does not equalize factor prices.[4] Furthermore, depending on demand patterns and the degree of factor substitution in production, it may well

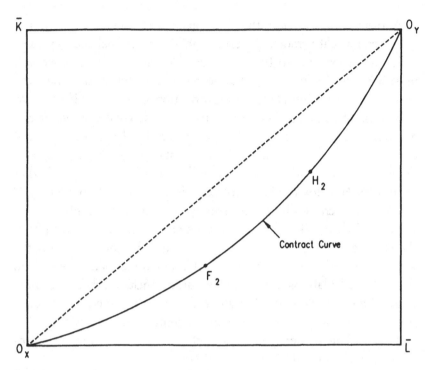

Figure 16.4
Edgeworth box diagram

be the case that free commodity trade widens rather than narrows the factor price differentials.

Now suppose that factor mobility (labor and capital) is allowed alongside trade in commodities. Labor will move from country F to country H and capital will move in the opposite direction. By the Rybczynski proposition, at the initial commodity trade price, there will be an excess supply of good x in country H and an excess supply of good y in country F. Exports of x from country H and its imports of y will further rise. Indeed, country H with its superior technology will specialize in production of good x. Thus factor mobility reinforces trade in commodities. In this model of international technological differences in certain industries, factor mobility and commodity trade complement each other.

Another phenomenon that can generate complementarity between commodity trade and labor mobility is external economies of scale. Being external to the individual firm, economies of scale still preserve perfect competition. Suppose for concreteness that there are external scale economies in the production of good x. If the two countries differ in absolute size but have identical relative factor endowments, Markusen (1983) showed that the larger country will export good x. As this good is more labor-intensive, the relative price of labor (w/r) in the free commodity trade equilibrium is higher in country H. Allowing labor to move from country F to country H will further increase the excess supply of good x in country H, via both the Rybczynski effect and the external scale economies effect, thereby generating an even higher volume of trade. Based on the work of Abowd and Freeman (1991) and Zimmermann (1992) and their own calculations, Faini and Venturini concluded that "the share of immigrant labor is positively correlated with the import penetration ratio" (p. 438), indicating complementarity between migration and trade. This evidence is presented in table 16.2, which is reproduced from Faini and Venturini (1993).

In a recent study on East-West migration, Layard et al. (1992) emphasize the role of trade in goods as an alternative to labor migration:

Given the difficulties posed by the prospect of very large-scale migration from East to West, and the risk that such large-scale migration could actually leave the remaining population in the East worse off, we need to

Table 16.2
Correlation coefficients between the share of foreign workers and trade ratios

	$M/(y + M - x)$
United States	0.22
Germany	
France	0.40
Spain	0.02

Source: Faini and Venturini (1993).
Note: x = exports; M = imports; y = output.

ask what alternatives are available. Ideally, policy should try to bring good jobs to the East *rather than* Eastern workers to the West. International trade ... *can* act as a substitute for migration. A free trade pact that ensures Eastern European countries access to the Western European market is the best single migration policy that could be put in place. In the amazing postwar reconstruction of Western Europe, the openness of the U.S. market was a crucial factor. Western Europe now has the opportunity of providing a similar service to the East.

The gains from trade in goods notwithstanding, we have pointed out that such trade can be a complement to labor mobility. It does not necessarily equalize wages and may even widen the wage gap, thereby generating more incentives for labor migration in the presence of technological advantage of one country over the other. Note also that the productivity advantage could merely reflect some superior infrastructure (roads, telecommunication systems, ports, energy, etc.), which is certainly the case in the East-West context. Hence, important elements of migration policy should be investment in infrastructure (possibly funded by foreign aid) and direct foreign investment, which tends also to diffuse technology and raise productivity. Once productivity gaps are narrowed, trade in goods can further alleviate the pressure for labor migration.

In view of the empirical falsification of the factor price equalization theorems,[5] Davis (1992) introduced Hicks-neutral differences in technology across countries, uniform over all industries. He tested the hypothesis concerning convergence of relative industry wages across countries. The evidence that he found "strongly rejected the hypothesis of increasing uniformity across countries in the relative industry wage structure," despite the ongoing trend of trade liberalization.

16.2   Substitution between Labor Mobility and Capital Mobility

Classical economic models suggest that factors of production will move, when not locally or otherwise constrained, from locations where their marginal product is low to locations where their marginal product is high. With frictionless factor mobility, eventually each factor of production generates the same marginal product wherever it is employed. Indeed, with identical constant returns-to-scale technologies everywhere and two factors (capital and labor), it suffices that one factor is freely mobile to equalize the marginal product of each factor everywhere.

To see this, consider the famous scissors diagram (figure 16.5), in which the marginal product of capital curves of the two countries (home and foreign) that comprise the world economy are depicted from opposite directions. Following MacDougall (1960), suppose that originally the world allocation of capital is at A, with the home country having a higher marginal product of capital than the foreign country. Now suppose that labor is stuck within national borders, but capital is internationally mobile. Then capital will flow from the foreign country to the home country until the marginal product of capital is the same in the two countries. This occurs at point E. Recall that, with constant returns-to-scale technologies, the marginal product of each factor depends only on the capital/labor ratio. Thus the home country originally had a lower capital/labor ratio than the foreign country, and the subsequent flow of capital that equalized the marginal products of capital brought about an identical capital/labor ratio in the two countries. But this implies also that the marginal products of labor are equalized as well. (Thus, even if labor were allowed to migrate from one country to another, it would not do so.) Similarly, mobility of labor in the opposite direction (i.e., from the home country to the foreign country) would have generated equal marginal products of capital, in addition to equal marginal products of labor.

Evidently, the observed international differentials in marginal products are enormous. The real wage in the United States, for example, is about 15 times higher than the real wage in India (see Summers and Heston 1991). The first explanation for this difference that comes to mind is the marked difference in skills or in human capital between American workers and Indian workers. After correcting for these differences, based on estimates by Krueger (1968),

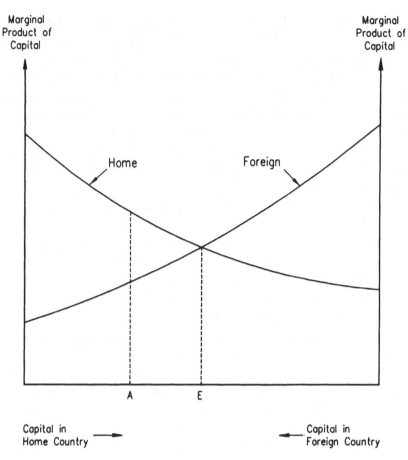

Figure 16.5
The allocation of capital between the home country and the foreign country

Lucas (1990) finds that the wage per effective labor (adjusted for human capital) in the United States is still three times higher than the wage per effective labor in India. Obviously, Indian labor can by no means enter freely to the United States so as to eliminate this observed wage differential. But when labor has a higher marginal product in the United States, it must be the case that capital has a higher marginal product in India. According to Lucas's calculations, the marginal product of capital in India is five times higher than the marginal product of capital in the United States. Why then, Lucas very correctly asked, does capital from the United States and other rich countries not flow into India and other less developed countries.

To some extent, one can resolve the puzzle by resorting to technological risk (e.g., Grossman and Razin 1984), economic distortions (e.g., Bhagwati and Srinivasan 1983), political and social unrest, and the like. Lucas, however, was able to suggest an alternative explanation to the puzzle about the lack of capital flow from developed to less developed countries, based on the new developments in growth theory.[6] According to this explanation, there is no difference in the marginal product of capital between the United States and India. Instead, there is only a productivity difference generated by an external economy effect of human capital. Lucas argues that investment in human capital not only augments the effective labor supply of the worker who made such an investment, but it also contributes to the productivity of all other workers and capital. Taking this *external* effect into account, Lucas suggests a resolution to the lack-of-capital flow puzzle.

The existence of an external productivity effect suggests that, even though capital has no incentive to move from rich countries to poor countries, labor nevertheless has a strong incentive to move from poor countries with low levels of human capital to rich countries with high levels of human capital.[7] Immigration quotas serve to check the brain drain. Lucas's explanation can be diagrammatically represented via factor price frontiers drawn in figure 16.6 with the rental price of capital (r) plotted on the vertical axis and the wage

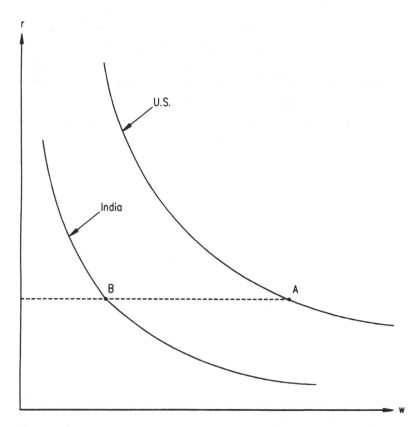

Figure 16.6
Factor price frontier

rate (w) on the horizontal axis. An external productivity effect moves the factor price frontier outward. Thus the United States and India can have the same rental price of capital even though the wage per effective labor in India is only one-third that in the United States. For instance, the United States could be at a point such as A on its factor price frontier, while India would be at B.

The human-capital-based model (and particularly the external productivity effect) is bad news for those who are looking for convergence in long-run productivity levels among countries (see Baumol 1986). If allowed to take place, the brain drain (induced by the external effect) will tend to increase the diversity in the level of per capita income across countries. In the presence of fixed pecuniary costs of migration (under the same proportional income differentials across countries) skilled labor has greater incentives to migrate than unskilled labor, thereby generating larger income diversity. On the other hand, the time cost of migration is relatively higher for skilled labor, curtailing its incentive to migrate.

17

Normative Issues of International Migration

For welfare analysis one has to distinguish between labor mobility and migration. By labor mobility we refer to the mobility of merely a factor of production (here indistinguishable from other factors such as capital), without any mobility of the consumption entity embodied in labor. Because an individual (household) providing labor services in another country is perceived as not changing national residency (a guest worker), that individual remains an integral element of the welfare calculus of the original country even while exporting labor services. Thus labor mobility creates no new conceptual issues of welfare evaluation. The set of people over which the social welfare function is defined does not change as a result of international labor mobility.

In contrast, labor migration is perceived not merely as an export of labor services, but rather as a change in the size of national communities. The migrant no longer belongs to the source country community and becomes a member of the destination country community. This raises a conceptual welfare issue in both the source country and the destination country. In evaluating the social welfare of the source country, should we consider the premigration or the postmigration population? Similarly, when evaluating the social welfare function of the destination country, should we take into account only the welfare of the veterans or consider the welfare of the migrants as well. Naturally, in evaluating alternative policies, a democratic society takes into account the welfare of all existing members at each point in time, regardless of whether they were born into this society or just recently joined it by migration. The conceptual welfare issue is about whether to take into account the welfare of those who may join or leave the society in the future. This issue is particularly relevant when evaluating a policy that is directly and significantly going to cause population shifts (e.g., naturalization policy, social security benefits to people who have left the country or are newcomers, etc.).

The reader may have noticed that the conceptual issue arising in the context of international migration is akin to the issue of population growth in a closed economy analyzed in chapter 5. When evaluating population growth policies, there is as well the issue of whether to take into account only the welfare of those alive at present or also the welfare of those as yet unborn.

Nevertheless, there are two important welfare evaluation asymmetries between population growth and international migration. First, by revealed preference, voluntary migrants are better off after migration than before, for otherwise they would have stayed in their home country. By contrast, it is a deep philosophical issue whether the yet-unborn child will be better off if not born at all. (Indeed, this issue is endlessly debated in many countries in abortion cases.) Second, with altruistic parents, the yet-unborn child is indirectly represented in the social welfare function of the existing population through the welfare of that child's parents, though only partially, because the child's utility per se is not an independent argument in the social welfare function of the existing society. By contrast, the migrant without altruistic relatives in the destination country is not represented in the social welfare function of the existing population in that country.

It is beyond the scope of this book to resolve this conceptual issue and offer an appropriate way of making interpersonal welfare comparisons (particularly between veterans and migrants). Instead, we follow Bhagwati and Srinivasan (1983) in identifying who gains and who loses from international migration, by how much, and how redistribution policies may be impeded by migration.

17.1   Gains and Losses from International Migration

The scissors diagram in figure 17.1 describes the allocation of people between two countries: a source country (SC) and a destination country (DC). We assume that the immobile factors are owned only by the country residents. Suppose that the initial allocation of people is at point A where the DC marginal product of labor (which is equal to the real wage) is higher than the SC marginal product of labor. If free migration is possible, people will migrate from the SC to the DC until the marginal products of labor are equalized at point B. The migrants earn a higher wage. Their net gain is represented by the area FNMK. Output in the DC is increased by an amount represented by the area AHMB, of which an amount represented by the area ANMB is paid to the migrants in wages. Thus the net gain of the veterans in the destination country is represented by the area NHM. Output in the SC falls by an amount represented by the area AFMB, of which the amount represented by the area AFKB was initially paid in wages to those who migrated. The net loss to the residents of the SC, "those left behind," is represented by the area FMK. Worldwide, there is a positive net gain, represented by the area FHM. But, as we have just seen, not all groups gain. The migrants and veterans in the destination country gain; those left behind in the source country lose.[1] In principle, there exists a bilateral transfer from the DC to the SC which can make both countries better off. Furthermore, looking only at the gain to the migrants, it by itself still exceeds the loss to those left behind. Therefore, the migrants themselves can compensate (e.g., by remittances) those left behind.[2]

Alternatively, the government in the SC typically imposes an implicit emigration tax on the migrants. This tax can take the form of denial of entitlement programs that were paid for in the past by the migrants (old age or retirement benefits); in other cases, due to capital and foreign exchange controls, the migrants cannot realize the full value of their assets which are left behind and so on.

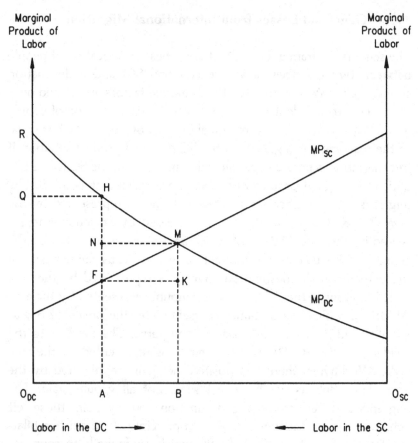

Figure 17.1
Gains and losses from international migration

Hamilton and Whalley (1984), attempting to quantify the implications of barriers to labor mobility between high-wage and low-wage countries, point out that the efficiency gains of the removal of immigration barriers are substantial. They suggest that this issue may be much more important to less-developed countries (LDCs) than the more conventional trade issues raised in the North-South debate. As pointed out in section 16.2, there is a perfect equivalence between labor and capital mobility under constant returns to scale, which extends also to the issue of welfare gains and losses among various income groups.[3]

17.2 Efficient Volume of Migration

By its very nature, international migration changes the population size of countries. It is therefore instructive to look at a benchmark framework in which there are no legal or other impediments to the determination of the population size of each country. Suppose a country can freely choose the number of its citizens or residents among a global pool of potential world residents. What is the most efficient migration size in this case? (We have already dealt with a similar question in section 5.1 of chapter 5, namely, the most efficient size of a population of *identical* individuals.)

The migration issue is a bit different. Suppose that the government, representing the established population, wishes to determine how many (homogeneous) migrants to admit. Suppose that the government can distinguish between the established population and the migrants. We employ essentially the model of chapter 5 (section 5.2) with some slight modifications. Suppose that the government wishes to maximize the utility of a representative member of the established population (veteran). Would-be migrants will come if and only if the bundle of a public good and a private good consumed in the destination country does not yield to the representative migrant a lower utility level than that migrant's reservation-utility level. This level is what the migrant enjoys in the source country.

In this case, the efficient migration level is obtained by maximizing

$$u^S(G, c_V), \tag{17.1}$$

subject to the resource constraint

$$F(T, n_V + n_M) \geq n_V c_V + n_M c_M + G \tag{17.2}$$

and the reservation utility constraint

$$u^M(G, c_M) \geq \bar{u}_M, \tag{17.3}$$

where

u^V = utility function of a veteran;

u^M = utility function of a migrant;

c_V =   private consumption of a veteran;

c_M =   private consumption of a migrant;

$\bar{u}^M$ =   reservation utility level of a migrant;

n_V =   number of veterans;

n_M =   number of migrants;

F =   production function of an all-purpose good;

T =   fixed amount of land; and

G =   consumption of a public good.

The control variables in this model are G, c_V, c_M, and n_M. (Recall that the number of veterans is fixed.)

In this case, it will still be efficient to attract migrants (by public and private consumption provision) up to the point where the marginal product of a migrant worker is equal to the migrant's private consumption, that is,

$$F_n = c_M. \tag{17.4}$$

Similarly, the Lindahl-Samuelson rule for the efficient provision of public goods still holds:

$$n_V(u_G^V/u_c^V) + n_M(u_G^M/u_c^M) = 1.$$

That is, the sum of the willingness to pay over the *entire* population (veterans and migrants) is equal to the marginal cost of the public good, which is one.

The only notable deviation from the results obtained in chapter 5 is with respect to the so-called Henry George rule, which states that the efficient provision of the public good is at exactly the level that can be financed by a 100-percent tax on land rent. Consider the interesting case in which the reservation utility level of the migrants is low enough, so that at the efficient migration size they enjoy a lower level of private consumption than the veterans, that is,

$$c_M < c_V. \tag{17.5}$$

In this case, the government will not tax away all the land rent but rather will leave some of the land rent in the hands of the veterans, so that they can privately consume more than the migrants are allowed. The land rent accrues to veterans only, and there is no compelling argument from the point of view of the government representing them to fully tax the rent away from the veterans in order to provide public goods whose benefits spill over to the migrants as well.

To prove this, note that it follows from (17.4)–(17.5) that

$$F_n(n_V + n_M) < c_V n_V + c_M n_M. \tag{17.6}$$

Subtracting (17.6) from (17.2) yields

$$F - F_n(n_V + n_M) > G. \tag{17.7}$$

Recalling that the left-hand side of (17.7) is equal to the land rent completes the proof.

17.3 International Migration and the Limits to Intracountry Redistribution

The modern welfare state typically redistributes income in one way or another from the rich to the poor. This may be done by a variety of means, such as progressive income taxation, cash transfers to the poor, in-kind transfers to the poor (food stamps, public housing, medical care, education, etc.), indirect subsidies of necessities (food, public transportation), and the like. Such redistribution makes a developed welfare state more attractive to poor migrants from less-developed countries, even when these migrants do not qualify for all the ingredients of the entitlement programs. Therefore, migration has strong implications for the welfare of the veteran residents in the destination country. Following Wildasin (1991), we shall illustrate these considerations in a stylized model with one immobile factor whose distribution is the underlying source of inequality between the two countries and with internationally mobile workers (veterans and migrants).

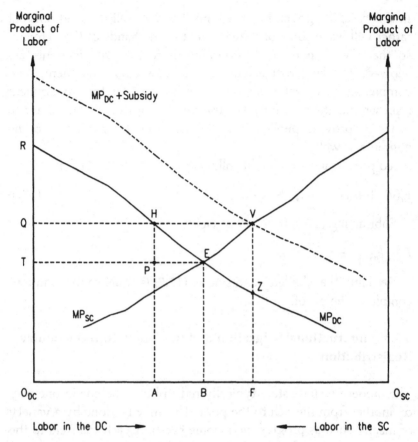

Figure 17.2
The allocation of workers between the destination country (DC) and the source country (SC)

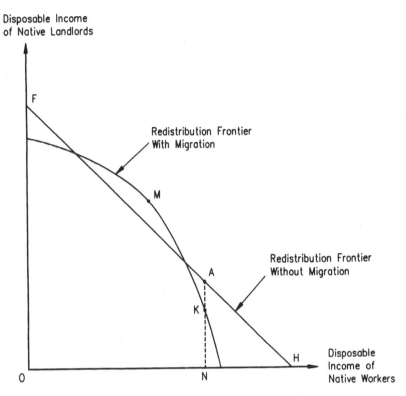

Figure 17.3
The income redistribution frontiers with and without migration

For this purpose we return to the model of section 17.1 which is
redrawn in figure 17.2, where the curves MP_{DC} and MP_{SC} portray the
marginal products of labor in the destination country (DC) and the
source country (SC), respectively. Suppose that the fixed factor is
land and that it is owned by immobile landlords, and consider the
income distribution in the DC between the landlords and the original
native workers. Assume that initially the allocation of (native) workers between the DC and the SC is at point A in figure 17.2 and no
migration is allowed. The income of workers is represented by the
area $O_{DC}QHA$ and the landlords' income is represented by the area
QRH. Suppose that this initial distribution of income is represented
by point A in figure 17.3. Suppose that redistribution takes the form

of a subsidy (possibly negative) to workers, financed by a lump-sum tax on landlords. Because we assume that the supply of labor of each worker is perfectly inelastic, this redistribution scheme creates no distortions, that is, the size of the national pie remains unchanged. Hence the income redistribution frontier is a straight line with a slope of unity (in absolute terms): the line FAH in figure 17.3.

Now, suppose that free migration is allowed. When no redistribution takes place in the DC (i.e., the subsidy to workers in the DC is zero), then AB workers will migrate from the SC to the DC. The wages in the DC fall from $O_{DC}Q$ to $O_{DC}T$ and the total income of the native workers in the DC falls from $O_{DC}QHA$ to $O_{DC}TPA$. At the same time, landlords' income rises from QRH to TRE. The total income of native workers and landlords rises from $O_{DC}RHA$ to $O_{DC}RHEPA$. Thus the income distribution point in this case, denoted by M in figure 17.3, lies to above and to the right of point A and outside the no-migration income redistribution frontier FAH.

Now suppose that redistribution takes place in the DC. Let us trace out in figure 17.3 the income redistribution frontier in this case. A subsidy to workers (veterans and migrants) in the DC raises the demand curve for workers in the DC from MP_{DC} to "MP_{DC} + Subsidy." The subsidy brings more migrants to the DC, raises the wage received by workers (natives, migrants, and "those left behind"), raises the total income of native workers in the DC, but lowers the net income of DC's landlords. (Note that the subsidy to workers is financed by a lump-sum tax on landlords.) The subsidy is no longer distortion-free, and the income redistribution frontier is no longer a straight line with a unitary slope. Recall that the wage of native workers in the no-migration, no-subsidy case was $O_{DC}Q$ in figure 17.2 and their total income was ON in figure 17.3. Now suppose that, with migration, we still want to preserve the income level ON of native workers. The amount of the subsidy that is required for this purpose is VZ in figure 17.2. A number of AF workers migrate to the DC in this case. Total income of landlords is equal to total output ($O_{DC}RZF$ in figure 17.2), less total wage income, including the wage subsidy (which is equal to the tax levied on landlords) received by workers ($O_{DC}QVF$ in figure 17.2). That is, total income of landlords in the DC is equal to QRH, minus HVZ. This income is obviously smaller than QRH. Thus the income redistribution frontier with migration passes below point A in figure 17.3; say, it passes through point K.

Migration therefore changes the income redistribution frontier in a nontrivial way. In a certain range, migration shifts the frontier outward and in some other ranges inward. With no redistribution, migration lowers the income of native workers and raises the income of native landlords. If a redistribution scheme attempts to preserve for native workers at least the income that they had before migration (and with no redistribution), it must make landlords worse off than they were in the premigration, no-redistribution case, and vice versa. In the neighborhood of K and to the left of it, both native groups (workers and landlords) are worse off than in the absence of migration. Therefore, both of them will opt for imposing immigration quotas or other restrictions on immigration. The modern welfare state is therefore more receptive (on economic grounds) to the idea of restricting immigration, a hypothesis that is yet to be tested empirically.

This framework brings up another nonaltruistic motive for foreign aid. The international trade literature has already brought to our attention the possibility that a country could sometimes become better off by giving foreign aid because the terms of trade may change in its favor (e.g., Samuelson 1951; Bhagwati, Brecher, and Hatta 1983). Within the present framework, gains through changing the terms of trade changes are absent, because there is only one tradable good. Nevertheless, the DC benefits from giving foreign aid to the SC if this aid serves to finance a subsidy to workers (especially would-be migrants) in the SC, thereby containing the migration from the SC to the DC, which migration was seen as imposing a toll on the redistribution policy of the DC. Indeed, as shown in Myres (1990), Hercowitz and Pines (1991), and Wildasin (1991), the foreign aid shifts outward almost the entire income redistribution frontier in the presence of free migration.

Notes

Chapter 2

1. In certain countries (e.g., England, the leader of the industrial revolution) there was a lag of several decades between the initial stages of the industrial revolution and the fall in fertility. One important contributing factor for this lag is the uneven spread of the economic gains resulting from the industrial revolution. Specifically, major portions of the population did not enjoy significantly higher incomes and higher education levels until the later stages of the industrial revolution. For more details, see World Bank (1984).

2. The total fertility rate represents the number of children that would be born to a woman if she were to live to the end of her childbearing years and were to bear children at each age at prevailing age-specific fertility rates.

3. At very high income levels, fertility shows a very weak tendency to increase with income, suggesting the very rich could also desire to have many children.

Chapter 4

1. Readers familiar with international trade theory will recognize the result obtained in this example. Because operating on the financial capital market requires that a lender has to find a borrower (and vice versa), it involves trade between individuals. Thus the absence of a capital market corresponds to the familiar autarky equilibrium of trade theory, where the relative prices (i.e., rates of return to investment) between autarkic individuals differ. Opening capital markets, that is, allowing lending and borrowing between individuals, brings about a common equilibrium rate of return. In standard trade models under usual assumptions, the equilibrium price after trade will lie in the interval between the two autarky prices. Compared to autarky, however, the output of one commodity will be lower in a trading equilibrium in the home country and higher in the foreign country, and the output of the second commodity will be higher at home and lower abroad. But there is nothing to preclude the loss of output of either commodity in one country

being more than offset by the gain in the output of the same commodity in the other country. Indeed, in the classic Ricardian world, England, specializing in linen, may produce more linen after trade than she and Portugal together did in autarky. Thus world output of linen may be higher after trade than in autarky. Similarly, opening up capital markets may raise rather than lower the total number of children. The authors are indebted to T. N. Srinavasan for pointing out this parallel.

Chapter 5

1. Sumner (1978, p. 107) maintains that average utilitarianism is incorrectly attributed to Mill, writing that "it seems to have originated early in this century among welfare economists."

2. The relation between the Benthamite and the Millian social welfare functions was also considered in the famous debate between Samuelson (1958 and 1959) and Lerner (1959a and 1959b). The focus there, however, was on optimal capital accumulation (or savings) when population growth is exogenous; see also Lane (1975), who discusses this issue in some detail.

3. This method of proof was suggested by T. N. Srinivasan.

4. In order to ensure that $c^{2L} > 0$, or equivalently, $\log(1 + c^{2L}) > 0$, it is required that $k/a < 2$.

5. Observe that the condition that $k/a > \log 4$ is consistent with the earlier restriction that $k/a < 2$ because $2 > \log 4$.

6. Notice that here again a nonlinear tax instrument may be required, namely, α and β as *functions* of c^1, n and c^2, in order to support the MOA.

Chapter 6

1. Malthus himself, in a subsequent edition of his *Essay*, alluded to this possibility, claiming that universal education could give people the foresight to check fertility. He maintained that improved living standards would lead to "new ... tastes and habits" for children before reaching the subsistence population level.

2. See also Eckstein et al. (1988).

Chapter 7

1. For a survey of the bargaining approach to the theory of the family, see Bergstrom (1993).

2. See Esther Boserup (1974) and Amira Grossbard (1978).

Chapter 8

1. See also Hirschleifer (1976) and Bergstrom (1989).

2. A standard theorem in the theory of taxation is that a tax redistributed to the consumer in a lump sum is welfare-reducing (see, for example, Diamond and McFadden 1974).

3. See James Mirrlees (1971) and Efraim Sadka (1976).

Chapter 9

This chapter is based on Lawrence Kotlikoff and Assaf Razin (1989), "Making Bequests without Spoiling Children: Bequests as an Implicit Tax Structure and the Possibility that Altruistic Bequests Are Not Equalizing." NBER Working Paper No. 2735. We thank Larry Kotlikoff for permitting us to use this material in the book.

Chapter 11

1. Mirrlees (1972) is an exception.

2. Cigno (1983) deals with the implications of altruistic parents for *inter*generational welfare of alternative policies with respect to family allowances.

3. Here we justify our assumption of complementarity between leisure and number of children by a heuristic appeal to the time intensity of raising children. Alternatively, we may formalize this argument by adding a time constraint à la Becker (1965) to the budget constraint (11.11) and by then specifying appropriate restrictions on the form of the utility function in order to ensure the complementarity property.

Chapter 12

This chapter is based on Marc Nerlove, Assaf Razin, Efraim Sadka and Robert von Weizscaeker (1993), "Income Distribution and Efficiency: The Social Security," *Public Finance* 47; 462–475. We thank Marc Nerlove and Robert von Weizscaeker for permitting us to use this material.

1. Capital is the only means of transferring income across time; hence a negative rate of return (i.e., $R \leq 1$) is quite possible in equilibrium. Obviously, $R = 0$ constitutes the boundary case where equilibrium dictates no transfer across time at all.

2. For the sake of simplicity, we assume that the tax does not apply to capital income; in any event, because we focus on the case where $b = 0$, there is consequently no capital income.

3. Recall that "institutional constraints" in our model mean that no enforcement mechanism exists that can obligate children to assume parents' debt left behind. It should be emphasized that this constraint is not as such linked to income inequality. Being possibly bequest-constrained is a result of the family's (and the social planner's) optimization process.

Chapter 13

1. The altruism function in Becker and Barro (1988) contains both the discount factor β and the number of children. The advantage of our formulation is that we can disentangle the effects of intertemporal (via β) and intratemporal (via the function $a(\cdot)$) altruism. This distinction is relevant for later analysis, where fertility is assumed to be endogenous. Our preference specification would be the same as that in Razin and Ben-Zion (1975) in certain cases.

2. It is straightforward to show that the growth rates of output and consumption (g_y and g_c) are positive when $\beta(1 + r) > (1 + g_n)^{1-\alpha}$.

3. This section draws on Razin and Yuen (1994).

Chapter 14

This chapter is a reprint of T. N. Srinivasan's survey, "Development in the Context of Rapid Population Growth: An Overall Assessment," (United Nations, 1993; except for his original section 3). We thank T. N. Srinivasan for permitting us to reprint his work.

1. A *few* of the surveys and reports are Birdsall (1988), Cassen (1976), Johnson and Lee (1987), Kelley (1988, 1992), Keyfitz (1991), National Research Council (1986), World Bank (1984), Royal Society, London, and National Academy of Sciences, U.S.A. (1992).

2. See also Boserup (1989) and Simon (1991).

3. See chapter 3 for an elaborate analysis of this trade-off.

4. Some of these externalities are internalized within the dynasty when each parent cares about the number and welfare of her children; see chapter 6.

5. See the part VI for a discussion of the interaction between trade and migration.

6. See also chapter 5.

Chapter 15

1. Hatton and Williamson (1992) give the following historical perspective: "In the century following 1820, an estimated 60 million Europeans set sail for labor-scarce New World destinations. About three-fifths of these went to the United States. By comparison, earlier migration from labor-abundant Europe had been a mere trickle and other nineteenth-century emigrations from, for example, India and China were also relatively modest. The only comparable intercontinental migration was the black slaves from Africa to the Americas and the Caribbeans. Indeed, it was only in the 1840s that the movement of Europeans into North America exceeded the Africans, and it was not until the 1880s that the cumulative total of Europeans exceeded African immigration."

2. Note that the United States started to impose immigration quotas in 1921. This marked the end of a century-long period of free mass immigration to the New World.

3. Including Portugal.

4. In 1983 about 30 percent of the Portugese population lived outside Portugal (see Organization of Economic Cooperation and Development 1985).

5. An even higher percentage of foreigners characterizes the labor-importing (oil-producing) countries in the Middle East. About two million foreign workers constituted more than 40 percent of the employed work force in 1975. In Africa, Ghana and the Ivory Coast employed about 1 million foreign workers in 1975, mostly from Mali, Togo, and Upper Volta. In Latin America, Argentina and Venezuela had about 2 million workers from Bolivia, Paraguay, and Colombia. Similarly, about 2–3 million illegal immigrants were living in the United States in 1980, about half of them from Mexico. They would have constituted about 8 percent of Mexico's labor force. For more details, see World Bank (1984).

Chapter 16

1. See Ethier (1985) for an earlier survey of these issues.

2. This graphic exposition is strictly correct for fixed unit-input-requirement coefficients (the a_{ij}s). It provides a linear approximation around the equilibrium factor-price point for variable unit-input-requirements.

3. In the $n \times n$ case this proposition is somewhat weaker, namely, $(\bar{q}^H - \bar{q}^F)(\bar{V}^H - \bar{V}^F) \leq 0$, where $\bar{q}^i$ is the autarkic factor price vector and $\bar{V}^i$ is the factor endowment vector ($i = H, F$).

4. Strictly speaking, factor price equalization can still result from free trade, if free trade leads to complete specialization in at least one of the two countries. We are indebted to Lars Svensson for this point.

5. Leamer (1984, p. 11) reports that a sample of 32 countries' wages in agriculture range from \$0.46/hour in India to \$2.04/hour in Denmark. As Leamer puts it: "Part of these differences might be explained by skill differences, but agricultural wages seem unlikely to include a reward for skills that is sufficiently variable to account for the data.... This observation encourages a search for assumptions that do not necessarily imply factor price equalization."

6. These developments endogenize the long-run growth rate through dynamically increasing returns (e.g., Romer 1986); see also chapter 13 of this book.

7. A similar observation about the direction of migration is made also by Galor and Stark (1991) in an overlapping generations model with immobile capital.

Chapter 17

1. If we distinguish between wage earners and landlords (or capitalists), then veteran wage earners in the DC lose, landlords in the DC gain, the left-behind wage earners in the SC gain, and landlords in the SC lose. Evidently, in the DC, landlords gain more than what the veteran workers lose, so that a compensation scheme could be devised, so as to make both veteran workers and landlords better off.

2. As pointed out in chapter 14, official remittances amounted to US\$ 65.6 billion in 1989; see Stanton-Russell and Teitelbaum (1992).

3. However, Helpman and Razin (1983) showed that in economies that produce differentiated products under increasing returns to scale and with monopolistic competition, foreign investment may flow in the "wrong" direction. Thus capital inflows may harm both the destination country and the source country. This was demonstrated by identifying two channels of influence that are special to such economies and that are not taken into account by private capital owners: the contribution of capital flows to total output through their inducement of changes in the scale of operation of individual firms and their direct contribution to consumers' welfare by changing the number of varieties.

References

Abel, Andrew (1988). "An Analysis of Fiscal Policy Under Operative and Inoperative Bequest Motives." In Elhanan Helpman, Assaf Razin, and Efraim Sadka (eds.), *Economic Effects of the Government Budget*. Cambridge: MIT Press.

Abowd, J., and R. Freeman (1991). "Introduction and Summary." In J. Abowd and R. Freeman (eds.), *Immigration, Trade and the Labor Market*. Chicago: NBER and University of Chicago Press.

Abramovitz, M. (1956). "Resource and Output Trends in the United States since 1870." *American Economic Review, Papers and Proceedings* 46:5–23.

Arrow, K. J., and M. Kurz (1970). *Public Investment, the Rate of Return, and Optimal Fiscal Policy*. Baltimore: Johns Hopkins University Press.

Asian Development Bank (1990). *Economic Policies for Sustainable Development*. Manila: Asian Development Bank.

Balcer, Yves, and Efraim Sadka (1986). "Equivalence Scales, Horizontal Equity and Optimal Taxation under Utilitarianism." *Journal of Public Economics* 29:79–97.

Barro, Robert (1974). "Are Government Bonds Net Wealth?" *Journal of Political Economy* 82:1095–1117.

Baumol, William J. (1986). "Productivity Growth, Convergence and Welfare: What Does the Long-Run Data Show?" *American Economic Review* 76:1072–1085.

Becker, G. S., (1960). "An Economic Analysis of Fertility." In Richard Easterlin (ed.), *Demographic and Economic Change in Developing Countries*. Princeton: Princeton University Press.

Becker, G. S. (1965). "A Theory of the Allocation of Time." *Economic Journal* 75:493–517.

Becker, Gary S. (1974). "A Theory of Social Interaction." *Journal of Political Economy* (November–December):1063–1094.

Becker, Gary S. (1993). "Nobel Lecture: The Economic Way of Looking at Behavior." *Journal of Political Economy* 101, 3 (June):385–409.

Becker, Gary S., and Gregg H. Lewis (1973). "On the Interaction between the Quantity and Quality of Children." *Journal of Political Economy* 81:279–288.

Becker, Gary S., and Nigel Tomes (1976). "Child Endowments and the Quantity and Quality of Children." *Journal of Political Economy* 84:S142–S163.

Becker, Gary S., and Robert J. Barro (1988). "A Reformulation of the Economic Theory of Fertility." *Quarterly Journal of Economics* 103:1–25.

Becker, Gary S., and Kevin Murphy (1988). "The Family and the State." *Journal of Law and Economics* 31(1): 1–18.

Bentham, Jeremy (1948). Rev. ed. of 1823. *An Introduction to the Principle of Morals and Legislation.* Oxford: Blackwell.

Berglas, Eitan, and David Pines (1983). "Clubs, Local Public Goods, and Transportation Models: A Synthesis." *Journal of Public Economics* 15:141–162.

Bergstrom, Theodore C. (1989). "A Fresh Look at the 'Rotten Kid Theorem'—and Other Household Mysteries." *Journal of Political Economy* 97(5):1138–1159.

Bergstrom, Theodore C. (1993). "A Survey of Theories of the Family." University of Michigan.

Bertola, Guiseppe (1993). "Factor Shares and Savings in Endogenous Growth." *American Economic Review*, forthcoming.

Bhagwati, Jagdish N., Richard Brecher, and Tatsuo Hatta (1983). "The Generalized Theory of Transfers and Welfare: Bilateral Transfers in a Multilateral World." *American Economic Review* 73:606–618.

Bhagwati, Jagdish N., and T. N. Srinivasan (1983a). *Lectures on International Trade.* Cambridge: MIT Press.

Bhagwati, Jagdish N., and T. N. Srinivasan (1983b). "On the Choice Between Capital and Labor Mobility." *Journal of International Economics* 14:209–221.

Birdsall, Nancy (1988). "Economic Approaches to Population Growth." In *Handbook of Development Economics, Volume I.* Amsterdam: Elsevier.

Boserup, Esther (1965). *The Conditions of Agricultural Growth.* London: Allen and Unwin.

Boserup, Esther (1974). *Women's Role in Economic Development.* London: St. Martin's Press.

Boserup, Esther (1989). *Population and Technical Change: A Study of Long-Term Trends*. Chicago: University of Chicago Press.

Bruno, M., and J. Habib (1976). "Taxes, Family Grants and Redistribution." *Journal of Public Economics* 5:57–80.

Cassen, Robert (1976). "Population and Development: A Survey." *World Development* 4(10/11): 785–830.

Cigno, A. (1983). "On Optimal Family Allowances." *Oxford Economic Papers* 35: 13–22.

Cox, Donald (1987). "Motives for Private Income Transfers." *Journal of Political Economy* 95 (June):508–546.

Dasgupta, Partha (1969). "On the Concept of Optimum Population." *Review of Economic Studies* 36:295–318.

Dasgupta, Partha (1984). "Ethical Foundations of Population Policies." Paper prepared for the Committee on Population, National Research Council, Washington, D.C.

Dasgupta, Partha (1987). "The Ethical Foundations of Population Policy." In D. Gale Johnson and Ronald D. Lee (eds.), *Population Growth and Economic Development: Issues and Evidence*. Madison: University of Wisconsin Press, 631–659.

Dasgupta, Partha (1993). "The Population Problem." In *An Enquiry into Well-Being and Destitution*. Oxford: Clarendon Press. Forthcoming.

Dasgupta, Partha, and Karl-Goran Maeler (1991). "The Environment and Emerging Development Issues." *Proceedings of the World Bank Annual Conference on Development Economics, 1990*. Washington, D.C.: World Bank.

Davis, Steven J. (1992). "Cross Country Patterns of Change in Relative Wages." In Oliver J. Blanchard and Stanley Fischer (eds.), *NBER Macroeconomics Annual, 1992*, Cambridge: MIT Press.

Deardoff, A. V. (1976). "The Growth Rate of Population: Comment." *International Economic Review* 17:510–515.

Deaton, A., and J. Muelbauer (1983). "On Measuring Child Costs in Poor Countries." Mimeo.

Denison, E. F. (1962). "Sources of Economic Growth in the United States and the Alternatives before Us." New York: Committee for Economic Development.

Diamond, Peter A., and Daniel L. McFadden (1974). "Some Uses of the Expenditure Function in Public Finance." *Journal of Public Economics* 3:3–21.

Domar, E. (1947). *Essays in the Theory of Economic Growth*. London: Oxford University Press.

Drazen, Allan (1978). "Government Debt, Human Capital, and Bequests in a Life-Cycle." *Journal of Political Economy* 86:505–516.

Eckstein, Zvi, Steve Stern, and Kenneth I. Wolpin (1988). "Fertility Choice, Land and the Malthusian Hypothesis." *International Economic Review* 29:353–361.

Edgeworth, F. Y. (1925). Review of Henry Sidgewick's *The Elements of Politics*. In *Papers Relating to Political Economy* 3:15–20. London: Macmillan.

Ethier, Wilfred (1985). "International Trade and Labor Migration." *American Economic Review* 75 (September):691–707.

Faini, Riccardo, and Alessandra Venturini (1993). "Trade, Aid and Migration: Same Basic Policy Issues." *European Economic Review* 37:435–442.

Forrester, Jay (1971). *World Dynamics*. Cambridge: Wright-Allen Press.

Frenkel, Jacob A., Assaf Razin, and Efraim Sadka (1991). *International Taxation in an Integrated World*. Cambridge: MIT Press.

Galor, Oded, and Oded Stark (1991). "The Impact of Differences in the Levels of Technology and International Labor Migration." *Journal of Population Economics* 4:1–12.

George, Henry (1914). *Progress and Poverty*. New York: Doubleday.

Goldman, S., and H. Uzawa (1964). "A Note on Separability in Demand Analysis." *Econometrica* 32:387–398.

Grossbard, Amira (1978). *The Economics of Polygamy*. Ph.d. Diss., University of Chicago.

Grossman, Gene M., and Assaf Razin (1984). "International Capital Movements Under Uncertainty." *Journal of Political Economy* 92:286–306.

Hamilton, Bruce, and John Whalley (1984). "Efficiency and Distributional Implications of Global Restrictions on Labor Mobility: Calculations and Policy Implications." *Journal of Development Economics* 4(1–2): 37–60.

Harrod, R. F. (1939). "An Essay in Dynamic Theory." *Economic Journal* 49:14–33.

Harsanyi, J. C. (1953). "Cardinal Utility in Welfare Economics and in the Theory of Risk Taking." *Journal of Political Economy* 61:434–435.

Harsanyi, J. C. (1955). "Cardinal Welfare, Individualistic Ethics, and Interpersonal Comparisons of Utility." *Journal of Political Economy* 63:309–321.

Hatton, Timothy I., and Jeffery G. Williamson (1992). "International Migration and World Development: A Historical Perspective." Historical Paper No. 41, NBER, Cambridge, MA.

Heckman, James, and Robert Willis (1976). "Estimation of a Stochastic Model of Reproduction: An Econometric Approach." In Nestor E. Terleckyj (ed.), *Household Production and Consumption*. New York: Columbia University Press (for NBER).

Helpman, Elhanan, and Assaf Razin (1983). "Increasing Returns, Monopolistic Competition, and Factor Movements: A Welfare Analysis." *Journal of International Economics* 14 (May):263–276.

Hercowitz, Zvi, and David Pines (1991). "Migration with Fiscal Externalities." *Journal of Public Economics* 46:163–180.

Higgins, G. M., A. H. Kassam, L. Naiken, G. Fischer, and M. M. Shah (1983). "Potential Population Supporting Capacities of Lands in the Developing World." Technical Report FPA/INT/513 of Project Land Resources for Population of the Future, FAO, Rome.

Hirschleifer, Jack (1977). "Shakespeare vs. Becker on Altruism: The Importance of Having the Last Word." *Journal of Economic Literature* 15:500–502.

Johnson, D., and Lee, R. (1987). *Population Growth and Economic Development: Issues and Evidence*. Madison: University of Wisconsin Press.

Kelley, Allen (1988). "Economic Consequences of Population Change in the Third World." *Journal of Economic Literature* 26(4): 1685–1728.

Kelley, Allen (1992). "Revisionism Revisited: An Essay on the Population Debate in Historial Perspective." Duke University, Center for Demographic Studies. Processed.

Keyfitz, Nathan (1991). "Population and Development Within the Ecosphere: One View of the Literature." *Population Index* 57(1): 5–22.

Keyfitz, Nathan, and Wilhelm Flieger (1990). *World Population Growth and Aging*. Chicago: University of Chicago Press.

Kimball, Miles (1987). "Making Sense of Two-Sided Altruism." *Journal of Monetary Economics* 20:301–326.

Knight, Frank H. (1921). *Risk, Uncertainty, and Profit*. Boston: Houghton-Mifflin.

Koerner, Heiko (1990). *Internationale Mobilitt der Arbeit*. Darmstadt: Wissenschaftliche Buchgesellschaft.

Koopmans, Tjalling C. (1975). "Concepts of Optimality and Their Uses." Nobel Memorial Prize Lecture. Royal Swedish Academy of Sciences, Stockholm, December 11.

Koopmans, Tjalling C., Peter A. Diamond, and R. A. Williamson (1964). "Stationary Utility and Time Perspective." *Econometrica* 32:82–100.

Krueger, Anne O. (1968). "Factor Endowments and Per Capita Income Differences Among Countries." *Economic Journal* 78:641–659.

Krugman, Paul (1990). "Increasing Returns and Economic Geography." NBER Working Paper no. 3275.

Kuznets, S. (1966). *Modern Economic Growth: Rate, Structure and Spread.* New Haven: Yale University Press.

Lane, John S. (1975). "A Synthesis of the Ramsey-Meade Problems When Population Change is Endogenous." *Review of Economic Studies,* 42:57–66.

Lane, John S. (1977). *On Optimal Population Paths.* Berlin: Springer-Verlag.

Layard, Richard, Oliver Blanchard, Rudiger Dornbusch, and Paul Krugman (1992). *East-West Migration.* Cambridge: MIT Press.

Leamer, Edward E. (1984). *Sources of International Comparative Advantage.* Cambridge: MIT Press.

Lee, Ronald, and Timothy Miller (1991). "Population Growth, Externalities to Childbearing, and Fertility Policy in Developing Countries." In *Proceedings of the World Bank Annual Conference on Development Economics, 1990.* Washington, D.C.: World Bank, 275–304.

Lerner, A. P. (1959a). "Consumption-Loan Interest and Money." *Journal of Political Economy* 67:512–518.

Lerner, A. P. (1959b). "Rejoinder." *Journal of Political Economy* 67:523–525.

Lucas, R. E. (1988). "On the Mechanics of Economic Development." *Journal of Monetary Economics* 22:3–42.

Lucas, Robert E. Jr. (1990). "Why Doesn't Capital Flow from Rich to Poor Countries?" *American Economic Review, Papers and Proceedings* 80(2): 92–96.

MacDougall, G. D. A. (1960). "The Benefits and Costs of Private Investment from Abroad: A Theoretical Approach." *Economic Record* 36:13–35.

Malthus, Thomas P. (1798). *An Essay on the Principle of Population and a Summary View of the Principle of Population.* Reprint, Baltimore: Penguin, 1970.

Markusen, James R. (1983). "Factor Movements and Commodity Trade as Complements." *Journal of International Economics* (May):341–356.

Meade, James E. (1952). "External Economies and Diseconomies in a Competitive Situation." *Economic Journal* 62:54–67.

Meade, James E. (1976). *The Just Economy*. London: Allen and Unwin.

Meadow, D. H., D. L. Meadow, J. Randers, and W. W. Behrens III (1972). *The Limits to Growth*. New York: Universe Books.

Mirrlees, J. A. (1971). "An Exploration in the Theory of Optimum Income Taxation." *Review of Economic Studies* 38:175–208.

Mirrlees, J. A. (1972). "Population Policy and the Taxation of Family Size." *Journal of Public Economics* 1:169–198.

Mundell, Robert A. (1957). "International Trade and Factor Mobility." *American Economic Review*.

Musgrave, Richard A. (1959). *The Theory of Public Finance*. New York, Toronto and London: McGraw-Hill.

Myres, J. (1990). "Optimality, Free Mobility and Regional Authority in a Federation." *Journal of Public Economics* 43:107–121.

National Research Council (1986). *Population Growth and Economic Development: Policy Questions*. Washington, D.C.: National Academy Press.

Neher, P. A., (1971). "Peasants, Procreation, and Pensions." *American Economic Review* 61:380–389.

Nerlove, Marc, and A. Meyer (1992). "Endogenous Fertility and the Environment: A Parable of Firewood." In P. Dasgupta and K. G. Maeler (eds.), *The Environment and Emerging Development Issues*. Oxford: Clarendon Press.

Organization of Economic Cooperation and Development (1985). *Employment Outlook*, September, p. 54.

Parfit, D. (1984). *Reasons and Persons*. Oxford: Oxford University Press.

Pearce, David, Edward Barbier, and Anil Makandya (1988). "Sustainable Development and Cost-Benefit Analysis." Paper presented at the Canadian Environment Assessment Workshop on Integrating Economic and Environment Assessment.

Pechman, J. A. (1966). *Federal Tax Policy*. New York: Norton.

Preston, Sam (1982). "Review of the Ultimate Resource." *Population and Development Review* 8:176–177.

Ramsey, F. P. (1928). "A Mathematical Theory of Saving," *Economic Journal* 38(1952): 543–559.

Raut, L., and T. N. Srinivasan (1991). "Endogenous Fertility, Technical Change and Growth in a Model of Overlapping Generations," Economic Growth Center Discussion Paper no. 628, Yale University.

Rawls, John (1971). *A Theory of Justice*. Cambridge: Harvard University Press.

Razin, Assaf, and Uri Ben-Zion (1975). "An International Model of Population Growth." *American Economic Review* 69:923–933.

Razin, Assaf, and Efraim Sadka (1993). *The Economy of Modern Israel: Malaise and Promise*. Chicago: University of Chicago Press.

Razin, Assaf, and Chi-Wa Yuen (1993). "Convergence in Growth Rates: A Quantative Assessment of the Role of Capital Mobility and International Taxation." In Leonardo Leiderman and Assaf Razin (eds.), *Capital Mobility: The Impact on Consumption, Investment, and Growth*. Cambridge: Cambridge University Press.

Rebelo, Sergio T. (1992). "Growth in Open Economies." *Carnegie-Rochester Conference Series on Public Policy* 36:5–46.

Romer, P. M. (1986). "Increasing Returns and Long-Run Growth." *Journal of Political Economy* 94(5): 1002–1037.

Rosen, Harvey S. (1988). *Public Finance*. 2d ed. Homewood, Ill.: Irwin.

Rostow, W. W. (1978). *The World Economy: History and Prospect*. London: Basingstoke.

Royal Society (U.K.), and National Academy of Sciences (U.S.) (1992). "Population Growth, Resource Consumption, and a Sustainable World." Unpublished manuscript.

Sadka, Efraim (1976). "On Income Distribution, Incentive Effects and Optimal Income Taxation," *Review of Economic Studies* 43:261–268.

Sah, Raaj (1991). "The Effects of Child Mortality Changes on Fertility Choice and Parental Welfare." *Journal of Political Economy* 99(3): 582–606.

Saint-Paul, Gilles (1992). "Fiscal Policy in an Endogenous Growth Model." *Quarterly Jorunal of Economics* 107:1243–1259.

Samuelson, Paul A. (1952). "The Transfer Problem and Transport Costs: The Terms of Trade when Impediments are Absent." *Economic Journal* 62:278–304.

Samuelson, Paul A. (1954). "The Pure Theory of Public Expenditures." *The Review of Economics and Statistics* 36:387–389.

Samuelson, Paul A. (1958). "An Exact Consumption-Loan Model of Interest with or without the Social Contrivance of Money." *Journal of Political Economy* 66:467–482.

Samuelson, Paul A. (1959). "Reply." *Journal of Political Economy* 67:518–522.

Samuelson, Paul A. (1975). "The Optimum Growth Rate for Population." *International Economic Review* 16:531–538.

Schultz, T. W., (ed.) (1974). *Economics of the Family: Marriage, Children and Human Capital.* Chicago and London: NBER.

Shah, M. M., G. Fischer, G. M. Higgins, A. H. Kassam, and L. Naiken (1984). "People, Land and Food Production: Potentials in the Developing World." International Institute for Applied Systems Analysis, Laxenburg, Austria. Mimeo.

Sidgwick, H. (1874). *The Methods of Ethics.* London: Macmillan.

Simon, J. L. (1982). *The Ultimate Resource.* Princeton, N.J.: Princeton University Press.

Solow, R. M. (1956). "A Contribution to the Theory of Economic Growth." *Quarterly Journal of Economics* 70:65–94.

Solow, R. M. (1957). "Technical Change and the Aggregate Production Function." *Review of Economics and Statistics* 39:312–320.

Stanton-Russell, Sharon, and Michael S. Teitelbaum (1992). "International Migration and International Trade." Discussion Paper No. 160, World Bank.

Stiglitz, Joseph E. (1977). "The Theory of Local Public Goods." In M. Feldstein and J. Inman (eds.), *The Economics of Public Services.* London: MacMillan, 274–344.

Stiglitz, Joseph (1987). "Pareto Efficient and Optimal Taxation and the New Welfare Economics." In *The Handbook of Public Economics.* Amsterdam: North Holland.

Stopler, W., and P. Samuelson (1941). "Protection and Real Wages." *Review of Economic Studies* 9:58–73.

Summers, Robert, and Al Heston (1991). "The Penn World Table (Mark 5): An Expanded Set of International Comparisons 1955–1988." *Quarterly Journal of Economics* 106 (May):327–368.

Sumner, L. W. (1978). "Classical Utilitarianism and Population Optimum." In R. I. Sikora and Brian Barry (eds.), *Obligations to Future Generations,* Philadelphia: Temple University Press.

U.S. Government Printing Office (1992). *Economic Report of the President.* February.

Vickrey, W. (1980). "Utility, Strategy, and Social Decision Rules." *Quarterly Journal of Economics* 74:507–535.

von Neumann, J. (1945). "A Model of General Equilibrium." *Review of Economic Studies* 13:1–9.

Weil, Philippe (1987). "Love Thy Children: Reflections on Barro Debt Neutrality Theorem." *Journal of Monetary Economics* 19:377–391.

Wildasin, David, E. (1986). *Urban Public Finance.* Harwood Economic Publishers.

Wildasin, David, E. (1991). "Income Redistribution and Migration." Working Paper No. 2, Center for Economic Studies, University of Munich.

Willis, R. J. (1980). "The Old Age Security Hypothesis and Population Growth." In T. Burch (ed.), *Demographic Behavior: Interdisciplinary Perspectives on Decision Making*. Boulder, CO: Westview Press.

World Bank (1984). *World Development Report, 1984*. World Bank and Oxford University Press.

World Bank (1989). *World Development Report, 1989*. World Bank and Oxford University Press.

World Bank (1992). *World Development Report, 1992*. Oxford University Press.

World Bank (1993). *World Development Report, 1993*. World Bank and Oxford University Press.

Woytinski, W. S., and E. S. Woytinski (1953). *World Population and Production: Trends and Outlook*. New York: 20th Century Fund.

Zhang, Junsen (1994). "Bequest as a Public Good Within Marriage: A Note." *Journal of Political Economy* 102(1): 201–207.

Zimmermann, K. (1992). "Industrial Restructuring, Unemployment and Migration." In A. Jacquemin et al. (eds.), *Europe and the Global Economic Interdependence*. (Forthcoming.)

Index

Printed in the United States
By Bookmasters